International Screen Industries

Series Editors:
Michael Curtin, University of California, Santa Barbara, and Paul McDonald, King's College London, UK.

The International Screen Industries series offers original and probing analysis of media industries around the world, examining their working practices and the social contexts in which they operate. Each volume provides a concise guide to the key players and trends that are shaping today's film, television and digital media.

Published titles:
The American Television Industry *Michael Curtin and Jane Shattuc*
Arab Television Industries *Marwan M. Kraidy and Joe F. Khalil*
The Chinese Television Industry *Michael Keane*
East Asian Screen Industries *Darrell Davis and Emilie Yueh-yu Yeh*
European Film Industries *Anne Jäckel*
European Television Industries *Petros Iosifidis, Jeanette Steemers and Mark Wheeler*
Global Television Marketplace *Timothy Havens*
Hollywood in the New Millennium *Tino Balio*
Latin American Television Industries *John Sinclair and Joseph D. Straubhaar*
Video and DVD Industries *Paul McDonald*
The Video Game Business *Randy Nichols*

Nollywood Central

Jade L. Miller

A BFI book published by Palgrave

© Jade L. Miller 2016

All rights reserved. No reproduction, copy or transmission of this publication may be made without written permission. No portion of this publication may be reproduced, copied or transmitted save with written permission or in accordance with the provisions of the Copyright, Designs and Patents Act 1988, or under the terms of any licence permitting limited copying issued by the Copyright Licensing Agency, Saffron House, 6-10 Kirby Street, London EC1N 8TS.
Any person who does any unauthorized act in relation to this publication may be liable to criminal prosecution and civil claims for damages.

The author has asserted her right to be identified as the author of
this work in accordance with the Copyright, Designs and Patents Act 1988.

First published in 2016 by
PALGRAVE

on behalf of the

BRITISH FILM INSTITUTE
21 Stephen Street, London W1T 1LN
www.bfi.org.uk

There's more to discover about film and television through the BFI.
Our world-renowned archive, cinemas, festivals, films, publications and learning resources are here to inspire you.

Palgrave in the UK is an imprint of Macmillan Publishers Limited, registered in England, company number 785998, of 4 Crinan Street, London N1 9XW. Palgrave Macmillan in the US is a division of St Martin's Press LLC, 175 Fifth Avenue, New York, NY 10010. Palgrave is a global imprint of the above companies and is represented throughout the world. Palgrave® and Macmillan® are registered trademarks in the United States, the United Kingdom, Europe and other countries.

Cover image © Glenna Gordon

Set by Cambrian Typesetters, Camberley, Surrey
Printed and bound by CPI Group (UK) Ltd, Croydon, CR0 4YY

This book is printed on paper suitable for recycling and made from fully managed and sustained forest sources. Logging, pulping and manufacturing processes are expected to conform to the environmental regulations of the country of origin.

British Library Cataloguing-in-Publication Data
A catalogue record for this book is available from the British Library
A catalog record for this book is available from the Library of Congress

ISBN 978–1–84457–691–3 (pb)
ISBN 978–1–84457–692–0 (hb)

Contents

Acknowledgments	vi
Introduction	1
1 History: Nollywood Rising	9
2 Nollywood in Nigeria: Production and Distribution	30
3 Nollywood, the Nigerian Product: Style, Format and Audiences	62
4 Organising Nollywood: Government Policy and Guilds	93
5 Nollywood's Global Circuits	120
Conclusion	150
Bibliography	160
Index	169

Acknowledgments

My sincerest thanks go to many individuals without whose support and guidance this book would not have happened. I would, first, like to thank the editors of this series, Michael Curtin and Paul McDonald, as well as the team at BFI Publishing/Palgrave. Michael has been a wonderful editor, guiding and advocating for this book every step of the way, and I thank both he and Paul for their insightful critiques and advice.

My research on Nollywood has been a journey, from its beginnings in my dissertation to its current version as a book in the BFI Screen Industries series. My deepest appreciation goes to my PhD advisor, Manuel Castells, for his support for me and this project and the invaluable advice and critiques he offered during the dissertation phase. I also must acknowledge the transformative education I received at the University of Southern California's (USC's) Annenberg School for Communication, the support of the school's many resources, the rest of my dissertation committee – Sarah Banet-Weiser, Elizabeth Currid, Adam Clayton Powell III and Jonathan Taplin – and the many productive conversations I had with other professors and my fellow graduate students at Annenberg.

While my support network gave me a base upon which to stand, this book would have gone nowhere without the generosity of many contacts in Nigeria. I began this project as an idea, knowing nobody in or even peripheral to the industry, bombarding every possible connection – from a former colleague from my days in the New York photography industry who had worked on an ad campaign for Nigerian beer to the mother of one of my father's students who had once worked at the US Consulate in Lagos. While I don't have room to name everyone who generously helped out in this regard, one contact went above and beyond professional helpfulness: Gbemi Olujobi, a Nigerian journalist who had recently earned her Masters degree at USC. Although we barely knew one another, she graciously met me in Lagos in my first days there and introduced me to the entertainment editor at her former newspaper, Jahman Anikulapo. I spent one of my first days in Lagos in his office as he called industry contact after industry contact, setting up meetings for me for the next day, and I am also thankful for his generosity. Gbemi visited with me many times to make sure I was doing OK in Lagos. I am grateful for her assistance and care.

ACKNOWLEDGMENTS

While they helped me begin in Lagos, I am also grateful to everyone in the industry who agreed to speak with me, giving me their time with no personal benefit to themselves. I was graciously invited to movie sets, to auditions and into private homes. I would like to thank everyone at Communicating for Change, the NGO where I lived in Lagos, particularly the handyman, Bube 'Isaac' Yahi, who agreed to accompany me on excursions that most others advised me against.

I am also thankful for the supportive environment of the Communication Department at Tulane University where I worked on this project as I completed a Mellon Post-Doctoral Fellowship, as well as the Mellon Foundation for making my time there possible. My good fortune continues in my current department of Communication Studies at Wilfrid Laurier University, where I feel myself truly among colleagues and friends. This research was supported by Wilfrid Laurier University and the Social Sciences and Humanities Research Council. I also thank my networks of supportive friends in the cities where I primarily wrote this: in Los Angeles, in New Orleans, in Toronto and in New York.

Last, but perhaps most importantly, I thank my parents, Dr Susan A. Basow and Dr Jay K. Miller, who instilled in me a love for knowledge, the confidence to pursue my goals and a fearlessness about interacting with the world. More than anyone, this book would not have come to be if not for their unwavering love and support, and I consider myself fortunate to count them as always on my side as my strongest supporters.

Introduction

At a Film Financing session as part of a recent Los Angeles Film Festival, a panel of five global film industry professionals convened a session intended for independent producers entitled 'Crossing Borders: Global Film Markets'. Throughout the discussion, the panellists, including a representative for international buyers and specialists in selling international distribution rights of Hollywood productions, painted a picture of a global system of media sales: rights being sold under similar terms to virtually identical buyers who happen to represent different territories which all function under the same system, and all operating under similar logics. They discussed the rationality, for instance, of splitting theatrical rights from television, online and DVD rights on the global film market; the global decline in DVD watching they attributed not only to piracy and other online viewing, but also to rising global consumer preference for one-time viewing. The picture they painted was of the world as a global market, split into territories for convenience of sales negotiations.

In the question and answer session, one attendee who did not identify herself rose to ask a question: 'What about Africa?' She noted that panellists had discussed distribution in the Americas, Europe, Asia and Australia, but hadn't mentioned Africa. The response from the five panellists was unanimous. 'We really don't sell to Africa,' said the moderator. She noted that theatrical rights might sometimes be sold in South Africa, but usually for a pittance, a drop in the bucket compared to sales made in other territories. Other countries in Africa, she noted, might get television sales, but probably would not. There is not enough infrastructure in any other countries in sub-Saharan Africa, she said, to guarantee making any money at all in those territories, rendering distribution efforts there pointless.

The moderator's and other panellists' comments in answer to this question were echoed at a banquet that same evening by Rashid Bahati, Senior Vice President of Business Development and Acquisitions for LeadDog Entertainment, a distributor of Black and African film. He also mentioned the lack of infrastructure in countries like Nigeria as a reason he had never sold distribution rights to Nigerian entities, nor bought them. Bahati said he once sent screeners (advance copies of a film meant for review purposes only) of three films to a distributor in Nigeria who had requested them. He never saw the

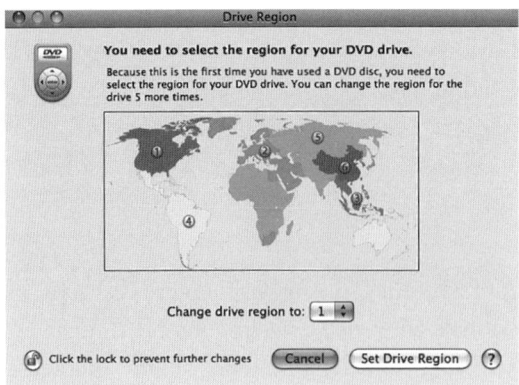

One view of the world as a potential global film market for formal DVD distribution

screeners nor heard back from this distributor again, leaving him to believe the screeners may have been 'pirated' or otherwise distributed without his authorisation. 'How can anyone enter into business deals with "unreliable" partners?' he asked.

These comments illustrate the experience of dominant global cultural industries from the perspective of what has traditionally been referred to as the 'global South'. The majority of the entire continent of sub-Saharan Africa, for instance, is mostly considered to be outside and tertiary to the well-oiled functioning of a global Hollywood, both as a source of production and as a site of distribution. That which emerges in the gaps between, in the absence of connectivity to global networks, will have no easy path to connect with, for instance, the complex funding and distribution networks of the dominant global cultural industries in a quest to grow. If we think of one dominant cultural industry network, with global Hollywood as its hub and other corporate national film industries as its nodes, we can also see the informal alternative cultural industry networks that exist on the flipside of and in gaps between those networks. This book interrogates the position and rise of new cultural industry hubs outside the traditional core networks in global cultural industries through an in-depth look at one case study: Nollywood, the burgeoning Nigerian movie industry that has taken off in sub-Saharan Africa and the diaspora.

NOLLYWOOD, THE CULTURAL PRODUCT

Nigeria is a vast and diverse nation, with over 250 languages spoken and approximately 170 million people, or a fifth of the total population of sub-Saharan Africa, living within its borders. The Hausa, the dominant ethnic group in Nigeria, populate the northern parts of the country, while the south, where Nigeria's largest metropolis, Lagos, is located, is dominated by the two next largest ethnic groups: the Igbo towards the east and the Yoruba, the larger of the two, towards the west. Since the early 1990s, Nigeria has come to be known for its prolific local production of 'video films', or movies made independently using video technologies and distributed for home viewing. There are similarly structured and interlinked video-based movie industries associated with all three ethnic groups, but the term 'Nollywood' is most usually used to refer to English-language movies, which are made in the south.

Unlike the tradition of African celluloid film, or Hollywood and Bollywood films, Nollywood movies are shot using video technologies (first analogue, now digital), and are primarily intended for popular home viewing on small screens, as opposed to theatrical (or film festival) distribution. Most are long – at least three hours in length – and many consist of at least two parts (e.g. Part I and Part II or more, purchased separately). Profits are usually made en masse over a catalogue of titles as opposed to from individual movies. Nollywood movies are a distinct cultural form, with, many argue, more of a connection stylistically to soap operas than to the sorts of cinema one might find at the international art film festivals that dot the sub-Saharan Africa cinemascape.

Nollywood may be unknown to much of what has traditionally been referred to as the 'global North', but throughout sub-Saharan Africa and the global African diaspora, Nollywood is not just known but is known as a ubiquitous dominant force. In Nigeria and in countries throughout sub-Saharan Africa, Nollywood has come to dominate screens, a move that has caused complaints of oversaturation of local screens in some smaller sub-Saharan African countries (see Ondego, 2008; *The Economist*, 2010). And, in some places, Nollywood has spurred local production in the 'Nollywood style' (see Krings, 2010, for example, on Nollywood's influence on Tanzanian video production). Nollywood's business model, a key focus of this book, has in some ways proved to be just as popular an export as the movies themselves.

NOLLYWOOD IN THE CONTEXT OF GLOBAL MEDIA FLOWS

While Nollywood is certainly a product of southern Nigeria, circulating first in the Nigerian market, nation-based classifications of media industries can be problematic. Critical enquiry into international communication has, for years, addressed direction in global media flows. Does media flow north–south, dominating world audiences? What about media that flow in the opposite direction, from south–north, via diasporic, niche, or other global flows? Or media that circulates intra-regionally, geolinguistically or via another south–south configuration? Media scholar Daya Thussu has termed these latter flows 'contra-flow', and argues for the increasing importance of such flows in understanding the dynamics of media production and distribution on a global scale. While acknowledging the multi-directionality of global media flows, I argue that differentiating between media industries based on nation-based classifications of origin (e.g. is this entire nation in the global North or global South?) is inherently murky and will begin to lose meaning the deeper one investigates ownership and investment networks.[1] If industries become ever more incorporated into 'global Hollywood's' corporate structure through investment and co-productions (see Arsenault and Castells, 2008), how 'contra' can this flow be? Instead, I argue that the economic and institutional structures producing media are the best way by which we can classify them, determining to what extent these industries are – or could be – a part of dominant global cultural industry networks.

If we think of movie production on a global scale, we can see that it is diverse, both culturally, in terms of production content, and economically, in terms of business structures and profit structures. Audiovisual entertainment industries exist worldwide, some quite robust, some quite profitable and some quite popular – and with varying degrees of connection to dominant global cultural industry networks, from dense to incredibly sparse. Mumbai, for instance, is the hub of a robust production, distribution and exhibition network specialising in 'Bollywood'-style films. Mexico City and Sao Paolo are hubs in the global telenovela industry, producing television content that rules prime-time in countries spanning five continents. And, of course, Los Angeles is the dominant industrial hub of a global network of film and television production and distribution. The production and distribution networks of these industries do not stand completely alone – all are globally linked in a number of ways. And, as any emerging hub becomes more popular, it is in the interest of the global film industry known as Hollywood to invest in and otherwise financially integrate it into their global interests: emergent cultural industry hubs vary in their level of official Hollywood connections and their own self-forged alternative global connections. Yet, while each hub is globally linked, it also represents a specific local creative milieu, responsive to local domestic (and regional) exigencies, and reflective of a number of very specific local conditions that have helped shape it.

Nollywood, the industry, reflects an extreme of disconnection and exclusion from these networks (though, of course, it is neither wholly disconnected nor wholly excluded) and serves as a site to explore the strength of what are arguably increasingly more important alternative global networks of production inputs and distribution: networks in which 'black' markets both feed and distribute content and networks in which opacity and informality both delimit potential Hollywood-driven growth and investment and simultaneously power the industry. Nollywood is an ideal case study in alternative media networks – for the level and breadth of its disconnect with dominant global networks of formal capital and cultural production, as well as its global profile and notable productivity.

Even as we look at the alternative global networks of Nollywood, the industry is clearly place-based, and the significance of location in Nigeria and in the global mega-city of Lagos can't be overstated. Lagos is simultaneously an overcrowded under-organised rapidly growing mega-city and a symbol of cosmopolitan wealth, global connections and the fast life in West Africa. Nollywood movies are, first, a local production of southern Nigeria and of Lagos, reflecting local culture in very specific ways – from its aesthetic to its industrial structure. And Nollywood movies are distributed globally and are connected to a number of globally linked networks, for both distribution and production inputs. Unlike many other global media industries, however, these networks are almost exclusively informal, and Nigeria (like most of sub-Saharan Africa as a whole) is mostly invisible (at least currently) to the dominant cultural industry networks as a potential site for productive input or even as a potential site for distribution. As such, this book is an exploration of the emergence of, and global networks forged by, an industry in a state of fragmented exclusion from the global 'Network Society'. How does this cultural industry, peripheral to dominant global networks in both its distribution and its industrial structure, yet central to alternative networks, relate to global markets and global networks? How do we define the spaces in which this industry is not peripheral but dominant, robust, vital and, indeed, central? And is it possible that, in its pervasive informality, opacity and decentralisation of power, Nollywood will continue to thrive – or at least function – in its alternative industrial structure and discreteness from dominant global cultural industry networks?

THIS BOOK

In researching this book, I observed as much of Nollywood's global and local workings as possible. This included the flashy side of Nollywood: industry banquets and premieres in Lagos and major Hollywood film conferences with Nollywood invitees. This also included what could better be termed 'scrappy Nollywood': everything from night-time shoots running off noisy generators in an after-hours office space to an open-call open-air audition for a sea of aspirants on the patio of an off-hours bar. I visited sites from an optical disc replication factory on the outskirts of Lagos to a Sony store catering to Nollywood professionals in Lagos's most expensive neighbourhood to the labyrinthine halls of government ministries in Abuja. I interviewed dozens of industry practitioners, from high-ranking Nollywood guild presidents and government ministers to aspiring screenwriters and small-scale video vendors. I did my best to draw as full a picture as I could of the breadth and depth of Nollywood's internal networks and connections to broader networks, as well as its sheer scale. In many ways, this book seeks to serve as a window, a view from the side and from inside a media industry in its early years, grown up in the specific conditions of a rapidly growing mega-city located in the global South.

While my research took me to Los Angeles, London, New York City, Atlanta, Boston, Accra and Abuja, the core of this story is based in Lagos, where the majority of this research was conducted. My initial forays into the industry were made through a few key introductions to major industry players, including the arts editor of a prestigious local newspaper, a high-ranking official in the Foreign Ministry and a contact at the US Consulate. These initial contacts helped to introduce me to key high-level informers, and any introduction quickly led me to many other potential interviewees, as is usually the case in Nollywood's personal connection-ruled industry.

In the first chapter, Chapter 1, I look at the formation of Nollywood, comparing what we know about its birth and rise to the existent literature on cultural industry growth, literature based nearly exclusively on industrial growth in the global North. If we look at Nigeria, Lagos and Nollywood as sites specifically disembedded from official global cultural industry networks – as in Hollywood's limited to non-existent distribution efforts there – how does cultural industry growth differ? In this chapter, I narrate the history of Nollywood, born in the early 1990s, augmented by interviews with those who were active in the early years of the industry, and compare Nollywood's story to some other examples of cultural industry growth.

In Chapter 2, I extend this look at Nollywood as an example of a cultural industry existing in a different environment from that dominating the existent literature: an industry impossible to conceive of separately from its location in global networks. This chapter presents the political economy of movie production and distribution processes currently at work in Nollywood, guided by interviews and observations with those working in nearly every corner of the industry from optical disc replication to special effects creation. The chapter deals in greater detail with the implications and legacies of Nollywood's birth from the murky area between black markets and 'legal' markets, particularly significant places of exclusion from the Network Society (the global 'Fourth World') where informality, black markets and even technological failure can be seen as endemic: (potential) building blocks as opposed to pure obstacles. This understanding of black market distribution and technological failure as part of a functioning system as opposed to a break in that system is a point of study first advanced by media anthropologist Brian Larkin in his ground-breaking work on the structures of northern Nigeria's Hausa-language video industry (2004, 2008) and I'm indebted to his approach here. I compare the functioning of Nollywood with the functioning of Lagos's famous Alaba electronics market, both operating in a global urban periphery while central to their own alternative networks and examine the ways in which marketers use informal business practices to resist formal investment and interference (foreign and domestic) in their dominance of the industry.

In Chapter 3, I address Nollywood texts. It is the appeal of Nollywood movies to domestic and international audiences that drives the industry, and this chapter looks at the sources of this appeal: the stories, styles, settings and themes of Nollywood movies. Onlookers have struggled to 'place' Nollywood as an industry, usually finding it to reside in both style and format somewhere between cinema and television. I take this chapter to place the industry myself, not only in style and format, but also in the context of other Nigerian artistic production. In addressing the uneasy relationship between Nollywood and the political project of Black African cinema, I argue that Nollywood's contribution to this politicised cinema project can come via its industrial structure, as it succeeded in creating a self-sustaining independent system of cultural production free from former colonial authorities. And this business model has itself served as a popular Nigerian export.

In the next chapter, I analyse the governance of the industry. One of the things for which Nollywood is most famous is its rise without the support or guidance of governmental policy. Instead, the industry grew in the gaps between official oversight and developed informal processes in lieu of most possible government-supplied infrastructure such as contract litigation or copyright protection. Chapter 4 looks at the ways in which a majority informal industry, born with no external effort guiding it, is governed and regulated. Supplemented with interviews with government ministers and guild presidents, I first address in detail the three government agencies currently possessing a charge to regulate Nollywood in some way: a censorship agency (National Film and Video Censors Board, NFVCB), a development agency (the Nigerian Film Corporation, NFC) and a copyright enforcement agency (the Nigerian Copyright Commission, NCC). I follow this with a case study of two (mostly unsuccessful) major governmental intervention initiatives that were pursued in recent years: a licensing framework for distributors and a licensing framework for practitioners. Last, this chapter looks at how the industry *is* governed, with guilds efficiently substituting for legal contracts yet not able to realise efforts to alter industry structure by formalising distribution. I conclude that, in an industry fuelled by the informal and running along alternative pathways, the most effective organisational tools are self-grown, just as the industry is itself self-grown and informal.

Chapter 5 is where the investigation of Nollywood as an industry is rounded out and connected to key questions about Nollywood's place in the global system. Chapter 5 addresses the global connections that mark Nollywood from production to distribution, both formal and informal. This chapter combs the entire production and distribution chain and identifies the ways in which the industry is globally connected. I analyse the many outposts that can be considered nodes of Nollywood throughout the world, and the many depots in Nigeria that can be considered nodes of the global Network Society in Nollywood/Lagos. The former can be seen in the many distribution agents and offices located in places like south and east London and the Bronx. The latter can be seen in the Sony equipment store in Lagos, selling equipment directly to most of Nollywood's top cinematographers, but also includes some more recent incursions of formal global capital into the diaspora-driven edges of the Nollywood industry, the only places in which it is able to invest. I look in particular at the case study of iROKOtv, a well-funded technology start-up, widely watched in the diaspora, hoping to become the 'Netflix of Africa', based on its carefully curated library of Nollywood content. This allows us to look at the immense disjuncture between the functioning of formal global capital and the logics of doing business in Lagos, in an industry run by a vast opaque informal network of small-scale entrepreneurs hostile to formality

In the conclusion, I bring all of these points together, looking broadly at Nollywood as an exemplar of cultural industry growth and functioning on the flipside – or outskirts – of the global Network Society: informal and following alternative networks, filling in the spaces between connections to the global Network Society and serving as an alternative media capital. I conclude that Nollywood, born of informality and continuing to thrive in conditions particularly inhospitable to the entry of major multinational entertainment firms and other formal global capital, owes its very existence to the huge gaps between connections to global networks.

In all of these ways, then, this book serves to interrogate the rise of new hubs and nodes in the global creative industries. Through an in-depth examination of Nollywood, a dominant popular movie producer for sub-Saharan Africa and the African diaspora, this book sets out to investigate the shape of networks and the differing realities facing creative industries growing in a state of highly fragmented and sparse connections to dominant global cultural industry networks. Nollywood, as a case study, offers us a chance to analyse the rise of a cultural industry from a state of relative exclusion from the global Network Society. This allows us to understand that which gives the industry strength and the implications of this research on debates surrounding global flows of culture, as well as debates regarding cultural industry formation.

NOTES
1. See Miller, 2010, for more on this in the context of the telenovela industry.

1
History: Nollywood Rising

Nollywood has become something of a trendy topic for features in the popular press in recent years, garnering profiles from CNN to *Esquire* to *The Economist*. The theme of many of these articles is the idea that Nollywood created itself, rising from virtually nothing in just the past twenty years, the product of local creativity and ingenuity in a place marked by bad news and lack. As is often the case in popular press articles, this characterisation is related to the truth but only scratches the surface, leaving out both the (rich) cultural history upon which Nollywood is based and the (minimal) relationship of most Nigerian industry to governmental support or protection. In this chapter, I look in greater detail at the formation of Nollywood, the industry, as an example of cultural industry growth in a very specific place, on the flipside of dominant global networks. In order to draw a fuller picture of Nollywood's history, we must look, first, at the specific political economic conditions and opportunities from which the industry emerged (certainly not 'nothing'), as well as the context through which we can view and understand the content of Nollywood movies and, then, the themes that emerge in this narrative. If we take this history and map it onto previously held truths about cultural industry growth, largely based on case studies from what has traditionally been referred to as the 'global North', we see clear areas of disjuncture and divergence. In light of the specific context of Nollywood's growth in Lagos and in Nigeria, this project allows us to look at cultural industry growth in light of the challenges and of the opportunities offered by location on the outskirts of dominant global networks and in a growing African mega-city: a context, perhaps, that is most relevant for cultural industry growth in the near future.

DEVELOPMENT OF NOLLYWOOD, 1990–2000: HUSTLE, HOPE AND HUBRIS

Nollywood, the industry, was born out of the combination of a number of conditions present in Nigeria at the beginning of the 1990s.[1] As background, it is important to note the significance of this timeframe. The late 1980s marked the advent of the World Bank-fuelled series of economic severity policies known as the Structural Adjustment Program (SAP). This fuelled rapid naira (the Nigerian currency) devaluation, plunging existent cultural industries into disarray and re-sorting even entertainment-seeking patterns in Nigerian society as a result of increased violence and theft, and an accompanying reluctance to leave the home. From this context, ironically coming shortly after a late 1970s oil boom-led dramatic *increase* in entertainment consumption (Haynes and Okome, 2000; Larkin, 2004), the other conditions relevant to Nollywood's growth also emerged.

First, there was the emergence of two different types of trained yet increasingly underemployed (and dissatisfied) pools of Nigerian creative talent. The first were actors, coming from a tradition of travelling theatre troupes among the Yoruba, who had for decades institutionalised a cultural tradition of acting as a paid profession, yet whose industry was experiencing a sustainability crisis by the early 1990s. The second were Nigerian Television Authority (NTA) employees. The NTA's policies at that time were squeezing trained soap opera creative workers off the air, from directors to videographers to actors. Added to this was technological opportunity: as the world was phasing out initial VHS technologies, Chinese and Malaysian businessmen and women were selling deadstock very cheaply to Nigerian electronics dealers. These elements (actors, soap opera workers and inexpensive new technologies) came together and formed the basis for something new in a moment of entrepreneurial clarity. This entrepreneurial moment was itself the product of specific political and economic conditions and a culture allowing for such dynamic progression. Before drawing from the themes of this story, let's first look in greater detail at the early years of Nollywood and the specific conditions of time and place, and of politics and economics, that provided both a window for the birth of the industry and the tools and opportunities it took to realise that opportunity. And before even that, let us begin with the story of Yoruba travelling theatre, a twentieth-century Nigerian popular entertainment phenomenon that predated, fed into and, in many ways, mirrors the Nigerian video boom of the past two decades.

Yoruba Travelling Theatre

We can begin with colonial Lagos of the early twentieth century: the milieu that gave birth to Yoruba travelling theatre. From the 1930s onward, Lagos was a magnet for aspirational migrants from a variety of backgrounds, and tiny Lagos Island, only a small corner of what is Lagos proper today, became a densely populated heterogeneous melting pot of diverse cultures, forming new societal norms (Barber, 2000). The groups flocking to Lagos at the time included former slaves returning from Brazil and Cuba, as well as anglophone countries, via Sierra Leone and significant rural–urban migrants. By 1931, new residents outnumbered those born in the area, and these new residents were hungry for educational and employment opportunities. Drawn by the promise of jobs, this new population was 'exceptionally diverse in terms of religion, class, occupation, and ethnicity' (ibid.: 23) and, perhaps most importantly for cultural production, was largely able to find waged labour. These jobs provided new workers with both leisure time and excess money, able to be spent on entertainment. Residents of Lagos, then, were open to money as a motor for their businesses and social lives, and were also open to any number of new foreign imports coming in through the ports. By the 1940s, amateur stagings of many different types of entertainment, from music to theatre, were seen (ibid.).

Cultural anthropologist Karin Barber attributes the birth of travelling Yoruba theatre in the late 1940s to the forces of urban expansion (Lagos tripled in size in just the 1950s alone), a post-war economic boom, a growth in education and anti-colonial nationalism that swept West Africa in the 1950s and 60s (Barber *et al.*, 1997). But, perhaps more than anything else, Barber *et al.* attribute the birth of the Yoruba theatre movement to the expanding cities, 'sites of entrepreneurship and innovation, the locus of new kinds of work … [where citizens] got used to paying for entertainment' (ibid.: 4–5), paying for tickets and sharing space in the audience with strangers.

The first major successful Yoruba theatre troupe film came from the godfather of the twentieth-century travelling Yoruba theatre troupe: Hubert Ogunde. Not only was his troupe different stylistically from the Yoruba theatrical performances that had come before (performing without masks, for instance, and introducing realism and dialogue into the plays), but his troupe also marked a change in the structure of the industry, eventually restructuring business models for popular entertainment throughout southern Nigeria and West Africa (Clark, 1979). Most importantly, Ogunde's troupe was the first to be supported solely via public patronage instead of that of elites (ibid.). This is important because it marks the emergence of a for-profit entertainment business structure in Nigerian-grown arts, a structure which directly paved the way for Nollywood's self-supporting business structure fifty years later. Ogunde introduced box offices, extensive written (posters and newspaper advertisements) as opposed to oral publicity, lighting and sound amplification, payment instead of apprenticeship for actors starting out and the promotion of actresses as stars and draws to a production in their own right (ibid.). We can see the parallels between these changes and the structure of theatre as business in the UK, Nigeria's colonial power. We can also see the offspring of these shifts in industry structure in the structure of Nollywood movies, incorporating a for-profit goal, written publicity, use of (relatively) contemporary technological equipment, payment on a per-job basis and a star system. Also significant was the reach of Ogunde's troupe into the recorded entertainment business, selling gramophone records of their performances in markets and record stores. Ogunde's troupe and the many similar troupes it spawned became a central part of southern Nigerian cultural production in the 1940s and ruled the entertainment scene through the 1970s, followed by an economic collapse-fuelled disintegration in the 1980s.

Nigeria's Yoruba drama troupes were composed of tightly knit bands of actors bound to one another in a family-esque unit. These troupes were extremely popular as they toured Yoruba-speaking areas, but, by the 1980s, the troupes were becoming increasingly large and unwieldy, and were having an increasingly difficult time making money from touring. As a fix, some Yoruba theatre entrepreneurs began filming their performances with 35mm and, more usually, 16mm cameras for later exhibition (Ogunleye, 2004). These exhibitions were usually at makeshift small-scale 'theatres': churches or meeting halls fitted for the showing with portable projection equipment. Members of the troupe were responsible for renting the venue, arranging projection, marketing and promotion and ticket sales, just as if it were a live drama troupe performance. Troupe members would almost always be present in order to ensure profits from ticket sales weren't falsified (ibid.). The first major Yoruba troupe film, Ola Balogun's *Ajani Ogun*, was made in 1976. As the oil boom boosted entertainment consumption in the late 1970s, a small number of filmed Yoruba hits followed, including Ogunde's *Aiye* (1979) and *Jaiyesinmi* (1983).

By the mid-1980s, these films had overtaken live theatre as preferred form of popular entertainment (Barber, 2000). While they were expensive to make, given the foreign post-production they necessitated, filmed performances were also popular among theatre troupes. For one, one film could feature star actors from a variety of productions, as a film was shot only once and didn't require the star's presence for an extended period of time. For a while in the 1980s, it appeared that Yoruba theatre troupe-driven films were set to become the new popular cultural form of choice in Nigeria. However, the economic collapse that came next severely delimited the ability of these troupes to finance such movies; live theatre was also in decline.

While some of these hits made the production of filmed theatre performances look promising to entrepreneurs, the reality was that film-making costs were too high for any serious profits to be made. All post-production occurred abroad, most often in London, as there were no facilities in Nigeria, and post-production costs (most notably, film processing) quickly dwarfed all other inputs to the film. It was similarly difficult to get funding and to distribute these Yoruba theatre-based films widely. However, production continued, though there was little thought that there was a sustainable industry hidden in the smattering of small-scale theatre troupe films.

VCRS, SOAP OPERAS AND THEATRE TROUPES ON SHIFTING GROUND

The second half of the 1980s introduced a number of particularly challenging conditions for the creation of any art forms in Nigeria, much less an expensive one requiring foreign exchange for post-production. These were the twin advents of economic hardships associated with the introduction of the World Bank-fuelled SAP and the spate of everyday hardships accompanying the Babanginda regime (see Haynes and Okome, 2000). In the SAP era, the naira underwent a rapid decline. Film-makers could no longer even hope to afford the expensive processing and post-production necessarily done in London. Any such entertainment would have to be remarkably inexpensive, as well as reliant only on a domestic production and distribution chain.

By the mid- to late 1980s, the Yoruba theatre troupes had moved on from 16mm to less expensive options. One was colour reversal stock (Adesanya, 2000). Colour reversal stock had the advantage of being much cheaper than film stock, and didn't need expensive lab development. The downside, however, is that the film could not be copied. The only existing copy in colour reversal is the original. This sole copy usually degraded quite quickly as it was screened multiple times. Less than ideal, colour reversal stock was considered a temporary fix for troupes and producers looking to keep costs down. Even with these savings, the plummeting naira led to further decline in film production as raising money became even more difficult and seriously impacted the sustainability of Nigeria's cultural movements, including Yoruba drama troupes and domestic soap opera production.

A number of other elements that marked these years also set the stage for the advent of Nigerian home video production. The Babanginda era was marked by increasing insecurity and violence in Nigeria's southern cities, including Lagos. Violence and insecurity were so endemic that people took to shutting themselves indoors from sunset to sunrise, abstaining from evening entertainment outside the home.[2] While this led to the death of most existent cinema houses in southern Nigeria, it opened space and demand for entertainment suited for home consumption.

As the era of the SAP and Babanginda began, there were still a number of popular soap operas produced, directed and acted in by Nigerian talent, on the air at the NTA.[3] However, in the early 1990s, a number of shake-ups hit and ultimately disrupted the robust Nigerian soap opera industry. For one, the economic decline meant less programme sponsorship by the major soap companies that had been their traditional source of support, and the advertising agencies that acted as the bridge between producers and the major soap companies were falling behind in paying (and in some cases not paying at all) the advertising funds owed to producers (Obaseki, 2008). At the same time, the NTA was pursuing a model of increased programme ownership. As producers balked at these conditions, the NTA also began getting particularly inexpensive deals for bulk buys of Latin American (primarily Mexican) telenovelas, squeezing out room for Nigerian-made productions during prime-time programming hours and filling the airwaves with nightly shows like the global Mexican-produced hit *The Rich Also Cry* (Igwe, 2009).

As the NTA was the only outlet, and only large soap companies such as OMO, Joy and Elephant were ready sponsors, outlets for soap operas were highly limited and growing increasingly so. Not only was the NTA's single station distribution suspected not to be meeting demand, but producers also believed that the NTA, acting as the sole gatekeeper, was keeping smaller and more daring entrepreneurs out (ibid.). Amaka Igwe, one of the prominent independent NTA producers from this era, reports that the disgruntled attitude of the top producers of the day was compounded by the new top-down NTA rules (meant to mitigate the squeezing of time slots) that, for example, restricted actors to acting in one NTA drama at a time, contributing to their exodus from soap operas (ibid.).

Against this SAP-fuelled background of disgruntled and squeezed-out soap opera talent on both sides of the camera, Yoruba drama troupes struggling to make money in the face of the falling naira and increasing insecurity came one more – vital – ingredient in the explosion of home video production. While these elements led to a glut of soap opera and Yoruba drama troupe creative talent, it was a glut of a different kind that opened up initial Nollywood development: the advent of VHS technologies purchased from Asian sources and dumped cheaply on the Nigerian market. Years before Nollywood was even born, a 1985 global technology report documented the boom in importation of television-based technologies that followed Nigeria's 1970s oil boom (Boyd and Straubhaar, 1985). Initially, VCR technologies were only the purview of the wealthy, but, even in 1985, observers were able to report some penetration to the middle classes and those lower classes 'seeking a means of earning a living from pirated cassettes' (ibid.: 13). Segun Olusola, a then managing director of the NTA, reported as early as 1983 that a few 'small local video production operations' had emerged, mainly taping performances of popular musical artists for resale (see ibid.: 64). He also reported in 1983 that 'video cassettes (blank, smuggled, pirated off-air or dubbed-off master copies) are available from roadside teenage vendors on all major roads in Lagos' (ibid.) and that the famous Alaba electronics market was already full of VCRs and tapes for sale. It was the beginning of the 1990s, however, that brought a concentration of VHS technologies en masse to Nigerian markets, as some of the technologies had become increasingly dated in the First World and used and deadstock VHS technologies became available at cut-price rates on the global marketplace. These technologies, including both older model VCRs and massive extraordinarily inexpensive shipments of blank tapes, were bought up by electronics vendors supplying remaindered technologies to developing markets. This is a familiar path for technologies recently upgraded in their initial markets. Technologies will first sell at full cost to initial markets, such as the USA, Japan, or the UK. Once an upgrade is introduced, the remaindered merchandise can be shifted to warehouses in global trading hubs like Singapore or Dubai, and can be sold wholesale in a lot to the highest bidder. These bidders are generally traders tasked with supplying goods to electronics markets in countries that are *not* in the first market. Nigeria was (and remains) a huge potential market for such products, as Lagos is a hub in the West African electronics trade. It was the advent of this increasingly low-cost technology flooding local electronics markets that gave birth to what we now know as Nollywood.

VIDEO MOVIES

By the late 1980s, Yoruba drama troupes had begun experimenting with video-based productions as a substitute for their celluloid films. Some Yoruba troupes delved into video production at this time, but their videos were essentially a single camera capturing a live performance, less creative than the cinematic production that preceded them, and created for sale to the small Yoruba-speaking middle-class population with access to VCRs (Haynes, 1995; Barber, 2000). By most accounts, these Yoruba video films are the most immediate predecessors of today's Nollywood films. Yet these video films were still entrenched in a business model that was based on both its drama troupe and celluloid roots. Even with the capability that videos offered for reproduction and distribution, the old model remained: multiple members of the drama troupe appearing in the movie would travel along with the official copy of it to exhibition halls and run all aspects of ticket sales and projection.

The break to the Nollywood model we can see today is credited to Kenneth Nnebue, an Igbo electronics trader dealing in imported used electronics equipment and blank VHS tapes. He noted not only the popularity of the Yoruba drama troupe movies in the Yoruba market, but also the economic implications of the new technologies being used. Those of Igbo descent, it is worth noting, have a reputation as being the most business-savvy of Nigeria's ethnic groups, seizing business opportunities from those places where nothing before existed. There is a saying in Nigeria to the effect that if a town has no Igbo living in it, there is nothing to be had there. As the Yoruba have a reputation as particularly culturally expressive among Nigeria's ethnic groups (though, of course, the Igbo

Kenneth Nnebue's *Living in Bondage* (1992)

and other ethnic groups in Nigeria have produced significant and well-regarded creative works as well), this combination of Igbo trader networks and organised Yoruba drama troupe talent would seem to be the perfect combination of two traditions of organisation: cultural and economic.

Kenneth Nnebue's first entry into the movie industry came in 1991 when he produced *Aje Ni Iya Mi*, a Yoruba-language video film, quite similar to those produced already by the drama troupes and aimed at Yoruba audiences. *Aje Ni Iya Mi* proved to be successful in the Yoruba market. Fresh from this success, it was in 1992 that Nnebue produced the video title almost universally cited as the first true Nollywood production: *Living in Bondage*, made in the Igbo language for 'a few hundred dollars' (Haynes, 2007b). *Living in Bondage* is considered a Nollywood classic, still widely viewed and the beneficiary of legendary success. The use of Igbo language opened up the video market to non-Yoruba and this movie is regarded as the catalyst for the explosion in video film production to come.

After the massive success of *Living in Bondage*, Nnebue returned two years later with the first English-language video film: *Glamour Girls*, released in 1994. Despite the success of his earlier movies, it was Nnebue's first foray into English-language production that opened up his and other entrepreneurs' eyes to the potential of the marketplace for English-language mass-market home videos made in Nigeria, now the backbone of the Nigerian movie industry.

Particularly in these initial years, video production in Nigeria was essentially open to any comers. The story of one small-scale producer, known popularly as Natty Bruce (full name Bruce Idigbogwu), who has been making movies for twenty years but has yet to make any profits – or, for the most part, even break even – from his own productions exemplifies the condition of this milieu. Natty Bruce, now living in Lagos, began trying to make movies in the 'bush' (the popular term for the countryside) in Igboland (as the southeast of the country, dominated by the Igbo ethnic group is known) even before Kenneth Nnebue made his first successful video for distribution (2009). Working as a DJ in a brothel, he was first inspired to make a movie in the mid-1980s after a chance encounter lent him the opportunity to see what a script looked like. Unschooled in every aspect of the movie-making process, Bruce utilised talent networks known to him: NTA workers from the local NTA station, those working in the local video production business (for hire for local weddings, funerals and banquets) and his own personal connections to a local community of martial arts enthusiasts more than happy to demonstrate their skills on camera for free. In terms of distribution, Bruce, too, followed the model he knew – that of public exhibitions – intending to create a master tape that he would show around Igboland (southeastern Nigeria). He was also able to utilise existent church and community centre networks for screenings, none of which made him back even his paltry initial investment.

Later, after Nnebue's innovations spurred an industry, Bruce was able to draw from others' successes. After seeing Nnebue's tactics, he realised he too could exploit networks of electronics traders and video 'pirates' (both nearly exclusively Igbo) for financing and distribution, and he eventually moved to Lagos to further pursue his dreams. While he eventually achieved a degree of fame as an action movie actor, has begun offering small-scale stuntman training courses to industry aspirants and has a central role in a number of guilds, Bruce has yet to achieve success or even a profit as a producer. It is, however, his ability to enter the industry with little training and eke out a living on its outskirts which speaks to the openness and penetrability of the industry throughout the stages of its development, perhaps particularly to an entrepreneur of Igbo descent. It may not be easy but it is possible with the right amount of hope, hubris and, most importantly, hustle. And it is his ability to draw from existent networks centred in Lagos that speaks to the magnetic self-increasing power of agglomeration and organisation.

Nnebue's foray quickly attracted an explosion in production as producers (much more professional than Natty Bruce) were drawn from the ashes of the

NTA's soap culture; electronics traders were drawn to add to their business model through funding, marketing and distributing these video movies. Both report being drawn by the lure of profitability, particularly in an era when many other business models were falling apart. Amaka Igwe,[4] for instance, the popular NTA producer and director, had begun working for the NTA only in 1990. By the time I interviewed her, she was a highly regarded member of the Nollywood elite, gracious and carrying herself with the gravitas that comes with years as an elder stateswoman of a popular and growing industry. In 1993, she was a young woman directing and producing her first top-rated soap opera, *Checkmate*. In that year, in the face of her and her colleagues' increasing frustration with changes at the NTA and the hardships brought by the SAP, Kenneth Nnebue approached her and commissioned her to write an English-language script for a new venture. She realised immediately that one could make twenty times the money in movies rather than soap operas, producing the same three hours of entertainment content (Igwe, 2009).

She was not the only one to realise this; many made the jump from soap operas to movies. Virtually all of the pioneering big-name directors of Nollywood came out of soap opera directors and producers of the early 1990s. It is not for nothing that many claim that Nollywood's closest stylistic cousin is the soap opera (Jedlowski, 2012; Haynes, 2010) rather than other film genres. In the beginning, says Igwe, there was no difference from the practitioner's standpoint between working on soap operas and working on films, though she says that has changed over the years with experience, evolution and training (2009). Thus, Nollywood was certainly not created completely from scratch. Yet when the NTA-as-the-sole-gatekeeper-of-limited-airtime model gave way to a diversity of independent producers (i.e. anyone who could raise the funds, or, as the Natty Bruce story illustrates, anyone who could hustle together a production with no real funds or connections), each able to find their own space in the marketplace (literally in stalls at the market), those producers were now capitalising on this same talent. In this way, initial penetrability and lack of entrenched business practices can be seen not only as an advantage, but also as one of the main assets marking networked cultural industry development in any context.

The impetus of the marketers (the distributors/executive producers are known colloquially as 'marketers' and are referred to as such throughout this project) was similarly financial. A man known as Gabosky (full name Gabriel Okoye) was one of these first few executive producers/distributors and, like almost all early marketers, began as an electronics importer. Though he is widely known as a Nollywood producer, much of his current business is still in the electronics trade. He strikes an imposing figure in his warehouse near the Alaba electronics market. When I visited his compound, I found myself being led through spacious and airy rooms in the quiet industrial outskirts of Lagos, past his shiny recent model Toyota SUV and through warehouse rooms full of shrink-wrapped mini-speakers and jumbles of stereo components. Unlike most marketers who dress in casual business attire – a collared shirt and cotton trousers, perhaps – Gabosky favours a degree of what Nigerians call 'swagger' in his personal appearance. He often wears a baseball cap or off-kilter fedora over a du-rag, and sometimes dons sunglasses in clearly un-sunny locations, an unusual ensemble for a Nigerian businessman. His entry into rooms often seems to be accompanied by a degree of fanfare; his SUV licence plate announces his arrival too, reading 'GABOSKY' and decorated with two interlinked Nigerian flags.

Gabosky produced two of the earliest and most popular Nollywood movies, still famous and successful today. He reports that his drive was simple: 'As a businessman, I know when I see something that will be a good business. When I saw there was a passion for home movies, it made sense' (2009). When he realised the potential suggested by *Living in Bondage*, he decided to invest in production himself. The workers on *Nneka, the Pretty Serpent* (1992), his first movie, were recruited from the NTA, where they had been soap opera and news producers. The movie was a financial success. Subsequent to this, Gabosky remained in both businesses: twenty years later, he still imports and sells European electronics and he still produces and distributes Nollywood movies. He has also spent time as a favoured distributor by the Nigerian Film and Video Censors Board (NFVCB) and other government initiatives because of his willingness to separate himself from the marketers. This favoured status has manifested itself by government designations that he head various initiatives to limit the power of the marketers, including an alternative guild and a very well-funded (though likely ineffective) initiative by a government-associated bank to start his own distribution network called G-Media.

Igwe and Gabosky are only two among many spurred by Nnebue's early successes with *Living in Bondage* and *Glamour Girls*. In 1994, the same year as Nnebue's English-language production, three video titles were sent for national approval to the NFVCB.[5] One year later, in 1995, the NFVCB received 201 video films and, in 1996, it received 250 video films. Video production levels climbed even further in subsequent years. By 2010, 921 video films were submitted to the NFVCB for review, and statistics on most of the first decade of this century feature similar figures. Unfortunately, recent changes within the NFVCB have led to a lack of accuracy and availability in such statistics since then. The trend of significant production, however, has been established, even if there are no longer reliable records.

It is worth noting that, as productions grew from existent talent bred in relatively legal and above-board contexts (NTA soap opera productions and Yoruba drama troupes), distribution and marketing grew from a different set of roots: the sellers of electronics (ranging from black to grey to white market) and existent sellers of cassettes and foreign movies. Many of these existent networks were those that made their money largely from black market and unauthorised content. Rather than being a shady or disreputable origin, in his seminal book on media in northern Nigeria, media anthropologist Brian Larkin (2004) points out that it was these networks of illegal and unauthorised distribution that enabled Nollywood's – and his focus, the northern Hausa video industry's – growth: without their existence, distribution networks would have had to have been formed from scratch. Chapter 2 deals in greater detail with the implications and legacies of these origins in the murky area between 'black' and 'legal' markets, particularly significant in the 'Fourth World', where informality, the black market and even technological failure can be seen as endemic – considering these qualities as potential building blocks as opposed to pure obstacles (ibid.).[6]

LAGOS AS A CREATIVE CITY

The tale of industrial development in Nollywood is a study in making something not from nothing, but from the unexpected – and not by design. Without governmental support or an overarching architect, Nollywood emerged as an industrial node in the spaces between more formal business endeavours. This stands as an example of creative industry development that flies in the face of much collective popular thinking on what makes creativity happen. Richard Florida may be the most well known of the armies of those writing prescriptions for cities wishing to become 'creative cities', home to the 'creative class' (2004). These prescriptions advise cities to create walkable arts districts with street cafés, industrial warehouses converted into live–work loft spaces and other amenities that appeal to an educated upwardly mobile class working in 'creative industries' from technology to publishing.[7] Is Lagos a creative city in Florida's definition of the phenomenon? (He particularly highlights rapid new technology dispersal and high tolerance for gay people in his formulas, two things in incredibly short supply in Lagos.) Did Surulere, the neighbourhood where many of Nollywood's directors are housed, abide by Florida-esque development and zoning advice, setting aside buildings for use by those working in the arts and creating arts walk evenings on the first Saturday of every month? Are Nollywood movie-makers part of Florida's touted leisure-oriented mobile creative class, attracted to Lagos because of its attractive quality of life and amenities? Such questions seem patently absurd (no, no and no, would clearly be the answers, as the lack of official planning, zoning, security and government oversight – and intense challenges of life in Lagos – render it as far from Florida's creative city platonic ideal of Austin, Texas, as could be), but this history leads us to look at *how* creative industries develop in different types of places. Can we think of Lagos as an archetypal creative city using a different set of terms? What does the explosion of Nollywood movies – and other art forms like Yoruba theatre before them – in Lagos tell us about the propensity for cities like Lagos to produce creative industries? What is it about Lagos?

Discourse on the 'creative city' has centred around ways that cities can enact hands-on policy to support the emergence of creative industries. Yet we can see here that it was, if anything, the lack of government attention that contributed to Nollywood's rise in Lagos. In her definitive study of Yoruba travelling theatre of the twentieth century, Barber (2000) limns the many factors that led Lagos to be a hub of Nigerian cultural production throughout the last century, as Nigeria moved from colonial rule to autonomy, and as Lagos itself grew to the magnetic megalopolis it is today. Both the main port of Nigeria and the main seat of the colonial government, Lagos provided both commercial and political opportunities that far out-paced that of outlying areas. Lagos, in Barber's telling, was a magnet for aspiration, rural–urban migration and cultural innovation, beginning at least in the 1930s, as its dynamic growth began to fast exceed that of other cities in West Africa. That initial magnetism had long-lasting implications that served as a basis for Nollywood's development in the same location.

This is a story of the city as creative milieu in its role as magnet to migrants from disparate backgrounds and place of freedom from restrictive social customs. And this story is echoed in the stories of other cities of creative milieus. Those who have theorised about why and how particular cities have served as incubators for creative production have tended to focus on cities from the global North, particularly Silicon Valley for technological innovation and Los Angeles for its film industry, both products of different ends of California at different ends of the twentieth century. The birth stories of these two creative milieus have much in common with that of Lagos as the incubator of Nigerian popular arts (both Yoruba theatre and Nollywood). All three stories emphasise each area as a place with a certain distance from conservative mores, a place that served as a magnet for people of diverse backgrounds to come and make their own way, realising entrepreneurial opportunities in a place previously thought to house few such chances. One theme pervades these varied individual tales (as opposed to the consultant-designed 'creative city'): openness. Informality, penetrability and even the opportunities offered by new technologies all speak to the same driver of creative industry growth: opportunity for new ideas, new people and unofficial, non-overseen transactions to enter, meet and grow. While informality and openness surround the birth years of all of these industries, the existent models of creative industry growth are based on stories of places like Hollywood and Silicon Valley: industries coming of age in a nation with a majority formal national economy and accessible legal infrastructure. For instance, while Hollywood wasn't a popular investment magnet in its initial years, it was growing in conditions that could hypothetically (and did, in fact) match up quite quickly to existent functioning formalised industrial processes. How do these models change if we consider creative industry development in the context of Nollywood?[8]

The story of this book is the story of the industrialisation and globalisation of a cluster of creative production growing up out of a somewhat similar setting to Hollywood, and to the many cultural hub cities of the 'global North' that went before it. The similarities lie in the informalities and the largely government-free mentality of a place initially off the global radar. However, the more important factors contributing to Nollywood's birth, growth and success are those areas in which Nollywood and Lagos are extremely different from the realities that have made up the bulk of economic geography studies or creative industries studies based on Hollywood, Silicon Valley and other Network Society success stories. Before drawing conclusions, let's first examine more closely those realities.

THE DISEMBEDDED 'FOURTH WORLD' AND THE GLOBAL ORDER

In his work (1998) on the rise of a globally interlinked world order based on access to and integration into globalisation processes and connective networks that he deemed the 'Network Society', sociologist Manuel Castells focuses also on those left out of this world order. He describes the rise of what he and others have referred to as the 'Fourth World', rising from the ashes of a now defunct 'Second World' (the USSR and its cohort of affiliated nations) and the 'Third World', which is seen by many as an increasingly meaningless grouping after the fall of the Soviet Union. The term 'Third World' has fallen out of favour not only because of its lack of specific significance in a post-Soviet world, but also because it is seen by some as a blanket term referring to entire countries as hopelessly challenged and existing in a constant state of underperformance and underdevelopment. While 'Fourth World' has stylistic similarities to this term, laden with negative connotations, it is also useful in the precision of its shifting definition: it refers only to those places at any given point that can be considered to be excluded from the amorphous Network Society. These places may be central to alternative global networks. The term 'Fourth World', then, refers to a state of exclusion from dominant global networks as opposed to static and specific places and nation-states at a permanent disadvantage. While the term is particularly specific and descriptive in the context of the subject matter of this book, I use it here only in quotes to signify the ways in which it is shorthand for the experience of exclusion as opposed to any static defined place.

The 'Fourth World' is a non-geographically discrete land of exclusion, on the rise with the advent of the connectivity of the Network Society (ibid.): exclusion from the possibility of making a living wage and isolation not just from a distant global elite, but also from the very members of the global Network Society living in the same city, perhaps even in the same quarter. For the 'Fourth World', unlike the Second and Third Worlds, is not constituted by nation-states; the individual 'places' constituting the 'Fourth World' can be conceived of as being as large as an entire region and as small as a hidden apartment of undocumented immigrants or a neighbourhood of urban poor in a global elite city such as New York, London, or Paris. As some segments of the world – those which offer value to global networks of power, wealth and information – are linked through global networks, their very physical neighbours are easily excluded, existing in the gaps between connections in the Network Society.

These characteristics[9] are particularly relevant to the Information Age, as global connections become the currency of the day. Sub-Saharan Africa itself can be considered a case study in exclusion. Africa as a continent and sub-Saharan Africa as a region are not totally excluded; indeed, there are elite in the major cities of every country who can be considered completely plugged in to global circuits, and the global oil, diamond and other precious metals industries are hard at work in pockets of the continent, linked to official global networks of sales, refinement and finance in their efforts to exploit the local natural resources. However, while some African citizens do profit from this, the money is not spread around widely. Africa as a whole is specifically disenfranchised by its 'fragmented incorporation' (ibid.: 91) into the global order and Nigeria is no exception.

Urban theorist AbdouMaliq Simone (2001) has developed a thorough theory of the complex play between the global order and the highly localised nature of the city in the African context. He makes the claim that no African cities are 'world cities' or 'global cities' in the sense of the traditional literature on the topic. Instead, urban Africa can be described as a series of localised informal networks operating on generally unsustainable platforms with their own informal networks of connections to the global. Simone takes as his starting point the history of cities in Africa: grown by colonial authorities for the primary purpose of transporting exploited local resources through to global networks. Yet, even in colonial times – and carried through to the post-colonial era – the African city is also a site of under-regulated spaces, spaces rife with informal and non-state-sanctioned opportunity. However, these new opportunities are limited – while some urban African residents can connect to the global order, there has never been restructuring of the global economic order to enable them to dominate as a collective whole. Instead, Simone's urban African cities house a vast sea of individual opportunities in their unsupervised realms, connecting some but never the city as a whole. The economy of the African city, in Simone's telling, is and has always been linked to global capital. Yet the urban economy's relationship to the global order has extensive gaps along with its connections, and it is in the gaps more than in the connections that urban African residents locate their own opportunities.

In places such as Lagos, we can see the specificities of this fragmented incorporation that contrasts dramatically with the global Network Society. The global Network Society has a tangible physical architecture embedded in the local: fibre-optic cables go from one physical location to another; business parks are built with direct information and transportation links to other hubs; motorways and high-speed trains bypass distractions as they link business centres to airports. This has been referred to as 'glocal infrastructure' (Graham and Marvin, 2001), as it is, by definition, first local in nature, a physical element of the city. Yet, at the same time, this piece of physical architecture is the very device that enables those nodes to connect to the global, and to bypass all of the purely local elements in between. It is in assessing this physical networked infrastructure that the experience of exclusion from the system best comes into focus. In much of the global 'Fourth World' not only are high-speed fibre-optic connections often an impossibility, but some more basic infrastructures also bypass localities: water, landline telephone connections, roads, security, electricity.

In Lagos, none one of these above-mentioned things can be relied upon. The majority of residents source water outside a municipal supply. Telephone wires are seen jumbled in heaps all around Lagos, fallen from their posts, dragging on the ground and tangled with one another. Businesses provide landline phone numbers to prospective clients mostly as a formality, as something that should be included on a business card. Without a mobile phone number as a supplement, one is unlikely to even get the phone to ring, much less contact someone at the business. Serious businesspeople will carry two or more mobile phones, one on each cellular network, to maximise the chances of getting a signal. Roads, too, are a reminder of infrastructural discreteness from global circuits in Lagos. Not only do enormous potholes bog down traffic, particularly in rainstorms, but also the road system appears to be largely untouched by changes or repairs since the mid-1970s, despite an exponential increase in the number of cars driving and decades of wear and tear (though it is worth noting that in the past few years, roads have begun to noticeably improve around Lagos thanks to Babatunde Fashola, governor of Lagos State from 2007 to 2015, particularly in wealthier enclaves). There are hardly any traffic lights and hardly any roads that are not clogged during the daylight hours. Okadas, or motorbikes, that weave in and out of traffic are a way of life: virtually anyone seen driving one can be paid around $1 to take passengers a short distance, and it is not uncommon to see middle-class businessmen exit their chauffeured car and hop on the back of one of the ubiquitous bikes in order to make it to a meeting on time. Okadas stand in for a formalised address system and maps as well, as the same $1 can hire an okada to drive in front of one's car, leading strangers from the better-known main road to their sought destination on a side street known only to neighbourhood residents.

It is security and electricity that are two of the biggest infrastructural disjunctures in Lagos, however. Electricity is so unreliable that practically every functioning business and the majority of middle- or upper-class urban households use generators daily to supplement government-supplied power at a great expense. A recent World Bank report estimated that 10 per cent of Nigerian companies' revenues are devoted to private power acquisition, including the cost of generators, their supplies and their operation (Foster and Pushak, 2011).[10] This cost also constitutes at least 3.7 per cent of the nation's GDP, but World Bank researchers estimate it to be two or three times that (ibid.). The implications of this lack of infrastructure not only impose extra burdens on the cost of doing business in Nigeria, but also bring into full focus the experience of disjuncture between daily life and connectivity to formalised global networks. It is in this context that Nigeria's home video production emerged and began to industrialise – a process that, for all of its similarities to the models of peripheral growth highlighted in existent renditions of creative industry development, has been and is still being performed under conditions quite different as a whole from that in most other case studies.

This theme comes up in studies of the rise of cultural industries emerging from the outskirts of or outside the global cultural industry networks and a look at these can illuminate the specific opportunities and challenges offered to Nollywood by Nigerian and Lagosian infrastructure. Economic geographers Dominic Power and Daniel Hallencreutz (2004), for instance, compare two well-known powerhouses in global music production: Stockholm, Sweden, a production hub for global pop music, and Kingston, Jamaica, a hub for independent producers and musicians taking inspiration in part from a local music scene. Both industries have only a small potential domestic market yet have been able to link up with global distribution chains, attracting attention and business deals from the global 'majors' (major labels). Yet, while Kingston's products have a higher collective commercial value on the retail market, it is Stockholm's musicians and producers that make the larger real collective profits (ibid.).

The reasons for this are manifold, but each reason leads back to one central theme: level of 'links between the local production system and the international circuits of capital, distribution, and effective property rights' (ibid.: 224). In other words, this study found that the level and quality of links between the local and the global determine economic value of each industry's cultural production. The links in this instance are virtual, in the sense of flows of cultural products and business deals, as well as quite physical: each of the major global music labels has a presence in Stockholm, all through wholly owned subsidiaries located in one particular Stockholm neighbourhood. In Kingston, in contrast, the Jamaican government and local industry heads have traditionally spurned the attempts of global major labels to locate offices there. As such, the city is virtually devoid of any entrenched global music industry interests. Power and Hallencreutz note that, while Kingston's music industry has a number of significant linkages to the global majors, there are many wide gaps between those links – and even the existent links are often under strain due to 'cultural differences' (ibid.). They conclude that Kingston's lower profitability compared to its collective-retail-value inferior Stockholm is attributable to these gaps: from slower adoption of new music production and distribution technologies to less internal organisational ability to protect themselves from intellectual property rights violations. On the one hand, we can note the positive effect that the distance between Jamaica's music industry and the global majors consistently may have on production and innovation, and the remarkably reliably high level of creativity evident in the series of globally popular musical genres that have emerged from the local music scene over the past few decades. The corollary to this is Jamaica's difficulties in reliably and consistently profiting from its innovative and popular musical production. If the goal is sustainable financial success on the level of global pop-stardom, it is in their disembeddedness from the global order where they have their biggest barrier to achieving this goal. On the other hand, that is far from the only possible goal of music production and many in the industry are satisfied with maintaining their autonomy.

In this way, we can see many parallels between this case study and the case study of Nollywood. Born of informality and continuing to thrive in an industrial structure particularly inhospitable to the entry of major multinational entertainment firms, Nollywood too exists in the gaps between connections to global networks. Nollywood, like Kingston's music industry, exists and derives much of its creative strength in a place of highly fragmented incorporation into dominant global cultural industry networks. This lack of formality means that financing and production is also unstable. When taken in the context of previous work done on cultural industry growth, and particularly in the policy recommendations cities commission to advise them on how to become hubs of creative production, we can see the gaps in previous theories and the very different conditions faced by cultural industries growing in a state of disembeddedness from the global Network Society.

The development of Bollywood, India's movie industry based in Mumbai, can also throw into relief different contexts in which creative clusters can industrialise. Like Nollywood, Bollywood's current production processes emerged from informality (though, in the case of Bollywood, that informality itself was born of a formal studio structure flourishing in the earlier part of the twentieth century). A 1997 Indian newspaper estimated that 40 per cent of Hindi films made in India in the 1990s were financed by 'dubious money' (Koppikar, 1997, cited in Athique, 2008). As in Nollywood, this includes so-called 'pirates' themselves investing in production and gradually being integrated into the system as financiers and distributors (Pendakur, 2003; Athique, 2008). In both industries, unlicensed distribution, VCR and other new technologies and informal distribution points – like small grocers – enabled growth in global markets without an influx of global capital. When mapping both industries, we can see the use of alternative networks with alternative hubs – such as Dubai or Jakarta – for supplies and distribution, as constitutive of an alternative infrastructure supporting an alternative growth. Just as Simone described in his analysis of African cities, those disembedded hubs, existing largely outside the global order, create their own alternative international circuits (more on this in Chapter 5). We can see too the power of growing demand for content that feels local in places not central to the global cultural industry networks. And we also see their birth from a rapidly growing mega-city. While Bollywood was birthed in Mumbai years ago, we can see that the pressure and creativity of the 'Fourth World' mega-city forms its own variety of incubator of explosive growth.

At the same time, Bollywood has become increasingly formalised since the late 1990s (Lorenzen and Taeube, 2006). Once the federal government changed the industry's classification in the Indian financial system to an investable industry, banks, global capital and increased partnerships with major media MNCs began to take hold. That the federal government was even able to accomplish such a shift with one fell swoop speaks to the power and reach of the Indian national government in its national industries. I argue that this increasing integration into dominant global cultural industry networks, fuelled by government decisions, renders Bollywood increasingly a part of those networks. And, as elaborated upon in the subsequent chapters, I believe the power of the marketers means such formalisation is unlikely to take hold in Nollywood in the foreseeable future.

CONCLUSION

In Nollywood's growth story, we can see the possibilities offered by the burgeoning industry's penetrability and lack of entrenched business interests. We can see Nollywood as exemplary of growth in the global urban periphery, in the sense of being periphery to the dominant global system. The product of a state of exclusion from dominant global cultural industry networks, and an example of the fragmented incorporation of the African city into the global order, Nollywood faces similar challenges in its relationship to the global movie industry to the challenges we saw the Kingston music industry face in its relationship to the global music industry. The gaps between connections to the global order offer space and room to grow in an environment of freedom and entrepreneurial flexibility and creativity. These same gaps offer challenges. Like Kingston's music industry, Nollywood experiences difficulties in acquiring formal funding, acquiring and utilising the newest of technologies and integrating effectively with the global networks that have the potential to maximise funding and returns.

In this way, we can see that the development of Nollywood is inseparable from its position as partially disembedded from the global order, a position that offers both opportunities and challenges. And the location of Nollywood in not only a city of fragmented incorporation into the global order, but also a nation – and a continent – that epitomise fragmented incorporation into the global order mark it as distinctive from industries that rose in a peripheral or frontier-esque city that still benefited from its location in the so-called 'global North'. We can see the emergence of Nollywood as a product of the opportunities emerging from existent cultural industries (Yoruba drama troupes and NTA soap operas), technological development (VHS) and SAP-induced changes in Nigeria, as well as a product of its specific Nigerian environment, itself an example of the condition of exclusion from dominant global networks. It is a story of making a functioning industry out of an architecture that might first appear barren to those understanding cultural industry development based on models that describe such growth in North America or Western Europe. It is a story of creativity and innovation on the other side of the global network of culture industries. I address next the current map of Nollywood, the industry: the production and distribution processes that have emerged, and how the industry functions in a simultaneous state of connectivity (to alternative and dominant circuits), fragmentation and disembeddedness.

NOTES

1. The history told here is, in part, informed by histories conducted by researchers who have gone before me, particularly Jonathan Haynes (1995); Jonathan Haynes and Onookome Okome (2000); Afolabi Adesanya (2000); Brian Larkin (2008) and Foluke Ogunleye (2004). I have independently verified much of this information and supplemented it through interviews with those involved first hand in the birth and development of the industry. I cite here facts I did not verify myself or that did not appear across a majority of written histories.

2. This feeling of insecurity and the measures taken against it are still in evidence today in Lagos.
3. As Haynes notes (2010), conceptions of 'high' arts versus popular arts as a subject worthy of study in the academy have meant that there are many extensive studies on Yoruba travelling theatre with little correspondingly done on NTA soap operas.
4. Who, sadly, passed away in 2014.
5. The National Film and Video Censors Board was established in 1993. Not only does it censor and classify films, but it also keeps what have traditionally been the best official records of Nigerian film and video productions. Despite the lack of governmental input into most of the industry, NFVCB approval has usually been considered vital by most, though recent upheaval has challenged this imperative. Until recent years, most producers submitted their titles for review, leading the NFVCB to be the industry's de facto record keeper and sole statistician. A change of leadership in the agency and its echoes in the past few years has led to these figures no longer being reliable – or even available.
6. This is not, of course, to romanticise disembeddedness. Nollywood producers repeatedly speak of how they would prefer their technology to work, greater accountability and greater transparency in the financing and distribution realms.
7. Critiques usually note the synonymity of this 'creative class' and gentrifiers.
8. This question has been asked by other scholars of Nigerian cultural production, such as Brian Larkin, seeking to redefine media anthropology from a Nigerian perspective (2004), or Noah Tsika, seeking to reimagine star studies with Nollywood as the key case study (2015).
9. '[T]he territorial confinement of systematically worthless populations, disconnected from networks of valuable functions and people' (Castells, 1998: 164)
10. In their 1989 report distributed by the World Bank, Lee and Anas found that private infrastructure provision (generator electricity combined with other infrastructural fixes) constituted 10 per cent of large firms' machinery and equipment costs and 25 per cent of small firms', suggesting that the cost for small firms could be much higher here as well. The World Bank occasionally commissions and/or otherwise publishes studies of this nature, but they do not collect all of this data repeatedly on a pre-planned recurrent basis. Therefore, 1989 is the last time infrastructure provision as part of firm cost by size was systematically measured. This twenty-five-year-old data is best used as a way to understand the possible extensions of the more current data on generator costs cited in text.

2
Nollywood in Nigeria: Production and Distribution

One of the most open events I attended as part of my research was an audition held in an off-hours bar in Surulere, the Lagos neighbourhood that serves as the hub of Nollywood's production companies, directors and professional associations. Outside, in the patio area of this bar, well over a hundred acting hopefuls sweated it out on folding chairs, waiting for their chance to approach the table of producers in groups of three, reading parts from the scenes provided to them. The intensity of the sun and the repetitiveness of the same scene being read out time and again by aspiring actors of varying skill led me to seek shelter in the actual bar for a time. What I found there was a very different scene. There was a sort of hierarchy. Outside, the industry hopefuls waited their turn, while inside the bar was a den of mid-level to well-known screenwriters, actors, producers and directors. As representatives from each guild are required to be present at each audition, the inside of the bar at this open-air audition became an excuse for Nollywood to physically meet one another. This was the elite or the sub-elite of Nollywood – everyone knew one another's name; some tables were more coveted than others. I fell in with a group of regularly employed actresses all smoking cigarettes, something 'respectable' women rarely do in public in Nigeria. They gossiped about trends in the industry (Soaps more reliable than movies! Bigger actresses getting more work once they lost weight!) and joked with the men in the room chiding them about their smoking habit. I was then invited from their table by a guild leader to go to talk to the table of guild presidents gathered in another even more exclusive room. The actresses winked and wished me luck, some inviting me to come see their soap operas shooting some time. Nollywood, in this context, was a tangible and familiar place, where, once introduced properly, one can feel oneself among friends. Of course, for those actors outside anxiously waiting their turn at the audition, Nollywood likely felt much less penetrable, much more closed. Despite the proclamation at the beginning of the audition that everyone's chances were equal and that decisions were to be made based on talent alone, when I saw the call-back auditions in a production company office the next day, I recognised nearly every actor from having spent time with them inside the bar at the audition, from seeing them on another movie shoot or in a completed movie, or from some other known Nollywood context.

Despite the low cost and rampant unauthorised distribution that marks the industry, Nollywood is a huge business with a well-defined structure and hierarchy, employing thousands. It has been variously estimated to make anywhere from $600 million (Oh, 2014) to $5 billion (over 1 trillion naira) (NBS, 2015) in annual sales, in inherently shaky estimates that valiantly attempt to incorporate global and unauthorised revenues via data collection channels that have been accused of unrealistic estimation in the past (see *The Economist*, 2015). Despite the rise of television viewing within Nigeria, and online viewing throughout the diaspora, the core of Nollywood, the basis for its sustainability and the focus of this book is at the heart of the industry: physical distribution of hard copies of Nollywood titles in open-air marketplaces.

Profits and expenses are a closely guarded secret by those involved in them, and few will publicly admit to experiencing great returns. This is in part to limit the risk of government authorities and business partners asking for a cut, but it speaks to the overwhelming culture of the industry: informal in the extreme, avoiding the possibility of documentation at every turn. For the most part, the distributors head the industry, and profits come for them in the context of quantity: made from collective returns over a wide catalogue of movie productions, as opposed to a blockbuster mentality of exceptional returns from any one individual production. It is the premise of this book that control over distribution and power are inseparable, both in Nollywood and in media industries worldwide, and that the dominance of the informal in Nollywood is key to understanding the industry's power structures and future.

The questions of what, exactly, informality is, and whether it should be celebrated have been subject to much scholarly debate, particularly in the context of media distribution studies, and Nollywood has been at the core of many of these arguments (see Lobato, 2010). There has been concern over the potential to exoticise and 'orientalise' Nollywood or Lagos via an overabundance of focus on and blind celebration of the informal in the industry (Gandy, 2005; Jedlowski, 2013a; Mboti, 2014). In part for these reasons, I wish to be very clear what exactly I mean by informality in Nollywood, and the ways in which it is a conscious choice in a global power play. In this chapter, I work to highlight the specific functioning of this informality within Nollywood's infrastructure and the ways it plays out in the industry. The basic intersecting constituents of informality in Nollywood, as spelled out in this book, are understood to be 1) *not documenting sales* or most other distribution figures in any publicly accessible or externally scrutinisable fashion, 2) *not utilising prosecutable legal contracts* for employment or other business relationships, 3) *not using agents* or other formal inputs such as accredited schools for talent recruitment, 4) *not pursuing copyright violations* via legal frameworks and 5) *privileging undocumented financing and distribution network*s and spurning alternatives (collectively not pursuing in good faith any of the four aforementioned areas of potential formalisation when opportunity presents). It may be noted that four of these five elements begin with the word 'not'. This is because our understanding of informality as an industrial feature worthy of mention exists only because of the existence of formality in these areas in other industries. Informality is only visible through comparison to formal alternatives and would otherwise be an unremarkable business practice. Informal media scholar Ramon Lobato defines this divide in a similar way: 'Formality refers to the degree to which industries are regulated, measured, and governed by the state and corporate institutions. Informal distributors are those which operate outside this sphere' (2012: 4). Without the existence of state and corporate oversight of business, we would not identify informality as a practice.

What draws these together is a lack of externally verified documentation and lack of reliance on external infrastructure (schools, courts, etc.). To be clear, the distinction between formality and informality is not a dichotomy but is rather a continuum, with no industry falling fully at either extreme. After all, even the most formal of media industries incorporate informal elements in aspects of labour recruitment (e.g. circumventing the labour market by giving a job to a friend's daughter) and labour relations (e.g. not pursuing a grievance in order to remain in good standing in the industry), while film accounting practices have been maligned as overly 'creative' and obfuscatory in nearly every industry selling movies. And Nollywood as an industry also features some formal elements in its production inputs and distribution outlets, such as its responsiveness to the censorship authority.[1] That said, the dominance and intersection of the above five elements in Nollywood's day-to-day functioning render the industry as *predominantly* informal as opposed to the *fragmented* informality that characterises many other global media industries.

In this chapter, I outline the processes of movie production and distribution in Nollywood, from financing to production to distribution, highlighting the relationship between distribution and power, and the informality, black and grey market networks and relationships of trust that are particularly relevant to this Nigerian creative industry – and, arguably, to any movie industries growing out of places largely excluded from the Network Society. In that vein, before going into the specifics on processes of movie production and distribution in Nigeria, I will be looking at Nollywood as growing out of a very specific place: Lagos, a rapidly expanding overflowing global mega-city. The structure of Nollywood reflects the specific architecture and shape of Lagos.

NOLLYWOOD, THE PLACE

'Where is Nollywood?' asked a neophyte on a Nollywood message board. The mirthful and mocking responses were plentiful. 'Nowhere!' said many, while others were more specific, citing places where one can, indeed, see Nollywood at work. One answer could be Idumota Market, a crowded chaotic marketplace on Lagos Island that was originally the centre of distribution and continues to sell large quantities (one street in particular is given over to stand after stand after stand of video film vendors). Another answer could be Alaba Market, a vast sprawling electronics market on the outskirts of Lagos that succeeded Idumota as the nerve centre of distribution and serves to house the head offices of many marketers. Surulere is another answer. This is the neighbourhood in mainland Lagos where most producers, directors and other creative professionals maintain offices and, in many cases, live. Far from the oil money-built towers of Victoria Island, Surulere is a middle-class neighbourhood populated by quiet residential streets of low-lying buildings and is home to most production offices and their post-production workspaces. Another answer is O'Jez's, a bar and restaurant in Surulere's National Stadium that serves as a meeting point and sometimes site of business deals. With the exception of O'Jez's, the offices and other workspaces of Nollywood in Surulere are unmarked and the streets are largely residential; besides the lively O'Jez's, most of Surulere's Nollywood workspaces will not lead to chance encounters for the uninitiated. Nollywood scholar Jonathan Haynes writes on the geography of Nollywood in Lagos, noting that the small amount of capital per entrepreneur has meant that the large spaces that mark other, more flashy movie industries – studios, theatres, large office complexes – don't exist here, and Nollywood is invisible to the street as it functions largely behind small unmarked doors (2007b). There are no soundstages or production studios here or anywhere else in the Nigerian movie business.[2] Another specific answer could be 51 Iweka Road, a building in Onitsha, a city in Igboland in southeastern Nigeria, in which many Igbo marketers base their business despite their presence in Lagos, housing an inordinate number of small production companies' offices in a row.

Despite international distribution and penetration throughout Nigeria, and despite its sister or parent offices in places like Onitsha, Nollywood remains centred on Lagos. Lagos is a growing global mega-city that is often cited as growing 'off the grid'. Possibly home to 21 million (Rosenthal, 2012), with less than a third connected to a public water supply as measured by Nigeria's statistical body (NBS, 2012), Lagos could be on its way to becoming the third largest city in the world, depending on how you count and who is counting. In understanding Lagos, the fungibility of the 21 million population figure is as important as the sheer size of the population it refers to. Just as with figures on Nollywood,

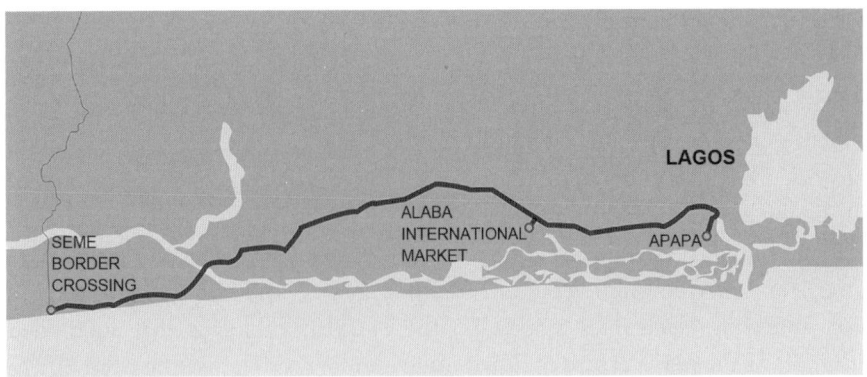

Alaba International Market, on the highway connecting Lagos's Apapa port to the Benin border at Seme

the contestation of Lagos's population statistic speaks to the culture of Lagos at large: mostly informal, undocumented and essentially unable to be counted and formalised by those who make their living counting such things. The production of such statistics is not just an academic exercise. Statistical proof of everything from population to sales figures has significant financial implications, directly affecting applications for everything from individual small business loans to national development grants to the terms of a national loan from the World Bank. The difficulties involved in producing statistics such as these mirror the difficulties involved in producing statistics about Nollywood itself, and the accompanying difficulty of investing in or even writing about the industry from an international vantage-point.

Alaba International Electronics Market is one location of Nollywood that epitomises the nature of the industry in its very structure. The sprawling market exists on the outskirts of Lagos. Journeying there in a taxi, one will emerge from the densely populated urban maze that is central Lagos into a dusty spread of low-lying disconnected buildings speckling the landscape, until Alaba itself is reached. Alaba is a city unto itself, with streets, churches, banks and apartments, though all look similar: low, dusty and constructed of inexpensive materials. The market, according to a rough and somewhat questionable estimate from over a decade ago, *may* be the epicentre of 75 per cent of West Africa's electronics trade, housing 50,000 merchants and netting $2 billion each year (figures, again to be taken with as many grains of salt as possible, are from Koolhaas *et al.*, 2001[3]). At Alaba, one can purchase anything from new flat-screen televisions to used generators to, of course, physical copies of movies.

Alaba (located on the side of the highway leaving Lagos, heading west for the Benin border) stands right where the largest Nigerian (and West African) electronics market could be expected to stand, directly between two sources of product importation: one formal (Apapa port) and one informal (the Benin border at Seme), as architects Koolhaas *et al.* pointed out in their look at Alaba as an urban phenomenon (ibid.). The location also separates Alaba from any government officials wanting to create 'order' or control the market in other ways. While markets like Idumota are in more vertical, densely populated areas in Lagos, Alaba can spread out as far as it would like without running into anything that the city would consider important enough to protect or pay attention to. The only efforts at delimitation come from within. Essentially 'dumped' (ibid.: 702) in the middle of nowhere, the market has thrived on official neglect, forging its own global network of connections out of a locale that was not only disconnected from the world order, but also from Nigeria and from Lagos itself.

Alaban infrastructure is much like that of Lagos: improvised and astounding. Koolhaas *et al.* (ibid.) reference a statistic that, even though it may lack veracity,[4] gives an idea of the scale and atmosphere of the market: that Alaba has the highest concentration of generators in the world. Each stall owner has his or her own 'gen' and many also have their own communication system. Merchants have private radiowave towers to ensure mobile phone service. Koolhaas *et al.* report that the merchants of Alaba, now institutionalised as an important centre for trade, have also collectively developed its surrounding areas, building a car park, local secretariat, fire station and electricity sub-station, as well as a local library, stocking all of the books and televisions in it.

This city and context form the backdrop for a number of specific conventions that guide the industry and Alaba serves as not only a hub, but also a metaphor for Nollywood. The next sections of this chapter will lay out in detail those specific conventions: how business in Nollywood works and how a movie goes from financing to distribution via informal trust-based networks with more connections to Nigerian black and grey market networks than to dominant global networks. These networks centralise power in the hands of the marketers, and the themes of creative improvisation and the power of informal fixes mark Alaba, Lagos and Nollywood alike.

INDUSTRY STRUCTURE AND PLAYERS

The backbone of Nigeria is its domestic circulation of physical copies of movies in open-air markets. These circuits of distribution are controlled by a group known in Nigeria as 'marketers',[5] but it would be more accurate to call them executive producers, distributors and financiers. The marketers for English-language movies are mostly from the Igbo ethnic group, the same group that pioneered English-language movies in the 1990s; their power is based in large part in their control over the opaque networks of open-air electronics markets

Kunle Afolayan's *Phone Swap* (2011)

through which Nollywood is primarily distributed domestically. Their distribution, like that of many straight-to-video (STV) industries, is predicated on the interchangeability of titles – a similarity between movies that renders none as a particularly risky investment. Also, like other STV industries, profits are made from quantity rather than bets on the quality of a few more creative, riskier movies.

Through the years, there has been much rancour and distrust between the marketers – sometimes referred to just as 'Alaba', for the market in which many are headquartered – and the creative arm of the industry, particularly among the well-known directors. Various efforts have attempted to capture power from the marketers and provide the creative arm with the possibility of bigger budgets and more creative control. While these efforts have been ongoing, in the past few years, these higher-profile directors and their allies have made some gains and have come to be known popularly as 'New Nollywood'. New Nollywood consists of a small group of internationally well-regarded Nollywood producers and directors making movies that are largely self-financed and that actively pursue distribution schemes that don't solely rely on physical distribution in open-air markets controlled by the marketers. New Nollywood movies are the type to be selected to represent Nollywood at film festivals or international screenings, as they feature bigger budgets, glossier content and a strategy of creative differentiation of titles. The strategies pursued often include splashy releases and multi-week runs at a small handful of high-end multiplexes in Nigeria's largest cities – or even releases in theatres serving the Nigerian diaspora in cities like London (Haynes, 2013; Ryan, 2013), pricier licences for television, online and aeroplane rights, grants, sponsorships, commissions and other methods to bolster budgets and manage their own distribution. Some of the highest-profile New Nollywood hits come from Kunle Afolayan, whose movies *The Figurine* (2009) and *Phone Swap* (2011) have proved popular with theatrical Nigerian audiences in Lagos and London alike, and have reportedly made back their high budgets plus a healthy profit. His most recent film, the 2014 production *October 1*, is a complete departure from the Nollywood aesthetic, full of sweeping panoramas, crane shots, orchestral music and high-definition slow-moving close-ups. The production budget (reportedly $2 million) is an exponential increase from even the New Nollywood range, raised from sponsorships from parties like Guinness, grants from the Lagos state government and the personal funds of Afolayan (SmartMonkeyTV, 2014); the film has been received accordingly, as it was picked up by Netflix and multiple film festivals. *The Figurine* and *Phone Swap* are more in keeping with the Nollywood aesthetic: the first a thriller about a cursed figurine and the latter a romantic comedy about two strangers who accidentally switch phones and become involved in one another's lives. Besides Afolayan, most of the better-known directors financing their own movies and actively pursuing international connections in distribution are also generally considered to be a part of New Nollywood: directors like Emem Isong and Tunde Kelani. While these movies are glossier, domestic audiences like and consume both types of movies; fans often give New Nollywood productions higher praise for 'quality', but they tend to watch both types. Neither avid fans nor popular stars can be sustained on New Nollywood content alone, as both consumption and labour rely upon access to a large pool of potential titles, larger than the output of New Nollywood (Njoku, 2015a).

Despite the level of international attention lavished on New Nollywood, the domestic market in Nigeria *is* the marketers' Nollywood. Jason Njoku, a British-Nigerian entrepreneur who is attempting to dominate the fledgling online market and who has pursued statistic production with religious zeal, estimates that 94 per cent of the Nigerian Nollywood market is still physical copy sales, virtually dominated by the marketers (2013b).[6] Given its dominance, this book takes the marketers' Nollywood as its main focus. However, I will acknowledge the different paths New Nollywood has taken, when appropriate, as a foil, a look at formal alternatives being pursued and reasons for their very limited success thus far. Unless otherwise specified, this book discusses the core of domestic Nollywood: the marketers' Nollywood. In this book, the term 'Nollywood' without qualifier refers to this, while 'New Nollywood' refers to the small handful of new efforts pursued by the better-known creative arm of the industry.

FINANCING MOVIES

Average budgets for regular Nollywood movies are often around $50,000–$65,000, though there are certainly movies made whose budgets fall either below or above these figures. The loans and grants upon which much global film production relies are usually unavailable to movie-makers in Lagos, due in part to lack of reliable distribution documentation. Instead, movies tend to be financed by the marketers, who serve as executive producers, financiers, marketers and distributors for each movie. Given their myriad powerful roles in the industry, one could say the marketers also run it.

Some movies go from inception to distribution under the direction of one marketer who is responsible for the whole movie, though other producers try to cobble together networks of investors, promising distribution rights, creative control and other incentives. While they dominate the scene, it is not just the marketers who executive produce. Independent producers, such as the New Nollywood contingent, can also sell their completed projects directly to marketers, and producers with more access to capital, either through personal connections or their own prior film profits, will often prefer to do this in order to retain more control over their product. Some of these producers most connected in Nollywood have developed their own distribution networks, linking with distributors in various markets directly, and it is this rare situation in which the most creative control can be retained by directors. If the completed film looks promising, a producer can immediately recoup his or her investment in the film by selling it and all the rights associated with it to a marketer, or, if the movie has a number of stars and seems a sure bet, can sometimes garner a 'pre-sales' guarantee which, in effect, finances a film entirely in advance. In an ideal scenario, the funder pays 50 per cent of costs upfront and 50 per cent at the end of production. In reality, however, movies are often plagued by rapidly disappearing and reappearing financing.

If the movie is not sold outright or funded wholly by the distributor, there is a royalty system in place in which the marketer pays the producer a percentage of each copy of a title sold. This system is not considered very desirable, as producers can rarely expect a fully truthful accounting of sales figures. No matter what system of financing is used, there tends to be a great deal of tension between directors and marketers, and deals are wrought with rancour and distrust – a phenomenon, it may be noted, that one can find in movie industries worldwide. Art and commerce are rarely a happy marriage in any context.

Unlike in many other global media industries, however, financing decisions are not based on any official estimates of sales potential, nor are they based on any degree of transparency in distribution plans. The only people who can truly feel confident in financing a movie are those who will also be in charge of distribution, and their decisions are founded on informal knowledge of the market based on their ownership and management of distribution outlets. In Nigeria, this means that the marketers, who began Nollywood, also run it, as their control over distribution of physical copies of movies through informal and opaque networks give them a level of power that is difficult to penetrate and even more difficult to usurp. As bandwidth issues preclude significant domestic online distribution, and as cinematic screenings are only existent for a handful of higher-end high-profile titles, those who dominate physical sales dominate the industry. In this sense, the marketers *are* Nollywood and any discussions of the past or future of Nollywood must recognise this group as a central locus of power. As Emmanuel Isikaku, former head of the marketers' guild, put it during his tenure, 'the man in the market interacting with the people in the market knows what makes commercial success' (Isikaku, 2009). In this way, financing is both informal and tied to grey market money (those who run the grey markets, selling goods with varying pedigrees, are the only ones who can confidently fund and distribute Nollywood). Like all else in Nollywood, informality and creativity born of necessity are the name of the game. Given the opacity and informality of this funding, it also must be noted that it could be of 'dubious' origin: with government checks on neither the industry's investors nor profits, it would be *possible* for those in need of such services to launder money through investment in movies. That said, there is no widespread and consistent link between any specific nefarious activity and Nollywood's funding, with the exception of the black and grey market distribution in which Nollywood's executive producers (marketers) may already be engaged.

PRODUCTION IN LAGOS

Decisions throughout the production are nominally up to the director but, when marketers fund the film, as is most often the case, they have the right to dictate everything from casting to plot. Particularly when such decisions are related to financial expenditures, they will tend to do so. In most cases, primary sponsorship of a movie also means participation in major production decisions. Marketers will often work repeatedly with the same director/producer or a small handful of trusted and reliable director/producers, as relationships of trust outweigh formalised contracts and negate the need for agents.

Scripts are sometimes written by the directors, but are also purchased from screenwriters, usually quite cheaply. Scripts must anticipate the finished product's future run-in with governmental censorship (the mechanics of which are discussed in greater detail in Chapter 4). This mainly means scriptwriters are incentivised to show a lack of visible sexual contact onscreen (though sex certainly figures heavily in plots) and are discouraged from over-reliance on witchcraft as a plot point (somewhat futile, as black magic is a popular and thus frequent plot element); there is also a call for negative consequences for immoral actions. These all seem to be reflective of the will of the general populace. Viewers will complain about too much sex, too much witchcraft, or not enough justice in the plot when they are noticed in movies, even though such elements may also enhance sales. Overt political statements are usually lacking in these mass-market productions (see Adejunmobi, 2007).

The scriptwriter's concept, the big-name star actor and the director usually begin the package. Once a movie moves closer to actual production, a cinematographer[7] is enlisted. The cinematographer will usually book the sound, sound mixers, lights and all relevant assistants. Non-star actors are usually enlisted through auditions. Auditions tend to be rather formal, well-attended affairs, with members of the leadership of each guild[8] expected to attend and make sure everything is operating in a respectable fashion.

Nollywood production is marked by velocity and low budgets. The average number of scenes shot per day is ten, with two to three weeks' worth of shooting on an average movie.[9] With one week of pre-production and one week of editing and packaging, a video film *can* actually go from inception to sale in four weeks, though three months is a much more common scenario and the occasional movie that may wind up on the international film festival or lecture circuit will take much longer. An in-demand worker can easily shoot two movies in one month. With low pay from any individual movie, workers make a living mainly through quantity, and some can be found working nearly every day, ending one movie project to begin another (or even trying to make some overlap between two shooting schedules work, a prospect usually fraught with stress and frustration for all involved). A standard theme in production in Lagos is the lack of reliable power supply. With the power from the public Nigerian Energy and Power Authority (NEPA) – often mockingly redubbed Never Expect Power Anytime and still referred to as NEPA, despite a relatively recent name change to PHCN[10] – exceedingly unreliable, the use (and failure) of noisy generators often plagues productions.

In terms of recording, Nollywood movies are often shot using new equipment imported from Europe or Asia and sold through official representatives of major equipment manufacturers, such as JVC and Sony (see Chapter 5 for more on this). Sony is by far the dominant supplier of equipment in Nigeria and its shop on Lagos's Victoria Island is frequented by most of the professional cinematographers.[11] Clients will order equipment and the store will have it shipped, usually from East Asia – most usually Singapore – or, at times, the Middle East, South Asia, or Europe. This, of course, makes the equipment that much more expensive, as taxes and shipping charges are then included, prompting many to request equipment be purchased on trips that acquaintances make abroad. While the purchase and use of these technologies connect Nollywood to the formal, documented global economy, the conditions of their use (following long waits for shipping and customs, much more expensive than the manufacturer's suggested retail price (MSRP) and reliant on interrupted power supplies) drive home Nigeria's and Nollywood's place in the global economy. From a site of heavily fragmented inclusion, global connections will usually be heavily mediated by the conditions of the 'Fourth World'.

Movie-making technologies in Nigeria have changed since Nollywood began on VHS in the early 1990s. After VHS came SuperVHS, followed by Betacam, then DV and then DVPro (Gabosky, 2009). If lighting is used, one professional cinematographer reports generally using 'RedHeads', Arri 2Ks, kino lights and 200 watt bulbs (Martins, 2009), all lights acquired through trade with the global economy – and frequently via official markets. These lights will usually be owned by the production company in charge of the movie, but if extra lights are needed or the producer does not have their own, these lights are easily rented from other production companies or via individual cinematographers not currently shooting. The nature of the industry – informal and trust-based – means that it is usually easy enough to find a trusted person with extra lights to rent; formal rental outfits have little place in Nollywood. And it is not just lights that are individually rented in this way. On one movie set I was on, a gun was needed as a prop. Throughout the shoot, I noticed a slight, silent young man sitting on a couch in the producer's office looking bored. He was the off-duty police officer who had been paid to rent his personal police gun for the duration of the night shoot, and he was present to make sure the gun, a valuable possession, was not mislaid. He watched with a blank unchanging expression on his face as various famous actors and crew posed for joking photographs waving around his work gun.

Post-production usually occurs in editing suites located in the production company offices of Lagos, and using digital editing tools, a stark contrast from the days of sending film for processing to London at great expense. Busy production companies will employ an in-house editor and have their own editing studio, but others can rent that same studio – and even that same editor along with it – on an individual basis. One production company in-house editor notes that, while editing a movie 'properly' should take at least thirty days, sixteen days is acceptable[12] and a week much too fast but not unheard of (Asu, 2009). Inexpensive but proprietary software packages EDIUS and Canopus DVStorm are among the standard editing tools. Some production companies will edit during shooting, but most won't due to the unreliability of shooting schedules and the associated expense of possibly renting out editing studios.

NOLLYWOOD LABOUR

There is little in the way of formal training in the industry and many workers have no training whatsoever, improvising along the way. Entry into Nollywood is generally based on family, ethnic, or other pre-existing ties. Some efforts to institute training programmes via movie-making schools have begun, but these have not yet become a reliable mechanism for feeding talent into the industry. It may be that schools are too formal an education for an informal industry. A notable exception is one-off training seminars offered usually to the more technical of workers. For instance, Sony, the dominant supplier of camera and sound equipment to the industry, leads periodic seminars on using its products, which it advertises through the guilds (e.g. the Nigerian Society of Cinematographers).

Actors aside, the most common way for people to get started in the industry is through apprenticeship for little to no money. It is commonplace in Nigeria for a 'big man' to train a number of 'boys' to work under him,[13] and it is no different in Nollywood. This tradition is thought to ensure loyalty on behalf of the underlings; the industry is full of people who got their start through loose personal connections. One mid-level producer I spoke with, for instance, runs a production company. The in-house editor at this company is the producer's former barber, who he trained and groomed to do editing. In this way, he says, 'I know he will always be loyal to me' (Producer 1, 2009). Most in Nollywood seem to have got their start in this way as opposed to coming into the industry already trained. Those who do enter the industry already possessing skills often acquired these skills in an informal fashion. One post-production special effects artist I interviewed, for instance, entered the industry with special effects skills, but these were learned mainly via free online tutorials on special effects software such as Video Co-Pilot, Cinema 4D and After-Effects, taken due to a personal interest in eventually working in the industry while he was in university studying something else. University education is common, though certainly not necessary in the creative arms of the industry: editors, producers and directors. Marketers, however, are not usually university educated, coming from a practical background working in the marketplaces from a young age; some of the rancour and distrust between the two groups is based on this difference alone.

Glossy promotion handed out at a premiere, the sort of formal event where Nollywood's elite congregate

Those that are university educated often report their parents' initial lack of enthusiasm about their chosen career path in the arts, a familiar story worldwide.

Guilds and trade organisations, explored in greater detail in Chapter 4, form the backbone of the movie industry in Nigeria. For guilds with many members and limited work (e.g. the Actors Guild), guild membership forms the framework through which creative workers look for and find work. In recent years, when the Actors Guild's offices were at the National Theatre, the National Theatre complex became a central location in the movie industry: calls for auditions would be posted at the Guild office, and an actress in the Guild's leadership claims that many would sit at the restaurants in the National Theatre complex all day long waiting (in her telling, usually futilely) to be 'discovered' by a passing director or producer (Ejenoboor, 2009). Now that the Guild has left the National Theatre for less central headquarters, this phenomenon is no longer in play.

Repeat collaborations and working relationships based on informal networks of referrals and trust are common. Despite the prominence of the guilds, people usually hear about jobs either from someone they have worked with before or from the recommendation of a friend. While there is no system of agents, the close-knit nature of the movie-making community means that a potential phone number is just a few phone calls away. If one wishes to contact an inferior, their number is easily found through personal networks. If one wishes to contact a superior, it usually must be done through an introduction, again through personal networks. Gathering places, like O'Jez's and the bar and restaurant in the National Stadium, can provide another opportunity to network one's way to the top. Industry events such as premieres, awards ceremonies and elaborate birthday banquets are the type of invitation-only places where big deals can be thrashed out. Bars like O'Jez's or its predecessor, Winnie's, which are open to the public, are less likely to yield dramatic results. They do, however, provide the chance to see and be seen; people always make an effort to hold their important meetings there, in order to be observed by others in the industry.

Many of those I interviewed requested we conduct our interview at O'Jez's and, in the course of the interviews, I would frequently see those I had met previously or hoped to speak to in the future. As I was interviewing one major producer at O'Jez's, also famous for his acting, we were constantly interrupted by his colleagues and inferiors in the industry. One young man approached us as he was departing, leaving his date standing off to the side. 'My girlfriend over there thinks she wants to be an actress. I know – crazy, right? But she's good – no, really, she's actually really good,' he began as he suggested the producer might know something perhaps. The producer I was with smiled benevolently and casually mentioned the address of an open audition the following morning to which the young man was welcome to bring his girlfriend. Not having sat with the couple, it would be impossible to know their dinner conversation, but one could presume it involved encouragement of one another to approach the famous producer – and that their very presence at O'Jez's that evening may have been related to the anticipation of seeing such a producer or director. In this way, O'Jez's can pave the way for opportunities and connections, but these are likely to be only superficial. The producer offered no assistance in getting the girlfriend a role and her audition among a sea of other hopefuls the following morning probably didn't lead to anything. If she was lucky, the audition might lead her to become slowly more integrated into the Nollywood labour community, however.

Though acting is hard to break into, Nollywood has an enviable, glamourous pantheon of stars.[14] Top stars can command significant fees per movie – up to half the budget of a movie for a true starring role by a big star, but their rates are usually less than that, especially when their role is more of a glorified cameo. In any case, reports of stars' fees are often exaggerated for public effect. In order to make a consistent living, even the biggest of stars must work frequently, shooting two or even three movies per month; those demanding extravagant fees have been refused employment en masse by collective action on behalf of the members of the marketers guild (FVPMAN) in recent years. Although it is a virtual necessity for a movie to have a star in it for it to be a good candidate for turning a profit, the marketers, in their collective actions, can hold the upper hand, as they control both financing and distribution. They can and will shut down production in the industry or blacklist certain workers if they feel their own power is being chipped away. And if others attempt to usurp their authority by employing such a blacklisted star, these rebels will be unlikely to be able to make much money from the movie due to their limited access to distribution networks. Stars can earn higher fees in New Nollywood fare, but there are not enough New Nollywood titles to sustain them; both the stars and the New Nollywood producers must maintain good relationships with the marketers.

It is here we can see the policing of the informal trust-based relationships that mark the industry: there *is* power and it is guarded jealously by a large, opaque bloc. These marketers are particularly important as we analyse the structure of the industry. The industry is *not* a disorganised chaotic collective. In the absence of control by legal institutions or large corporate studios, control is enforced by a mass of small enterprises bound together by strong informal ties. Informality does not mean disorganisation. What I mean by informality, instead, is an industry that is opaque, undocumented and that has no recourse to *legal* institutions to structure it. As will be explored in further detail in Chapter 4, Nollywood's labour is, in fact, quite organised. What I mean by organisation is accountability, structure (such as the audition process in which each guild submits a representative) and potential for collective activity, such as shutting down production or refusing employment to a transgressing individual. Nollywood's organisation comes not just via personal relationships but even more via voluntary guilds, guilds with no public documentation or relationship with governmental oversight, yet guilds that are taken seriously. In this regard, the industry is both informal and organised.

In all of these ways, we can see informal connections and trust as the building blocks of the industry, giving it both the freedom to grow and the strength to stand. While informal connections and trust also form the basis for many of Hollywood's working relationships and those of most other contractual employment-based creative industries worldwide, what is distinctive about Nollywood is that this is the *only* currency. There is, effectively, no possibility of recourse to contracts or a legal system as back-up, and there are no talent agencies. The strength of informal trust-based connections as a building block emerged as a contrast to the experience of legal infrastructural informality – lack of legal frameworks, for instance, through which to form and police legally binding agreements; this does and will continue to shape the industry. Furthermore, the industry's location in a state of significant exclusion from many formal global networks has and will continue to shape it. Payment often follows the same logic. It is rare to receive payment upfront, though the more cachet a creative worker has, the more likely they'll be able to demand such a scenario as a condition for employment. Average creative workers are only paid after production and it is quite common that these fees are subject to disputes – sometimes not paid at all.

DISTRIBUTION

Nollywood movies, despite their sometimes haphazard-seeming production, are incredibly popular and widely distributed. They are consumed in a variety of formats, in a variety of settings and make their way to their final destination via a wide variety of paths, mostly informal. While Nollywood movies are distributed globally, we will focus here on the logics of their domestic (Nigerian) distribution, and this is mainly physical distribution via open-air marketplaces. International distribution will be addressed in greater detail in Chapter 5.

Theatres

Nollywood productions are not shot on film and are designed for direct home entertainment release. Some argue that this very aesthetic – the aesthetic of the small screen – is embedded in each shot of Nollywood movies, full of facial close-ups and usually lacking panoramas or other elements of cinematic visual language (Jedlowski, 2012; Haynes, 2007b). This lack of cinema culture is bemoaned by many working in distribution. New Nollywood, in particular, invests heavily in building cinemas and getting screen time at the few existent local cineplexes. While the few western-style multiplex cinemas in Nigeria tend to show Hollywood films at prices only accessible to the elite classes,[15] in the past few years, a small number of theatres have emerged screening select higher-end Nollywood fare from digital copies. If such cinematic release is utilised, ticket sales at these venues will contribute to the overall take of the movie. For the movies able to benefit from this distribution venue, this can be very significant income. However, as it now stands, these few movie theatres have made little structural change in the industry and sales of physical copies of movies are still key. New Nollywood's highly touted cinema screenings have contributed to the ability to fund their own movies, but have not significantly altered the industry overall.

Were there to be a formal cinema culture – cities full of silver screens, box offices and official reports of daily ticket sales, it would mean a complete upheaval of power relations in Nollywood; it seems unlikely that marketers would be able to maintain their hold on power for long. The very core of the marketers' current power is their unique ability to profit from the distribution of physical copies of movies in the country, due to their control over distribution networks. Cinematic distribution would open up room for others to control distribution, making possible the type of formalisation, documentation and transparency that would enable bank loans, foreign investment and other challenges to the marketers' sovereignty.

The extreme informality of distribution within Nigeria, marked by lack of cinemas, is seen by many in the New Nollywood part of the industry – as well as outside it – as an impediment to future industrial growth. Formalised distribution would diversify potential investors, enabling larger budgets, but formalised distribution would also change what Nollywood is. The marketers that gave birth to the industry and now run it would no longer be in control. Their focus on quantity instead of quality and their mastery of domestic marketplace distribution networks would likely give way to stylistic and industrial conventions that accrue to media industries supported by bank, corporate and foreign investment and integration into dominant global cultural industry networks.

That said, regular Nollywood is still screened in public in a few ways. Video parlours may also be set up informally in some neighbourhoods. These tend to be small, cramped spaces in marketplaces with a single television, sometimes only 14 inches (about 36cm) wide, screening the latest movie at admission prices calculated in cents as opposed to dollars. Even more informally, one family in a given neighbourhood may run their generator at night and charge neighbours a nominal fee to come and watch a movie at their dwelling, so as to spread out the cost of electricity and electronics ownership among a wider network. Profits from any of these screenings do not, of course, go back to the producers apart from the sale of a single copy – and even then only if it is an authorised copy. In the same vein, there are informal rental outfits known as video clubs. The head of a video club will buy a Nollywood movie at street value and rent it out to club members at around 30 naira (15 cents) per rental period – often a couple of days long. These clubs are independent operations with no regulation or oversight and all profit from rentals goes to the club owners.

Licensing for Television, Internet and Airline

While the possibility of increased domestic cinematic distribution has galvanised New Nollywood and its supporters, it is only one piece in the puzzle of non-physical distribution avenues that New Nollywood can attempt to piece together in the domestic market. Producers can also seek income from sales of licensed rights to televised, online and airline screening. Televised viewing is common among viewers in Nigeria, particularly on satellite television. Online and airline screenings, however, are accessible to a much smaller part of the population, as discussed in subsequent chapters. While these three outlets are available to domestic Nigerian viewers, the rights for these tend to be sold at an international level and as an afterthought to physical sales. If pursued, online and airline rights are generally packaged together and sold to businesses managing them at a global level. The leader and largest of these companies is iROKOtv, an originally British start-up funded with significant international capital, with offices currently in multiple countries, including South Africa and the USA.[16] Similarly, most money to be made from television, if pursued, is routed through satellite television companies, the largest of which, M-Net, has a collection of Africa Magic branded channels and is based in South Africa and run by a significant global media corporation, Naspers. Given the global nature of the major players in these rights, Africa Magic and iROKOtv, I will discuss the architecture of these deals in more detail in Chapter 5. However, I will give a brief overview of them here in terms of their relationship to domestic producers.

These rights are sold by both the marketers and small New Nollywood segment of the industry, but they are more important to the latter, as they lend independent producers the opportunity for more independence from the marketers. This opportunity has been piecemeal, however, and the marketers still circulate the vast majority of domestic content. Even combined, these rights are generally not enough to constitute the budget of an entire movie. Internet rights (packaged with possible airline rights) have gone up in recent years as iROKO introduced higher payments for content as part of its strategy for gaining market dominance. iROKO pays $3,000–$22,000 depending on quality and popularity. Africa Magic has raised their prices as well and will pay $4,000–$8,000 for high-profile movies, though they still pay less for more generic fare – even as low as $600. In either case, money paid for internet/airline rights added to television rights will not cover the movie's entire budget. It is only the big-budget titles that will garner the high end of payment for these rights, meaning they will never cover the full budget. The main exception to this is movies commissioned by Africa Magic for their channels. Budgets for these are on the low side, however, and these are often considered by viewers as similar to any other made-for-TV movie: sufficiently entertaining but not quite the real thing. Much online distribution and televised distribution (particularly on free-to-air channels) is unlicensed and sends no proceeds back to the original producers.

Video Sales

Despite the existence of these other means of distribution, and the potential they offer New Nollywood and other independent artists to control their own content, the core of Nollywood is physical. Most Nollywood movies are primarily and first distributed through domestic physical sales of videos. Video sales are dominated by the marketers, who control not only the production of movies and hiring of personnel, but also the informal distribution networks that snake through the country's crowded marketplaces. Despite New Nollywood's realised efforts in self-funding and self-distributing via cinema, internet, or satellite television, the majority of Nollywood titles are products of directors working with or for the marketers.

Once the master cut of a movie has been edited, it is delivered to the marketer, who then delivers it as soon as possible to the disc replicator. He or she must have a good relationship with the replication factory in order to go to the front of the queue and ensure a timely release. There are only approximately fourteen licensed replication plants in all of Nigeria, most of which are in the greater Lagos area. Despite the factory-level size of such plants, the informality of all business in Nigeria and low level of governmental oversight mean that unlicensed and technically illegal plants also exist. Both the unlicensed plants and some of the licensed plants are said to engage in mass-scale factory runs for unauthorised parties engaged in illegal distribution.[17]

Video compact discs (VCDs) dominate as a replication technology. VCD is a video reproduction technology that has lived almost its entire life in the developing world. Introduced by global technology corporations JVC and Philips in 1993, the VCD was originally intended to be a digital successor to VHS (Wang, 2003; McDonald, 2007). However, in initial markets like Western Europe and North America, the VCD didn't present enough clear benefits to bring about a market shift. Compared to VHS, the VCD offers slightly better sound and approximately equivalent picture quality, rendering it not obviously superior – and, at the same time, the VCD format requires a single movie to be spread out over at least two separate discs as VCDs can each only carry 72 minutes' worth of content (McDonald, 2007). Once DVDs were introduced, just a few years later, it was clear DVDs, not VCDs, would be the successor to VHS in North American and European markets: compared to the more expensive DVD format, VCDs have lower sound and picture quality, and carry fewer capabilities for special features and storage.

The VCD did not disappear, however. The benefits of the VCD, blurry in initial markets, come into focus in developing markets. One key benefit of the VCD technology is that it is incredibly inexpensive to reproduce (and has none of the copyright protections included in DVDs). And, while a VCD is marginally better

Transerve Disc, one of the largest disc replication factories in greater Lagos

quality than a VHS in 'perfect' conditions, a VCD that is eight unauthorised copies removed from the original, and has been laying in the extreme heat for months fares much better than would a VHS in the same circumstances. China was the first market to seize upon this low-cost reproduction technology, amenable to unauthorised reproductions of content and hearty in the face of less than ideal storage options (Wang, 2003; McDonald, 2007). As Chinese factories churned out low cost VCD players and inexpensive VCD content, VCD reigned as the successor to VHS, first, in Asian and, eventually, also in African markets, where it was embraced for similar reasons. While Asia has now begun the shift to DVDs, VCDs still dominate the market in Nigeria. While the low cost and reproducibility of VCD surely contributes to its continued reign in Nigeria, the style of Nollywood movies – viewed on small screens and more likely to include close-ups on actors' faces than sweeping panoramas – means that picture fidelity is also not as important as it might be in an action movie or epic originally shot for cinema screens.

Transerve Disc, one of the largest optical disc replication plants in Nigeria, is representative of the changes that have taken place in duplication and distribution over the course of Nollywood's short history. Transerve began operating in 1994, producing VHS tapes. VCD production capabilities were added in 2004 and, by 2005, VHS technologies were ripped out, replaced with all-VCD replication facilities. The managing director and CEO described this move as a response to 'a sudden shift in the market' (Orakpo, 2009). Factories often manufacture VCDs from scratch – polycarbonate resin – in Nigeria, keeping import costs down. DVD technology has been adopted at home by some wealthier Nigerian families, but VCD is still the technology of the masses and, as such, it still dominates domestic distribution and disc replication.

When a pressing is finished, the factory returns the shipment of pressed VCDs to the distributor who then packages them with the appropriate graphics they have printed elsewhere. Separating the production of the graphic packaging from the production of the disc is meant to limit the potential for authorised disc replicators to turn around and 'pirate' the content in their time off. If someone replicates unauthorised VCDs from the master, they will still be at least a little bit late to market if they wait to acquire the graphics for unauthorised replication.[18] Orders range between runs of 1,000 and a few hundred thousand, with frequent orders for second pressings. Factories maintain contracts with a number of clients, agreeing to produce a certain volume at reduced rates and shorter turn-around times for each client per year if they agree to do all of their reproductions with the same factory. Other distributors, however, negotiate for every run, comparing deals with a number of firms, but likely sacrificing either timeliness or price (ibid.).

Once the marketers have combined the VCDs with the sleeves imprinted with authorised marketing materials, they send them through their distribution network. A new week's movies are usually released by marketers on Mondays and subsequently sold by individual small businesses in the networks of Nollywood's domestic physical circulation: video stalls and shops in bazaars and open-air markets, fanning out further to small grocery or dedicated video stores and street hawkers. Distribution networks are usually first focused on a few main hubs in Alaba (the Lagos market) and Onitsha (the city in the Igbo-dominated southeast that is home to a large number of production companies), and spread out from there to smaller cities and, eventually, villages. Outside Lagos and Onitsha, marketers often also have direct connections with distributors in other major Nollywood distribution centres, particularly Aba, Kano and, sometimes, Accra in Ghana. Marketers will send copies to each hub from Lagos by trucks and buses, and traders in surrounding areas will, in turn, come to pick up copies at each sub-hub. Traders may pick up copies from Aba, for instance, and take them to nearby Port Harcourt. Isikaku reports a desire on behalf of the powerful national marketers to exert control over some of the smaller hubs – controlling, for instance, Port Harcourt directly – but wholesale access to these arms of the industry is all that is needed, and money is made from wholesale as opposed to direct retail in connecting to smaller and more remote areas.

Proprietors of the small-scale retail outlets will pick up (or receive delivery of) the week's titles from their regular distributors and sell them on commission, returning unsold copies. This feedback helps marketers to have an up-to-date (at least weekly) sense of demand, and this, along with their print runs with their replication factory, is information they keep closely guarded. There have been attempts by FVPMAN, the marketers' organising guild, to collectively space out movie releases in order to counteract periodic 'gluts' in movie releases. FVPMAN has also cut down on production at times to address the same issue.

The distribution networks described here are held together by trust and informality, as well as ethnic and family ties, as opposed to legally binding contracts – as are virtually all Nollywood institutions, a necessity in an informal economy. This tradition of vast networks of informal distribution outlets rather than large retailers (e.g. large chains of formalised shops to be found in shopping malls) is both the source and product of the marketers' collective power. As they are the only parties able to efficiently move official products through nationwide distribution networks, the only parties able to have any knowledge of sales and the only parties to have first-line access to profits, we can see how control of these networks of informal (undocumented) distribution is inseparable from power in the industry, as illustrated in Figure 1 (on p. 53). Access to and control of distribution networks is a source of power in nearly every media industry, whether it involves ownership of networks of television or radio stations, or exclusive deals with major online distributors and chains of multiplex cinemas. When those distribution networks are undocumented, however – when no one but the controllers of those networks (in this case, the marketers) can even know sales figures – that power is almost impenetrable, since no one else is likely to be willing to invest substantially without knowledge of sales estimates and returns. The marketers, both beneficiaries and architects of this system, are fully aware of the ways in which these business practices reserve power for themselves and limit opportunities for outsiders. In this way, informality in distribution is less a 'challenge' for a burgeoning industry, as it is often described in development assessments, but, rather, a conscious and active strategy by networks of small-scale savvy entrepreneurs to discourage competition from better-capitalised challengers.

Average Nollywood movies often sell 50,000–200,000 authorised copies domestically in open-air markets, while a blockbuster can sell nearer to 1 million copies (Njoku, 2013a). The pricing of Nollywood movies is a complicated affair and reflects the innovative ways the marketers have dealt with competition from unauthorised distribution of Nollywood and foreign movies alike. The easiest way to explain it is to say that newly released Nollywood movies sell in Nigeria in VCD form for around 350–400 naira ($1.75–$2) wholesale per full

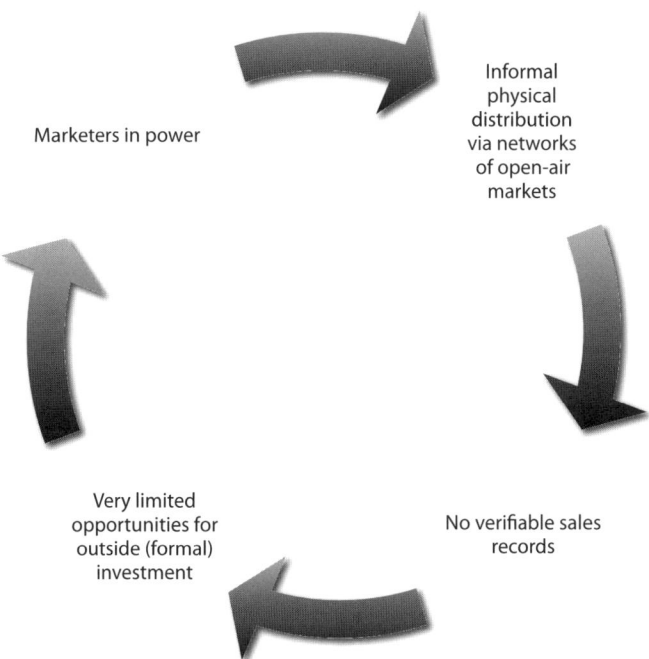

Figure 1 The power cycle of informality in Nollywood

movie, and that this has been a steady price over the years. That isn't the full tale, however. Over the years, the marketers have put considerable effort into addressing unlicensed distribution in their pricing strategies, with two main techniques meant to lower their prices so much that unlicensed distributors are disincentivised to compete.

First, they began splitting movies up into more and more parts, priced more cheaply, leaving little content remaining on the metaphorical cutting room floor. In some cases this has worked to pique audience interest further in the branded title. In others, it has resulted in dialogue-packed movies bloated to twice (or more) their anticipated scripted running time. For years, wholesale prices for Alaba movies ranged from 150–200 naira per copy (about $1), with 300–400 naira (around $2) charged 'retail' in the streets. To maximise revenues, titles were frequently split into two parts, so those wishing to follow a story from start to finish would wind up buying both parts (hence a 300–400 naira or $2 total wholesale).

In recent years, this has ballooned, leading to situations as drastic as splitting a movie into eight parts and charging 43 naira (21 cents) wholesale, per copy (Njoku, 2013a). In other words, this means a wholesale price of 43 naira for a brand new movie in its initial release in its original packaging. The cost of

Common breakdown of movie into multiple parts, with each part split between two VCDs

production of a VCD has been estimated at 26 naira per copy leaving 17 naira (9 cents) per copy gross profit for this hypothetical disc. However, we must recall that most buying Part 1 would likely also buy Parts 2–8, so overall revenue from the movie would actually be the same as if the movie were sold in just two parts. The overall price would be similar for consumers, but the cost of VCD production would render unauthorised distribution of this title less attractive, as margins would be shaved. To be clear, this is just one extreme in pricing. Most movies are still sold in fewer than eight parts – more like two, three, or four. In either instance, this reflects a marketer trend towards cutting prices and extending the number of 'parts' to better compete with unlicensed distribution.

Another strategy is a rather brutal windowing system, in which the prices of titles that have been out for three or more weeks dip down to just 50 naira retail, or 25 cents. This is known as the secondary market for the movie, similar to a second run for film industries using a windowed cinematic release strategy. For a hypothetical popular movie selling 100,000 copies domestically in the first three weeks, this can mean up to 10 million naira ($50,000) in initial domestic profit, with a possible 2 million naira ($10,000) domestic licensed take coming from an additional 200,000–300,000 secondary copies sold wholesale. These secondary sales wholesale at an astounding 10 naira (6 cents) per copy, and are sold in the markets for 50 naira (30 cents). Making over $10,000 on intellectual property being sold at 6 cents per copy is a powerful challenge to unlicensed distribution, though the scale of the figures cited here were given by a producer whose titles tend to sell well and she notes that this would be a best-case scenario for her. The average lesser-known Nollywood movie will not see returns near this scale. However, the practice of initial versus secondary domestic sales periods, and the ability to make money from each, applies down the line. Both this windowing practice and the multi-part release strategy serve as challenges to unlicensed distribution – not through the threat of police raids or court battles, but through squeezing legitimate profits so as to actually compete on price with unauthorised distributors who did not need to fund the production budget.

Unlicensed Distribution ('Piracy')

Indeed, piracy is also a mainstay of the video distribution system, although I will mostly refer to it here as unlicensed or unauthorised distribution, in order to remain value neutral. Once a movie hits the streets, it is easy for an unauthorised party to replicate the movie on his or her own and return to the streets selling an unlicensed copy which sells for the same price as the first-tier domestic market original (though the past few years have seen the advent of hyper-compressed twenty-in-one discs for the same price, another stage in the battle between original financiers and unauthorised distributors); audiences do not seem to actively differentiate between legitimate and unauthorised copies, or to prefer one to the other. As Larkin illustrates in his media anthropology of northern Nigeria (2004, 2008), in a nation where there are virtually no outlets for legitimate sales of Hollywood movies, unauthorised distribution is not seen as much of a criminal activity, and there is little public shame in purchasing or selling 'pirated' products, especially as this may be the only way to access a title. Throughout even Lagos, the centralised distribution hub, it is quite common to see a legitimate retailer operating one or two storefronts away from a permanent unauthorised retail shop. With no recourse to the ineffective police forces – and sometimes with overlapping business interests – the two neighbouring retailers may even be friendly with one another.

Despite the public proclamations of the marketers that unauthorised distribution is decimating the industry, the marketers are not collectively clearly operating on the legal side of copyright law in all of their business dealings.

Instead, one might say that they operate in a grey area, making agreements for certain rights for movies and then over-stepping them, and hiding profits. The core of the marketers comes from a background of electronics trading, including the trade of unlicensed distribution of foreign movies. As Brian Larkin illustrates (2004, 2008), their success comes in part from using the same distribution networks they built for unauthorised distribution of Hollywood, Bollywood and kung fu movies years before, and is augmented by their ability to operate behind closed doors and out of sight of any potential regulators. Indeed, the very things most of the visible prominent Nollywood figures bemoan – lack of transparency, lack of formality, inability for outsiders to calculate returns before or after the making of a movie – are the very same things that are an original and persistent source of industrial strength. They are the same things that keep marketers in power and evade investment or co-option by forces outside the industry. As I illustrate in Figure 1 (p. 53), this power circle is difficult to penetrate as long as distribution remains centred in circulation of physical copies. Marketers maintain physical distribution through their opaque and informal networks of open-air marketplaces. The informality of these marketplaces (the lack of documentation of sales figures, print runs and ownership) is the very device that makes it nearly impossible for banks or foreign corporations to invest, leaving the marketers at the helm of the industry that they built in the 1990s, even in the face of much interest from within and outside in formalising. While this formalisation would bring bigger budgets and opportunities for the realisation of more creative artistic visions, none of these are outcomes desired by the marketers. As such, they are able to maintain their hold on power by their very informality. It is virtually impossible to usurp their hold on the distribution of physical Nollywood within Nigeria's marketplace network. A few years ago, Jason Njoku of iROKOtv, the upstart online distributor, attempted to supplement his online distribution by cracking physical distribution himself. Within less than a year, he posted the following to his business blog:

> Our DVD adventure in 2013 was a fine balance of over-ambition and poor execution. Tried to replicate what Alaba had managed in 20 years in a mere 6 months across 4 cities (London, JoBurg, NY and Lagos). Failed. Miserably, now I have a renewed respect for distribution chops of the Alaba boys. We will have to disrupt those boys another way. It cost us something like $250,000 at least before we came to our senses. (Njoku, 2014b)

Larkin (2004, 2008) presents a nuanced and highly influential study of the entrenched role of unauthorised distribution networks and technological breakdown in Nigerian video film business models. Non- and quasi-functional equipment and systems for production and distribution can be considered more than quirks in the system: they are so standard and expected as to be endemic – a part of the structure. As he puts it, 'If infrastructures represent attempts to order, regulate, and rationalise society, then breakdowns in their operation, or the rise of provisional and informal infrastructures, highlight the failure of that ordering and the recoding that takes place' (Larkin, 2004: 290–1). Not only is technological breakdown and 'pirate' distribution part of the Nigerian infrastructure, Larkin notes also that Nigeria itself 'has become progressively disembedded from the official global economy… [and] ever more integrated into a parallel, unofficial world economy that reorients Nigeria towards new metropoles such as Dubai, Singapore, and Beirut' (ibid.: 293) and derives up to 70 per cent of current GDP from the 'shadow economy' (ibid.: 297). As such, we can see Nollywood as an opportunity to examine the emergence of industrialised creativity in what might be considered a state of disembeddedness from dominant global cultural industry network/s. In the face of such exclusion, we can see a creative industry that not only took root, but that is also still functioning and producing without significant formalisation or integration into dominant global networks of cultural industry financing and distribution.

For such a young industry, Nollywood is subject to constant speculation on the shape of its future and various plans to shift that future in one direction or another, coming both from within and outside the industry. New plans to 'formalise' in one way or another are near constant, including cinema construction schemes and various licensing initiatives put forth by the government and guilds. Some of these new ideas die before they are born while others persist but only affect a small subset of the industry during their tenure – a handful of powerful producers, most frequently. As with most cultural industries, the real power of the industry is centralised with those that control distribution. In Nollywood, this will tend to mean the marketers. Locating power in creative industries is key to understanding their functioning, and understanding the marketers as the nexus of power here is key to understanding Nollywood's persistence in informal infrastructure. This informality can be a source of industrial strength as opposed to a weakness to be overcome – at least from the perspective of the marketers. This persistent informality can mean that integration into dominant global cultural industry networks is inherently limited.

CONCLUSION

The functioning of Nollywood as an industry is inseparable from its location in Lagos, in Nigeria, in sub-Saharan Africa and in a place of fragmented exclusion from the global Network Society, sometimes referred to as the 'Fourth World'. Alaba's rise in the outskirts of the urban core – in the urban periphery, one might say – mirrors Nollywood's rise outside the global core. In both settings, a functioning industrial order was created from an architecture of informality and alternative self-created infrastructure. In Alaba, we can see these individual fixes through the sea of mobile phone towers and personal generators blanketing the landscape, a landscape previously a barren area on the side of the highway to Benin. In Nollywood, we can trace this thread throughout the industry. Financing, for example, is usually done by the eventual distributor in the absence of reliable sales estimates or accountability. Production relationships are built on trust, not contracts, and entry to the industry is rarely housed in formal schools, as apprenticeships acquired through personal connections rule. The aesthetic of Nollywood movies is born from the experience of shooting in Lagos: full of improvisation. Even the foreign equipment used (e.g. Sony cameras, editing software) is mediated through an atmosphere of exclusion: difficult to acquire and only usable with limited intermittent electricity.

Another commonality is that both Alaba and Nollywood share a deceptively organised governance. While both are mostly ignored by Nigeria's and Lagos's actual government, both are indeed governed: self-governed. In Alaba, we can see this through the libraries, firehouses, schools and other social infrastructure built by the massive collective of small merchants housed in the market. These merchants are held together by the urge for self-preservation as well as the Nigerian tradition of self-organisation. In the same way, we see Nollywood's marketers (some of whom are also the very same small-stall owners of Alaba) controlling the industry with the firm hand of confident self-organisation. They maintain star salaries at a manageable level, control gluts, create stars and maintain distribution networks that rapidly disseminate new cultural products to the most remote of Nigeria's hamlets. Although they are threatened by illegal distribution practices, they are also strengthened by them, particularly those of their own genesis.

At the same time, it is important not to over-romanticise the transformative potential of Lagos. As journalist George Packer put it, 'if there is an element of American frontier capitalism in the unregulated informal economy of Lagos, there is much less opportunity to make hard work pay off' (2006). That those in Nollywood did so is a testament to their tenacity and creativity in structuring this industry, made from building blocks others may have seen only as lack: 'lack'[19] of effective contract enforcement, 'lack' of copyright enforcement mechanisms, 'lack' of theatres, 'lack' of investment capital. Yet, as Haynes points out (2000), celebrating ingenious methods of coping with breakdowns in order can be not just counter-productive, shifting attention away from change, but also patronising. Celebrating the ingenuity of Nollywood movies with low production values, lighting, sound and editing can seem, as Haynes puts it, 'glib':

something easy to do from a position of comfort, 'secure in the possession of a "high" camera … immune to embarrassment by shoddy productions' (ibid.: 17). Similarly, geographer Matthew Gandy critiques much celebration of Lagos's ingenuity, particularly that of Koolhaas *et al.*, noting the very real problems posed by structural weakness in Nigeria and deriding the celebration of informality as a fix against them (Gandy, 2005). Gandy cautions us to be clear that the informality that is being celebrated in such academic works is not the choice of the people. Rather, it is the 'result of a specific set of policies pursued by Nigeria's military dictatorships over the last decades under IMF and World Bank guidance, which decimated the metropolitan economy' (ibid.: 42). And Nyasha Mboti asks us to consider the other-isation we engage in when we paint Nollywood as the foil to 'normal' practices (2014).

I argue here not for a celebration of informality, but rather I suggest a serious examination of the relationships of power and formality in networks of global media industries. I suggest we recognise that certain actors benefit from formality and others benefit from informality. Just as many Nigerians would prefer formalisation, others – such as the marketers – actively and consciously resist it in every business dealing in an effort to maintain autonomy over industries they created themselves. On a global level, if we assess the current structure of global media industry networks, we see that media industries producing heterogeneous content have increasingly homogeneous ownership relationships. Formalised domestic industries tend to be controlled by identifiable major corporations that have global investments and co-ownership relationships. In an effort to diversify, these global media corporations, headquartered in locations from Los Angeles to Tokyo to London to Mumbai to Sao Paolo, are increasingly invested in one another, be it through partial ownership stakes, distribution agreements, or ongoing co-production relationships. In order to become a part of these networks, industries must have significant levels of formality, with reliable documentation of sales figures.

In Nollywood, we can clearly see the relationship between marketers' access to (and control of) informal distribution networks and their control over the industry, and we can also see how the big-name producers of New Nollywood and their supporters would like to gain more control over profits through their control over more formalised and documented distribution. Formalisation of distribution (starting with the use of documentable distribution and creation of sales figures, leading to the ability to access significant sources of external funding) would alter in Nollywood in many ways. As marketers would lose power, banks and foreign corporations could begin to invest. We can see this potential in part in the recent investments that online distributor iROKOtv has received on the back of its transparent, fully documented revenue and viewer accounting, as discussed in greater detail in Chapter 5. In looking at informality, while noting its limitations, it is important also to acknowledge the way in which it delimits foreign investment and incorporation into formal global media industry networks.[20] It is also vital to acknowledge the ways in which informality and non-documentation are conscious and active business strategies marketers use to resist governmental and corporate efforts to dethrone them and more closely control the industry.

NOTES

1. See Chapters 4 and 5 for more in-depth exploration of these.
2. Some television shows do have soundstages, mostly built for specific shows. I visited the set of an all-West African reality show, akin to *American Idol*, and found it to be shot in a brand new high-end soundstage, sponsored by the show's South African owners and corporate sponsors. No Nollywood movies were shot there, nor were there any plans to rent it out to the infamously low-budget Nollywood productions in the future. The disparity between the slick international corporate pan-African reality show production and the Nollywood movies I saw being shot was striking.
3. I cite these to give scalar perspective, but do so reluctantly, as I attempt to neither reinforce the production and circulation of 'statistics' of essentially unmeasurable figures nor replicate the culture of quantification often imposed by institutional onlookers on informal contexts.
4. And comparing global generator density is perhaps the epitome of figures that could never be reliably counted.
5. The term 'distributors' will be used in this book to denote anyone who distributes Nollywood movies. I will use the Nigerian term 'marketers' to describe the specific class of industry workers that executive produces, markets and distributes Nollywood movies, and belongs to the industry-structuring guild FVPMAN. All marketers are distributors, but there are some who attempt to distribute without being a member of the marketer community.
6. Despite his assuredness, I would still caution readers to take that percentage point as a qualitative as opposed to quantitative assessment: the industry *feels* (to an observer personally invested in circumventing such sales) like it is 94 per cent physical copy sales, but no one has actually *measured* it.
7. While these are technically videographers, they are referred to as cinematographers in the industry and I will refer to them here as such to minimise confusion when quoting Nigerian sources.
8. As discussed in greater detail in Chapter 4, most job functions in Nollywood are represented by a guild; guild membership is so widespread it can be taken as a given for anyone working extensively in the industry.

9. A popular cinematographer suggests that ten to fifteen days is the bare minimum for a movie, while a 'good' movie will take twenty-one days of shooting and some producers will attempt to get away with just four to five days (Martins, 2009).
10. PHCN stands for Power Holding Company of Nigeria, but has often been redubbed to Problem Has Changed Names.
11. Isaac Martins, a top cinematographer, claims that the dominance of Sony is due to the Lagos shop's entrepreneurial managers' efforts to better understand the Nigerian production system.
12. He breaks this down as twelve days of picture cutting, two days for the director to turn this into a director's cut and two days to lay sound.
13. In Nigeria, a wealthy successful man is usually referred to as 'big', and underlings and servants are often referred to as 'boys', no matter their age.
14. See Tsika (2015) for a book-length study on Nollywood's star system.
15. Though surging crime rates shuttered most cinemas, a handful remain. They still haven't proliferated, however: they are the exception rather than the rule. The Muslim North is a different story entirely, with male-only open-air cinemas common. Nollywood as defined in this book, as well as in the industry, has little intersection with the North's cinema system.
16. They no longer have a British office, moving recently from London to New York as more of their investors were in the USA.
17. Sometimes as part of an attempt to have the facilities running for twenty-four hours a day, to maximise their productivity: official production by day and black market production by night. See Wang (2003) for more on this phenomenon.
18. In the marketplace, authorised and unauthorised movies are often indistinguishable from one another.
19. I use quotations for the word 'lack' because these are only seen as lack because of the normalisation of the alternatives.
20. In Chapter 5, I discuss Nollywood's alternative global networks, drawn on informality.

3

Nollywood, the Nigerian Product: Style, Format and Audiences

A woman looks on in horror as the witchcraft she used to ensure her fiancée's loyalty backfires and he dies a violent death before her eyes. His ghost then returns to haunt her until she takes her own life in a mixture of regret and despair. A man trades identities temporarily with his less fortunate but fertile twin in order to impregnate his wife and finds himself unable to return to his comfortable life, leaving him in a state of despondency. His ensuing machinations leave multiple lives in an utter shambles. A fifteen-year-old girl marries against her parents wishes and proceeds to spend the next few years in an abusive marriage, suffers severe pregnancy complications and ultimately takes her own life.

Nollywood movies do not hold back on shocking plot points or dramatic consequences for actions. The movies are stylistically identifiable, recognisably southern Nigerian and West African, both in form and in detail. In light of the focus thus far on the history and current structure of the industry, it is important to consider what drove the original growth of Nollywood and what continues to fuel the industry: the popularity and appeal of Nollywood as a cultural product. The resonance Nollywood movies have with the Nigerian viewer, the West African viewer and viewers throughout the rest of sub-Saharan Africa and the African diaspora is the true motor of Nollywood's explosive growth. Sold in the open-air markets of sub-Saharan Africa alongside pirated Hollywood, Bollywood and Asian martial arts movies, viewers consciously make the decision time and again that Nollywood movies are their cultural product of choice.

Nollywood's style and form drive its success, but they have given rise to disagreement in how to discuss – or how to 'place' – Nollywood in both style and format. Onlookers, from journalists to Nollywood directors to academics, have variously placed it in the category of cinema, video, television, theatre and some combination thereof, and this placement has implications for how the industry is understood. This chapter examines the styles, format and consumption of Nollywood, in the context of African cinema, global televisual content and the Nigerian popular arts. I suggest we can also see Nollywood's business model as a product in itself, as it can be thought of as Nollywood's collective inherent political position; it has itself circulated widely, inspiring and enabling related cultural creation in pockets across the continent and in the Nigerian diaspora. First, however, let's take a closer look at Nollywood texts.

GENRES, THEMES AND SETTINGS

With plots ranging from action-packed thrillers to love stories to traditional dramas involving village life, Nollywood movies take on many forms. Though diverse, they tend to be united by stylistic conventions that include an emphasis on dialogue, involved side stories and multiple climactic plot points spread out over the course of what can, at times, be a lengthy storyline, sometimes taking six or more hours to unfold via multiple separately sold parts. The plots of Nollywood movies tend to be sensational and full of startling twists. Good and bad news enter dramatically and often engender sizable reactions. Plots are rife with shocking revelations (e.g. someone is pregnant, has a terminal illness, is someone's long-lost father) and the length of the movies allows for many turns and twists before conflicts are resolved. In this way, plots are multi-climactic, much in the spirit of a multi-episode soap opera or telenovela (see Adejunmobi, 2015). Also as in the plots of their soap opera cousins, changes of fortune feature frequently, with rags to riches (and perhaps back to rags again) tales and drastic alterations in status an often-used plot convention.

Settings

Nollywood movies pull from both the traditional and the modern in their iconographies, and present the two side by side in ways that connect with viewers living lives connected to both as well. Movies are set either in the city or the countryside (representing either village life or the bush. These two tropes are so well known that some urban viewers report watching village movies exclusively to connect with perceived traditional 'African' culture (Becker, 2013). Popular satellite television network Africa Magic has devoted an entire channel just to content set in cities for those drawn to such content (this channel is known as 'Africa Magic Urban'). Village settings are places at once traditional yet inextricably linked to the modern world in a number of ways. For instance, village scenes set in modern times are likely to include televisions, brand name products and mobile phones. At the same time, they are also likely to feature an iconography that leaves viewers feeling connected to a perceived shared past: traditional clothing, groups of women pounding yams, yards full of dust and goats. City scenes feature the specific iconography of modern West African urban life, with Lagos as modern teeming metropolis. Urban exteriors are set on the distinctive streets of Lagos or the gated courtyards of up-market houses, while interiors feature familiar symbols of modernity in West Africa: tiled floors, metal railings on interior stairways, traditional printed fabrics for curtains, overstuffed, extravagantly tufted leather sofas and, perhaps, among young characters, posters of African or western pop stars. These elements have led English scholar Jonathan Haynes to refer to Nollywood movies as 'familiar in the wrong ways and strange in the wrong ways' (2000) to the eyes that book many international film festivals. Rather than a movie in western festival-ready form, featuring African details (an art film-paced drama, perhaps, with lead characters wearing Nigerian prints or set in a traditional village), they are a movie in popular African form, featuring details of cosmopolitan life (a melodrama-filled sequel full of mobile phones and SUVs, and governed by relatively conservative morals).

We can see the presence of Nigeria in nearly every scene in Nollywood movies, and this presence can serve as one of the movies' primary draws – something Haynes points to in his analysis of the ever-present awareness of Lagos in Nollywood movies (2007b). This presence is, in part, a product of the realities of production. Budget sizes mean that Lagos (or an unspecified generic neighbourhood found in Lagos) is often the shooting location; the time period is usually the present or unspecified – and, if the past is represented, it may look the same as the present (ibid.). Almost all shooting is done on location, as Nigerian soundstages (used in Nigerian television production) are too expensive, and the locations are usually crew members' apartments, repurposed production offices, the expensive houses of well-to-do Nollywood investors, or the city streets (or, for country settings, 'out in the bush'). Constructed sets for movies generally consist of a spare room transformed into, for instance, a necromancer's lair via a cursorily painted backdrop and a few odd props, such as a table covered with gold foil and halved gourds. In this way, the very aesthetic of Nollywood is tied both to the experience of life in Lagos and the structure of the industry (see ibid.).

Similarly, limited time for editing, multi-part release plans and last-minute production schedules can, at times, contribute to a story-telling style marked by lengthy plot interludes with little action, extended dialogue and the unsettling entrance and exit of storylines tertiary to the main plot of the film. While bigger-budget New Nollywood productions are generally carefully planned out and edited, much of the rest of Nollywood operates on an aesthetic marked by velocity and last-minute improvisation on behalf of directors. Full scripts tend only to be given to leads, with those in supporting roles only receiving copies of the scenes in which they will appear, as producers see no reason to incur the photocopying expenses for minor characters (Ejenoboor, 2009). As a result, some background actors may be unaware of their role's relation to the overall plot, contributing to a disjointed feeling found in some productions.

Genres

Genres in Nollywood can be thought of as being as wide as 'urban' or 'village', but they can also be as specific as the general plot of one successful movie repeated time and again in a formulaic series of successors. While the term 'genre' itself can often constitute a general plot formula, genre is particularly likely to constitute a fill-in-the-blanks sketch in Nollywood movies. One of the more involved Nollywood genres is the epic. Epic movies are usually set in the past and feature some approximation of 'traditional' village life, sometimes featuring famous wars or historical figures. *Battle of Musanga* (1996), for instance, a popular early Nollywood epic, is a historical narrative centred around the locally contested influx of colonisers and Christianity into an Igbo village in the mid-1800s. Epics can be fully fictional as well. *Igodo: Land of the Living Dead* (1999) is another classic Nollywood epic, but the conflict it features is between multiple generations of villagers and the very real spirit world in the countryside around them. In *Igodo*, a boy is predestined for greatness, but local evil-wishers have him sentenced to death on trumped-up charges. In response, the spirits curse the land and visit revenge upon the village. The movie portrays the great pains taken by villagers to reverse the curse, sending representatives to attempt to appease the spirit world in different ways.

Indeed, black magic appears in many Nollywood movies, particularly in dramas, whether set in the village or the city. One subset of black magic movies deals with spiritual beliefs come to life. In a typical tale, a protagonist may fail to heed a warning or superstition and anger a spirit, or may cross the spirit in some other way, such as making it jealous. The spirit then rains curses and misfortune upon the mis-doer and those around him or her. The hero must understand the curse and undertake certain tasks to placate or destroy the angered spirit. This loose formula has persisted from the village-set movies of Nollywood's early days through to some of the most high-end New Nollywood movies, such as Kunle Afolayan's highly lauded[1] release, *The Figurine*, in which a group of young adults obtain a cursed figurine, which seems to wreak havoc in their lives years later (though the ending of the movie leaves it up to the viewer to judge whether the bad fortune befalling key characters was actually due to the figurine or just to the machinations of a lead character who wished to frame the figurine for some of his own actions).

In urban settings, a movie focused on black magic may instead feature an urban protagonist attempting to attain something desired – usually financial gain or the loyalty of a desired romantic partner – via nefarious methods, resorting to individual or group black magic rituals to achieve their goals. They almost always come to regret these decisions. One of Nollywood's first hits, *Living in*

BlackBerry Babes (2011)

Bondage, set the stage for this theme in its depiction of the misfortunes experienced by a man who resorted to black magic – killing his wife as part of a ritual – for financial gain.

Urban dramas often follow the same theme outside the realm of black magic. A particularly popular subset of these aspirational urban dramas is what some call the 'city girl' (Adenugba, 2008) or 'ghetto life' (Ayakoroma, 2014) sub-genre, in which the choices of covetous young urban women, often involving prostitution, are portrayed as ruinous. This prostitution-oriented sub-genre began with Nollywood itself, in popular early titles *Glamour Girls* and *Domitilla: The Story of a Prostitute* (1996), and has continued through to current times with megahits like *Jénífá* (2008) and the many *Jénífá*-branded spin-offs it spawned. *Jénífá*, whose compelling and charismatic main character is drawn into potentially ruinous prostitution[2] when she arrives to begin university in Lagos, would also fit into the 'university student' or 'campus life' sub-genre of dramas. These movies explore the temptations of black magic, prostitution, gold-digging relations, or other 'bad' behaviour that may entice students when they arrive at university and attempt to attain status. University student movies may feature male or female protagonists and involve bad choices outside of the sphere of prostitution. Popular recent satirical hit *BlackBerry Babes* (2011), for instance, explores the choices of female university students obsessed with obtaining the status accompanying ownership of a new model BlackBerry smartphone: while some of the characters are shown to sleep with specific older male benefactors, they don't enter the world of actual prostitution until the last movie in the trilogy (*BlackBerry Babes Reloaded*, 2012). Instead, they spend much of the plot

A scene from *Last Flight to Abuja* (2012), a bigger-budget action movie

relishing the power they wield as they extort, swindle, rob and double-cross their many lecherous prospective suitors.

Continuing these urban explorations of unsavoury behaviour secretly underlying rapid gain in wealth or status are thriller or action movies, which allow audiences an insight to a seedy underworld, following crime networks and those fleeing or trying to thwart them. Teco Benson is one of the more popular directors in this genre. His titles – such as *Mission to Nowhere* (2007), in which police seek the murderer of a wealthy politician's wife, or *State of Emergency* (2004), in which the protagonist must thwart the plans of former military men turned terrorists – epitomise the genre, as could recent bigger-budget New Nollywood hit *Last Flight to Abuja* (2012), which unravels the events that led to passengers being on-board a particular aeroplane that crashes.

While movies featuring black magic, misbehaving youths and crime may be sensational, many Nollywood movies have a more intimate scope. Romances and family movies are two genres that focus on the travails and resolution of interpersonal conflict, in both rural and urban settings. These genres often have smaller casts and fewer locations than their flashier cousins, and are also both often targeted specifically at women. Romances follow the troubles of star-crossed lovers who often eventually make their relationship work – either against all odds, after a period of reflection on their values, via a series of unlikely events that bring them closer together, or after one lover learns an important lesson about their mistreatment of their partner. Or, a romance might feature two characters competing for the affection of a third. Family movies similarly focus on interpersonal conflict shared between a few characters, but tend to be set in the home and feature internal conflicts, like two brothers fighting to head the family after a father's death (see *Brothers War*, 2013).

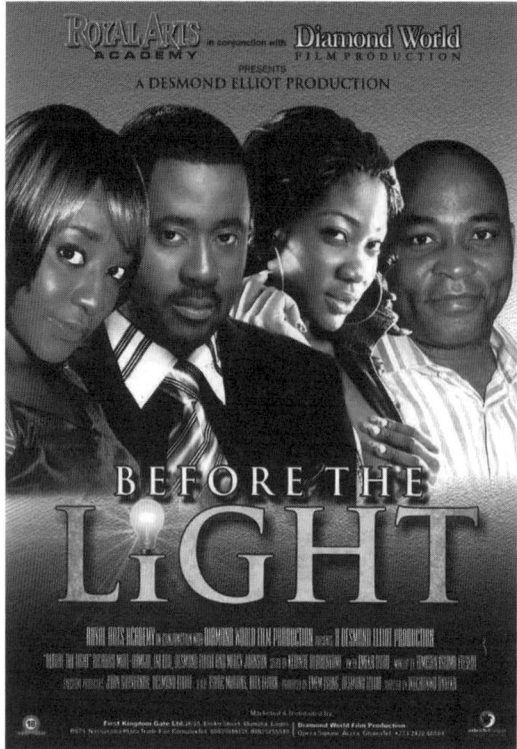

Before the Light (2009), a family movie, traces the conflict between a child's stepmother and biological mother

Comedies are a broad genre that has produced a number of much-loved genre-specific stars. These movies have a number of tropes; one popular formula is the fish out of water, involving the cultural clashes of rural–urban migrants, or Nigerians abroad. Another Nollywood classic, *Osuofia in London* (2003), is an example of this. In *Osuofia*, a poor, unlucky and unworldly villager learns his wealthy brother has died in London, and he goes to London to try and claim his fortune. He meets his brother's fiancée, a British woman, and his brother's solicitor, who are both out to swindle him. Much of the movie revolves around humorous situations resulting from his unfamiliarity with city life and British customs; he succeeds, in the end, in outwitting the swindlers and returning to Nigeria with the fortune and his brother's fiancée as a wife. (In a later sequel, the British wife plays the comedic fish out of water as she tries to fit into Osuofia's village as his second wife.)

While comedies, dramas, epics, romances, thrillers, action and family movies are all archetypes under which movies might be labelled, genres can be thought of as very specific formulas, with one popular movie spawning generations of imitators, such as the slew of very similar 'city girl' prostitution movies that followed the success of *Glamour Girls* in 1994. We can also think of popular movies

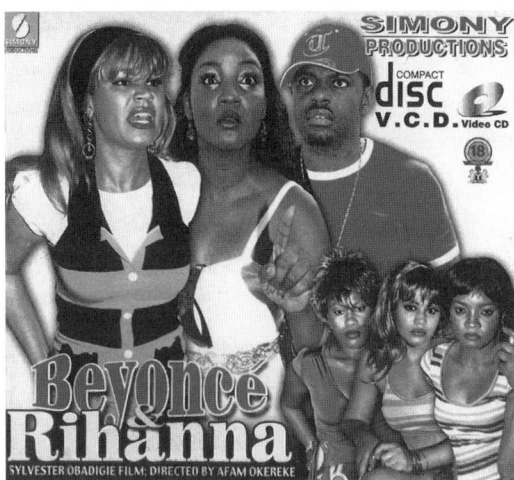

Beyonce and Rhianna (2008)

as spawning imitators, not through plot similarity but through unauthorised appropriation. In the absence of copyright enforcement, movies can adopt anything they want as branding with impunity. For instance, the popularity of *Osuofia in London* meant that the actor that played the Osuofia character is now frequently billed as 'Osuofia' in subsequent movies, though the actor is the only common factor – producer, director, character, plot and setting are completely different (Tsika, 2015). The original producers may or may not be behind this effort. In any case, they have more important things to do than chase down whoever has used their intellectual property in this way, and usually do not see it as a significant threat to their contemporary efforts. Not only do characters and movies sometimes share names with unrelated past hits, but they also sometimes share names with unrelated international pop superstars. *Beyonce and Rihanna* (2008), for instance, is a popular title about two Nigerian women who happen to be named Beyonce and Rihanna, who are fighting over a man named Jay while aspiring to best one another in a singing competition. Other titles acknowledge their use of international pop stardom in their plots. *Lady Gaga* (2012) is a popular movie about a Nigerian woman who intentionally dresses and acts like international pop star Lady Gaga in her quest to become famous and popular herself. The iconography of international pop stardom, in these cases, is just one more component of modern Nigerian life available for use by movie-makers.

Themes

Nollywood movies reflect Nigerian values. Marriage, faith, duty, fidelity and family, for instance, are usually lauded, and many plots are structured to reward those who value these and punish those who blindly pursue material goods to the detriment of their families or faith. Morality and religiosity are esteemed: pastors are often given exalted status, and the devout are usually particularly well regarded. The emphasis on morality appeals to many who feel a disconnect with the sexual or materialistic overtones and morally dubious endings in western movies. In addition to family and faith, Nollywood movies also tend to highlight justice: punishment for wrongs is a central theme. Though unscrupulous behaviour and black magic can sometimes lead characters to wealth, Nollywood movies are quick to show that this behaviour will ultimately lead to characters' downfall.

This focus on black magic reflects the widespread belief in Nigeria – and across much of sub-Saharan Africa – in the everyday realities of black magic and witchcraft. In Nigeria, these stories may hold particular appeal. Nigeria is marked by the extraordinary differences between immense oil wealth, accompanied by private jets, foreign boarding schools, luxury cars and phalanxes of security, and the daily lives of 'ordinary' Nigerians, many of whose full-time job salaries are never quite enough to afford sufficient food, shelter, medical care and transport to and from work for them and their family. While this disparity in wealth marks many countries in the developing world, Nigeria's version is particularly distinctive because of the closeness between wealth and poverty in Nigeria, chronologically, geographically and in terms of social ties. In Nigerian cities, wealth and poverty are side by side with one another with no satellite slum cities on the outskirts of a wealthy core. Similarly, the patronage relationships between employers and employees and the vast size of Nigerian families mean that it is often a short path of social and familial connections between the rich and the poor. Perhaps most striking is the rapidity with which some families have beaten the proverbial path from rags to riches. While some wealth in Nigeria is certainly gained honestly, popular opinion would seem to believe otherwise. Those that have achieved wealth, be it from oil, importation, or connection to political office, are often viewed with a mixture of awe and suspicion as such paths are frequently marked by bribes, cronyism and other forms of corruption. The rapid enrichment of individuals and their families through oil wealth and political favour, as well as piracy, 419 scams[3] and other dubious sources have led to the status of wealth as seeming unnatural and the product of a mix of luck, tenacity and the ill-gotten and very real blessings of black magic. From this perspective, we can see the roots of Nollywood's frequent preoccupation with portraying the misery visited upon those who resort to such paths to achieve success. And this performance of justice – reward for piety and penalties exacted for deviance or hurting loved ones – appear not just in Nollywood, but also have marked other iterations of Nigerian popular culture.

NOLLYWOOD AND 'AFRICAN CINEMA'

Nollywood is just one type of Nigerian mass cultural production. In Nigeria, one of the most populous nations in the world (and the most populous nation in Africa), there is a lot of room for popular culture to achieve very large-scale domestic popularity, and the NTA soaps and Yoruba travelling theatre troupes discussed in Chapter 1 are examples of other Nigerian mass cultural forces that have enjoyed domestic success. Nigeria has been the source of a wide variety of other well-known cultural output as well, from musicians like Afrobeat king Fela Kuti and millennial African pop superstars D'Banj and P-Square to the famed tradition of Onitsha market pamphlets to writers famous on a global scale, such as Chinua Achebe, Ben Okri, Wole Soyinka and Chimamanda Ngochi Adichie. Across a wide variety of media, Nigeria's cultural output has been prolific and influential, both within West Africa and on a global level; Nollywood is only the latest Nigerian cultural product to circulate globally.

When Nollywood is discussed as a movie industry, however, it is often not in the context of these other Nigerian popular culture products, but instead against the backdrop of African cinema, as Nollywood is a key and prolific producer of Nigerian (and, hence, African) movies. Nollywood's fit with the tradition of African art cinema is a bit more difficult than its fit with other Nigerian popular arts. Nigeria has contributed to African celluloid film output over the years, though never by more than a few titles in any given year (as is the case with most countries' celluloid film production in sub-Saharan Africa). While direct connections between the development of Nigerian celluloid movie production and the development of Nollywood video production are limited, it is worth reviewing Nigerian cinematic tradition in order to better understand Nollywood's position vis-à-vis what is usually known as 'African cinema'. After all, both Nollywood and Nigerian celluloid productions are 'Nigerian movies' and a brief look at celluloid film production from countries across the African continent can shed greater light onto the significance of Nollywood movies, products of a distinct industrial structure and with distinctly different stylistic tendencies. First, let's examine the roots of African film production in the colonial era.

Colonial African Movie Policy and Its Aftermath

Beginning in 1939, the UK established Colonial Film Units in their colonies, which produced educational films meant to inform colonial subjects about health and comportment standards, including titles such as *Post Office Savings Bank* (1935), *Mister English at Home* (1940) and *Infant Malaria* (1935) (Diawara, 2007), while other films, like *Daybreak in Udi* (1949), have scripted narratives meant to encourage 'modern' behaviours (in the case of *Daybreak in Udi*, the behaviour in question is visiting a maternity hospital to give birth rather than

Scene from *Daybreak in Udi* (1949), an example of a British instructional colonial film in Nigeria

doing so at home). In an effort towards cost reduction in the making of these films, a small number of local African trainees were given western-style instruction in film production, preparing them to work on these films. This training, first, went on in regional institutes set up for this purpose[4] and, later, in London, as these training centres were shut down, relocated to one central base in London and renamed the British Overseas Film and Television Centre (BOFTC). Though some anglophone Africans received training at the BOFTC, there was no great movement towards African-led film-making in colonial British Africa and, therefore, little need for film policy; the number who received such training was quite small.

There was no movement towards African-led film-making in colonial French Africa either, with no African involvement in movie production at all and no tradition of instructional movies produced in-country. The only official French policy regarding film in Africa during colonial times was the Laval Decree, issued in 1934. The Laval Decree stipulated that any prospective film shoots in French colonies had to be submitted to French colonial authorities for prior approval, a policy meant to discourage subversive messages which, in effect, also discouraged film production in general (Thackaway, 2003) and the hiring of African creative workers on films shot in francophone Africa (Diawara,

1987). As different as British and French film involvement in their colonies may have been, their approaches differed even more widely after their colonies achieved independence.

The sweep of independence through anglophone Africa left the British with virtually nothing in the way of organised initiatives relating to movie-making in former colonies. In contrast, throughout francophone Africa, France began to actively support cinema through a number of policy initiatives. In 1961, the Consortium Audiovisual International (CAI) was founded, as were, in 1963, the Ministry of Cooperation and its Bureau du Cinema, with the goal of offering financial and technical assistance to African film-makers in their former colonies. While these efforts originally supported newsreels and documentaries, the focus quickly shifted to artistic expression (Okome, 1995).[5] While some of this money was required to be spent on French technicians and post-production in France (Thackaway, 2003) – and other less pure motives have been suggested[6] – a main stated goal of these efforts was aid to the arts after years of colonialist domination. The results of this continued initiative have been striking and long-reaching. French support has been integral to much of what is now collectively known as 'Black African cinema'.

Post-colonial African Cinema

African cinema in the post-colonial era has often been conceived of as a project at a near-continental level. Films are made on a one-off basis in countries across sub-Saharan Africa. Rather than building sustainable mass entertainment industries spanning Africa, the goal has been largely aesthetic and political. In his widely read book, *Black African Cinema*, Nigerian film scholar Frank Ukadike was among the first to tie together the cinematic output of what he called 'Black Africa'. In his conceptualisation, Black African cinema can be seen as a broad class with its initial goal a more realistic portrayal of African life than seen in pre-independence films, made largely by colonial powers, either for or about the colonised populace (1994). In this vein, this filmic production – Black African cinema – is often received as inherently political in its collective nature, even as it is differentiated along linguistic (e.g. francophone vs anglophone) and ethnic lines. In many ways it is a cinema produced for a select world stage rather than a mass audience.[7]

If one is to examine the industrial structure of what has traditionally been termed 'African cinema', however, one will often find a structurally troubling reliance on former colonial powers, particularly France. Funding and distribution deals for these celluloid films indicate a process fraught with difficulty; each film can take years – in some cases it's even decades – to come to fruition. And, while focused on political aims, these films have been made with correspondingly little attention to sustainable business models or to the potential of spawning a popular mass entertainment industry. France's involvement in Black African film-making in the post-colonial period is marked by both pre-production French aid and the tendency for France's Ministry for Cooperation and Development to purchase the non-commercial distribution rights at an inflated price for screenings at French cultural centres (Armes, 2006). 'This is, in a very real sense,' noted film scholar Roy Armes, 'a cinema of which France is the principal producer and consumer' (2006: 55).

While the films produced through these French efforts are widely well regarded, the structure and support that produce these films can be seen as paternalistic. While there are no political content restrictions, as there were in the days of the Laval Decree, French civil servants are still likely to decide whether or not particular films are made and which subjects are valid, especially when the independent economic viability of these African 'art' films in the free entertainment marketplace is not very robust. And, it must be noted, the majority of these films are not widely screened in their 'home' country, if they are distributed there at all.

In other words, movies may be made in francophone Africa featuring themes and messages relevant to political struggle, but their dependence on French sources for funding and distribution is near complete. Despite their grappling with issues important to Africans and their often critical stance towards the French and colonial authorities, the production of these movies has still been dependent on the French. Even though these funding organisations frequently demonstrate a preference for politically resistant content, having former colonial authorities undertaking the role of gatekeeper makes some chafe. Senegalese film-maker Ousman Sembéne, often referred to as the 'father of African cinema', has termed the situation to be 'an economic dependency which, as such, gives the West the right to view Africa in a way that I cannot bear' (cited in Slome, 1996).

Even since 1980, when French aid was decentralised and associated film institutions relocated to Africa, African films that win funding must at least fit in to European perceptions of what African film is or could be. Though European institutions with a role in African film-making don't interfere with content or censor films, their influence persists in their very industrial structure. For instance, Armes points out, no matter what language films are produced in, there needs to be a script produced in a major European language in order for it to go through competitive funding processes. Similarly, film-makers with a base in Paris will be better able to navigate the demands of French funding agencies (Armes, 2006), a structural hurdle not put in place on purpose, but one that has significant implications on the content produced there. While this system does not encourage film-makers to alter their message, it does delimit diversity in both style and voice. Not only does the system encourage films to be stylistically comprehensible to European funders and audiences, but film-makers with a European or North American education and resources to base themselves in Europe also have a better chance to make their voices heard than moviemakers hailing from more modest backgrounds. For instance, with a few notable exceptions such as Sembéne, nearly all celebrated francophone African film auteurs, lauded in film festivals and the academy, came from well-to-do backgrounds and went to film school in Europe or the USA (ibid.). While there is no overt pressure to change messages, there are a number of more subtle structural elements in this patronage system that delimit diversity.

Nigerian cinema, like that in other anglophone African countries, never relied on the French funding machine (or the British, for that matter) to the extent that francophone Africa did, and could be considered more independent as a result. Yet these films still maintained a level of reliance on the state or international partners, whether through national film bodies or international funders. The most celebrated of Nigeria's celluloid production, for example, would be difficult to classify as truly independent. For instance, *Kongi's Harvest* (1970), widely considered the first full-length non-documentary celluloid Nigerian movie, is a Nigerian–Swedish–US co-production, and was followed by *Bullfrog in the Sun* (1971), a Nigerian–German–US co-production (Ukadike, 1994). Both still relied heavily on their foreign partners; and, it must be noted, there was never an explosion of Nigerian cinematic production of this variety.

It was the Yoruba drama troupe films in which Nigerian filmic production was most self-sufficient and had the most potential as a stand-alone industry, as these movies were funded and distributed via Nigerian channels. Yet, shot on celluloid film, this project was unsustainably expensive for the distribution channels upon which it relied. Copies of celluloid travel more slowly and more formally than the videos that succeeded them, making distribution on a truly mass scale an unlikely proposition. Yoruba theatre troupe films had the potential for sustainability in the funding and distribution paths they drew, but never achieved the moment of entrepreneurial clarity that would lead them to be distributed on such a mass and profitable scale as Nollywood. It is also a key point that Yoruba drama troupe films were not received on the world stage as part of the project of Black African cinema. African film scholar Frank Ukadike, for instance, characterised them in 1994 as 'an enterprise born out of greed and lack of concern for cinematic creativity … truly second-rate entertainment' (149), as they were seen as a pale imitation – little more than a record – of live Yoruba theatre performances.[8]

I argue that Nollywood's main contribution to the project of African cinema (and that of other similar video industries) can be seen as its industrial structure, and its independence and autonomy from external funding and green-lighting channels.⁹ Establishing its own sustainable global networks without the oversight of the state (see Chapter 4), multinational corporation (MNC) capital (see Chapter 5), or foreign altruistic or art-minded bodies, it is possible that Nollywood is achieving in structure some of the aims of African celluloid film in content: independence and a distinctive identity separate from its former colonial authorities. As veteran executive producer/marketer Emmanuel Isikaku put it:

> the Nigerians believed from day one in sponsoring things from *their* pockets ... In other African countries they make movies with money from international agencies. I don't have to wait for any NGO to give me money. I can do it myself. (2009)

Similarly, Moradewun Adejunmobi argues that it is the very commerciality of Nollywood and its corresponding responsiveness to local audiences (a necessity when budgets are based on sales) that render the industry as particularly vital and politically important (2007). This is not to diminish the value or importance of African celluloid film production: it continues to illuminate African concerns, settings and artists, and to diversify art cinema as it has been doing for decades. Rather, this is to assert that Nollywood is not separate or excepted from the issues of African cinema. Though rarely if ever political, Nollywood movies achieve some of the aims of Black African cinema in their very industrial structure. And, unlike much African cinema, Nollywood movies achieve wide circulation in their home country.

THINKING ABOUT NOLLYWOOD CONTENT

If Yoruba drama troupe movies were critically received less favourably than the films that make up the traditional canon of African cinema, video production has been taken even less seriously from a critical perspective. When Nollywood first emerged in the 1990s, it was ignored or panned by existent film-makers, film critics and film scholars, and considered unimportant in the context of the more 'serious' production being created by celluloid auteurs. With the exception of a few, like Nigerian film scholar Onookome Okome, the majority of scholarly work done on Nollywood has come from outside African film scholarship (Haynes, 2010). Even today, some of the loudest of Nollywood's critics are African film-makers offended by being lumped in with these popular movies with low production values, insulted by these movies being taken just as seriously as their own (Okome, 2010).

The project of film festival/art house/grant-driven African cinema has largely been a political one, dealing with issues of identity, colonialism and authority. Nollywood movies – set in modern landscapes, with visual and plot styles similar to soap operas and with no overt political statement for the most part – do not fit into what has come to be known as African cinema[10] or, for that matter, art cinema in general.[11] While I argue that the realities of Nollywood's funding, production and circulation can be considered the backbone of its role in furthering the project of Black African cinema, we can also look to the content of Nollywood movies for new spaces in which to understand Nollywood's relationship to what has traditionally been known as African cinema. Nollywood is best viewed as a category separate from that of African art film, lying between celluloid and television, and occupying a space between 'traditional' and 'modern' cultures in society. Karin Barber, the Yoruba theatre scholar, deems this space the 'popular arts' (1987). Rather than following imported elite stylistic conventions or continuing and preserving a static traditionalism, the popular arts – which are not candidates for folk art preservation or for grants from high art-promoting bodies – fill a huge and growing demand. As the world urbanises, drawing migrants from rural settings to urban centres, there is a particularly large and growing demand for such cultural production that walks the line between modern and traditional, and between the familiarity of local artistic traditions and the (often deeper) familiarity of global visual culture.

The form of Nollywood movies, even, places them squarely between the traditional and modern, in a space reserved for popular media. The length, for instance – often three hours or more as a standard to tell a single story – certainly differentiates them from the films that populate international film festivals and cinemas worldwide. The characteristics of Nollywood plots and narrative structure, as well as its intended home on television as opposed to theatre screens, contribute to its classification, perhaps, as 'small-screen cinema', sitting between television and film (Jedlowski, 2012). In this way, the Nollywood movie is discrete from both the Hollywood film and traditional Nigerian oral art forms, yet is connected to both.[12]

Indeed, the format of Nollywood movies has left people struggling for the words with which to describe and 'place' it. Scholars have varyingly used the terms 'video film', 'small-screen cinema' and 'video movie', among others, in attempts to ground Nollywood's description, at least in part, in its video-based production and its small-screen viewing. In this book, I have tended to refer to Nollywood content simply as movies, referring to them in regards to their loose shape as opposed to their format, in a search for the broadest descriptor possible. This goes along with the stylistic conventions of Carmela Garritano, who refers to Ghanaian movies, her topic of study, as 'video movies', as the term encapsulates the intentions of those movie-makers with no cinematic aspirations (2013). That said, the term 'videofilm' or 'video film' also seems to epitomise the hybrid qualities of Nollywood, acknowledging the video format alongside connections to soap operas, melodrama and STV movie content as well as film; the term 'video film' has become increasingly popular as a descriptor. Others, most notably a group of well-known New Nollywood directors, have created the label 'New Nigerian Cinema' to describe their content, emphasising connections to the tradition of African cinema and distancing themselves from video or small screens. This moniker suggests that video is a format of necessity, utilised only on the path to true expression realisation – movies shot on celluloid and viewed in cinema houses – and encapsulating the intentions of only a subset of the industry as a whole.

Even the name 'Nollywood' itself offers problems in its framing. While the first use of the name is unclear, it became widely used after a *New York Times* article; the implications of its subsequent use have been both a boon and thorn in the industry's side (see Haynes, 2007a, for a full-length essay on the topic). While the term has lent the industry significant built-in clout in popular press and even academic articles, the use of the –ollywood rhyming sobriquet places Nollywood in the same ideoscape as Hollywood and Bollywood, the two best-known –ollywoods on a global level. To compare Nollywood to either of these two is to suggest that Nollywood is a poorer, smaller imitator of these cinema-based film industries, which both feature large budgets, flashy effects and blockbuster logics. Rhyming makes Nollywood appear to be an industry of lack, which leads many mass market journalists to ask what lies behind its persistent 'inability' to produce movies that appear similar in scale and form to the glossy Hollywood or Bollywood features intended for cinema screens.

As we can see, however, Nollywood is a popular art that is more 'televisual' in both form and format, a term used by Moradewun Adejunmobi to illustrate ways in which Nollywood's form and consumption has features more in common with television than cinema (2015). Nollywood's televisuality references its relentless strings of sequels, its multi-climactic plots and the ample side stories sliding in and out of movies, resembling soap operas in form; viewers engage in patterns of recurrent interrupted viewing that resemble the way audiences consume daytime television (ibid.). Adejunmobi suggests that the appeal of Nollywood movies is in their similarity: 'they are valued not for offering a unique storyline but for being the newest and latest interpretation of a familiar story' (ibid.: 123).[13]

This similarity between titles is a feature of STV industries worldwide, an art form rarely studied by scholars, even though the majority of movies released worldwide are released STV.[14] STV generally refers to the collection of martial arts movies, action scene vehicles, erotic thrillers and tweaked versions of hit films with less famous actors that populate late-night television screens, cheap movie bins and the back catalogues of movie aggregators the world over.[15] In style, financing and industrial structure, STV is an industrial logic separate from cinema-based film industries and exists alongside cinema-bound films in every market.

Media scholar Ramon Lobato describes STV as an industry that functions on the logics of interchangeability. Movies must sit comfortably and clearly in a specific section of the video market (such as martial arts or erotic thrillers). As he puts it, 'this is a film culture that doesn't expect or even desire the exceptional; the important thing is that the film covers the right generic bases' (2012: 25). The logics of commercial cinematic film industries revolve around a single film standing out from its peers. Investors bet that a particular film will be a remarkable hit and experience correspondingly remarkable returns, but they must make many bets, in the knowledge that only a few of their expensive investments will pan out and that the returns from the winner will hedge and justify their failed bets. In order to stand out to financiers and audiences alike, commercial cinema-based film-makers hope to have something distinctive to achieve their financial goals: maybe a unique script, astounding special effects, or a compelling star performance. This strategy can be seen in the marketing: in interviews, a film's principals usually discuss how the film is different from other films in its genre. The logics of STV are very different. Too much distinction or uniqueness could be detrimental here. In an industry marked by quantity as opposed to quality per title, and with limited marketing efforts per movie, the motivation is for each movie to be reasonably interchangeable with others in its genre. When viewers have a huge catalogue to pick from, and when investment money has no desire to take risks, STV producers would be considered the most masterful and therefore the most successful if they produce content that stays as close to the genre formula as possible, with a few tweaks, giving viewers what they want and near-guaranteeing (moderate) returns (ibid.). It is an industrial logic based not on gambling on risky content with the possibility of great returns but on similar products consistently meeting modest expectations.

This is an industrial logic embedded in the format of the movie. Movies shot on film and bound for cinemas pursue a different formula for success than movies bound for home video sales. Though Nollywood shares many industrial features in common with STV, when viewed in the context of other STV industries worldwide, Nollywood glitters and shines. Its stars, its fame, its global reach – unlike STV action movies, for instance, which pale in comparison to the Hollywood films they mimic – Nollywood stands on its own on the world stage. As Noah Tsika put it in his study of Nollywood stardom, 'no other film industry in the world has developed a bona fide star system using only VHS and VCD' (2015: 70). Nollywood can be considered the world's foremost STV industry, based not on budgets or returns (it would not be in the lead in those categories), but rather based on its stature and, just as importantly, its glamour.

Indeed, instead of viewing a pale Nollywood through the lens of African cinema, we are better off understanding Nollywood through the lens of the popular mass creative movements that actually spawned it, as outlined in Chapter 1: Nollywood's most direct predecessors, televised domestic soap operas and Yoruba travelling theatre, as well as the global STV and televised melodrama industries. Viewing Nollywood content through the lens of soap operas, arguably Nollywood's nearest stylistic relative, brings us to a staple in the narrative form of Nollywood, telenovelas, Bollywood and soap operas alike: melodrama. It is no coincidence that the latter three were all popular entertainment in pre-Nollywood Nigeria. Melodrama, it has been noted, is a common trope in everything from Chinese to Egyptian cinema and television, all important cultural product exporters regionally (Haynes, 2000). In other words, if a movie or televised production is widely exported and consumed on a mass scale in an international context, it is common for it to incorporate melodrama. The irony is the near absence of melodrama in the arts showcases that make up international cinema. As Jonathan Haynes put it, 'popular melodramatic forms get filtered out almost entirely by the politicised paradigm of Third World cinema and by the aesthetic criteria that determine the access of foreign films to the art cinema circuit in the West' (ibid.: 24).

APPEALING TO NOLLYWOOD'S AUDIENCES

As we can see, Nollywood, the cultural product, has complicated intersections with a number of artistic traditions: Yoruba drama, soap operas, telenovelas, STV and African celluloid film, to name a few. To its audiences, however, Nollywood stands very much on its own. Simultaneously representing links to a sense of African-ness and to global urbanism, Nollywood has become the fabric of daily life throughout sub-Saharan Africa and the loosely defined African diaspora. Fervent fans of Nollywood watch daily. And those that distribute Nollywood have put energy into capitalising on this fervour. Nollywood's marketing budgets are quite modest compared to those of celluloid film industries. This is characteristic of the logics of STV industries: titles that benefit from their formulaic nature in the marketplace will necessitate much less in marketing budgets than a blockbuster, meant to break records and get just-a-few-times-a-year cinemagoers out of the house to make this 'the one' (though New Nollywood pursues more blockbuster-style industrial logics).

Nollywood Audiences in Nigeria

Nollywood is alive in the streets of Lagos. Information about Nollywood productions blankets the streets, particularly in the form of newspapers sold by the ever-present street vendors that seem to fill each tiny gap in traffic in Lagos's streets, walking between every lane of vehicles, hawking everything from sweets to cold beverages to Nollywood movies and gossip magazines. Posters and handbills can be seen widely, most frequently consisting of shots of the most recognisable actors' faces in particularly dramatic expressions. Indeed, it is extremely important for a movie to have recognisable actors on its posters and on the cover, even if their appearance in the movie is essentially a glorified cameo. Stars sell the movie and they sell other things too, including the many products for which they serve as spokespeople (Tsika, 2015), as well as newspapers. Jahman Anikulapo, editor of the Arts section of Nigeria's top newspaper, notes that 'if you don't put a picture of a Nollywood actor or actress on your paper, you don't sell' (2009). And, indeed, there is almost always a small picture and blurb about some Nollywood gossip in Nigeria's most respected news publications.

The market for Nollywood movies within Nigeria spans classes, though some who view themselves as wealthy and worldly mark themselves as cosmopolitan or sophisticated by their professed preference for Hollywood over Nollywood movies. One wealthy young woman with whom I spoke, who has lived with her family in both London and Lagos, watches Nollywood movies, but told me her family would be 'gutted' if she ever became romantically involved with even a very famous Nollywood actor, thinking it beneath her upbringing. All the same, rural and urban, young and old – Nollywood movies appeal to a wide swathe of the population. Whole families watch Nollywood movies together and movies are made to offend few.

Though no thorough Nielsen-esque studies of consumption patterns have been (or could be easily) performed, one can readily find people watching movies at home with their families at night or as background while performing chores during the day, just as one can find people watching Nollywood movies while at work or clustered in marketplace video parlours during the day, both public and private spaces. While online distribution within Nigeria only accounts for a minute portion of domestic viewing (see Chapter 5 for a more extensive discussion of online distribution in and outside Nigeria), online distribution produces some of the most reliable statistics on viewing patterns. Popular online Nollywood portal iROKOtv reports that its prime viewing hours within Nigeria for online content are during prime business hours: 11 a.m. to 4 p.m., a stark contrast from its figures on its online viewers watching the same content in the USA, Asia and Europe, markets which peak from 6 p.m. to midnight (Njoku,

2014c). This suggests that the online viewing public in Nigeria are people with desk jobs (a receptionist or front desk guard, for instance) that include electricity and internet connectivity that are more reliable than those in residential buildings. This timeframe also may reflect prime household chore time for housewives, who watch without their families in the upper middle-class and wealthy households in which online viewing is possible. In either case, these figures on online viewing offer rare solid statistical evidence suggesting that viewing one movie after another, and viewing while doing something else, is part of the fabric of daily life in Nigeria – whether it is online, on television, or on VCD.

Nollywood, like almost every other movie industry in the world, is, at heart, a domestic industry. Just as those working in the production of telenovelas call foreign sales the 'gravy' on top of the main course of domestic distribution, and just as US-based studios continue to produce culturally specific comedies, baseball-themed movies and other films with limited appeal abroad, Nollywood too is almost exclusively focused on the production side on appealing to the domestic market. Significant profits made from foreign sales tend to go to movies that are also hits on the domestic market. After all, in estimating a hypothetical movie's take, one New Nollywood producer suggested that even a very popular movie with strong international potential would get at least 70 per cent of its take from the domestic market (Isong, 2014). Not only is this market a concern, but domestic markets comprised of particular ethnic groups are also a focus in movie production. Renowned New Nollywood director Tunde Kelani repeatedly refers to the Yoruba masses as 'my audience', saying he produces films in the Yoruba language more than English 'because that is what my audience wants'. His English films 'flop', he said (likely an exaggeration as many of his films have enjoyed great success), because Yoruba audiences demand Yoruba-language films (2009). Similarly, successful New Nollywood producer/director Emem Isong views production of some movies in the language of her ethnic minority group as a great source of strength in her production efforts. As she has little competition, movies aimed at this group are nearly guaranteed sales (2011). And, in her assessment of the Ghanaian video industry, Carmela Garritano examines the ways in which production in the Akan language thwart piracy by limiting the market to a very small area (2013).[16]

That said, English-language production is the bread and butter – or perhaps we should say the pounded cassava or jollof rice – of the industry. These movies feel less culturally specific than those in regional or ethnic group-specific languages like Yoruba. The familiarity they have can reach across ethnic groups. It is also worth noting the role of English language in Nigerian popular culture in general. It is the language of both domestic soap operas and much imported international content, including Hollywood fare. Nollywood movies' English-language production helps place them in a familiar cultural context of modernity.

Nollywood's International Audiences

Nollywood fans outside Nigeria remain tuned in to the Nigeria-based industry. Interviews with Nollywood fans in the USA suggest that diaspora fans keep up to date in three main ways with the movies coming out in Nigeria each week. Local African grocery stores and other African video shops may put up posters in their stores or in nightclubs popular with young Nigerian-Americans or other African expatriates, announcing new releases. These posters will likely be made by the US distributor from whom the shop acquires its movies. These movies usually arrive in Atlanta shops, for instance, within a week of their original Nigerian release date.

Fans might also find out about a new movie online. Online distributors, such as leading streaming portal iROKOtv (more on this company in Chapter 5), put significant effort into publicising their content and creating a buzz among their subscribers for new high-end titles they have acquired. Over and above the subscription platform's own ads, fans may also keep up via the extremely popular fan news and gossip sites, or even internet message boards, attracting visitors from many different continents and posting news about and reviews of popular movies and stars. Younger fans also report knowledge of new Nigerian movies coming from the Facebook or other social media fanpages of their favourite stars. A star might announce the release of a new movie in which she stars. The news would reach a global audience. However, with no immediate access to the movie, fans might be particularly likely to search the myriad sites featuring unauthorised screenings of Nollywood movies online. Fans report that it usually only takes a day or two from the initial release date for a viewer to rip and post a copy of a newly released Nollywood movie online.

English-language production is also a significant driver of Nollywood's appeal in international markets. The paths of the recent African diaspora dictates most of the locational patterns of Nollywood's distribution, though Nollywood is also popular in places like Haiti, Barbados and St Lucia in the Caribbean, where most fans are many generations removed from their African heritage. Part of the appeal of Nollywood is the way in which it recalls the experience of being in Nigeria or West Africa. The fare of US- or Europe-based Nigerian producers who make their own versions of Nollywood movies tends not to be as popular as that produced in Nigeria – because of both their perceived lack of 'authenticity' and, at least equally importantly, their lack of Nollywood movie stars, as these stars live and primarily work in Nigeria. Bronx-based diaspora movie seller Rabiu Mohammed notes that the audiences buying Nollywood movies in the diaspora buy them *because* the movies remind them of home. 'People want to watch because it makes them think of Africa,' he notes, and adds the obvious corollary: 'Movies made here make them think no such thing' (2009). The African-ness of Nollywood is wrapped up in its place of production: a movie made by Nigerian expatriate actors, producers and writers, but made in the USA, misses the essential Nigerian-ness and African-ness that draws audiences in the first place. Interviews with Nollywood fans in the Nigerian diaspora suggest the same motivations for preferring Nigeria-made content to Nollywood fare made in the diaspora. Diaspora fans say they are watching Nollywood movies to feel connected to Nigerian culture, and both the physical setting of these movies in Nigeria and the presence of Nigeria-based Nollywood stars is key to their enjoyment of these movies (Atlanta Fans 1 and 2, 2011).

Nigerian-ness is often conflated to African-ness among diaspora audiences furthest removed from the country. In her work on Nollywood viewing in Barbados, film scholar Jane Bryce notes that audiences generally don't have an understanding of the specific geographies at play. Ghana, for instance, is often estimated by those she interviewed to be an area within Nigeria, regions of Nigeria are not differentiated and Nigeria itself is generally subsumed by the catch-all moniker 'Africa' (Bryce, 2013). Nollywood movies are marketed in Barbados simply as 'African movies' and people don distinctly Nigerian styles learned from movies and call them 'African' fashion (ibid.).

Similarly, even urban Ugandan viewers in Kampala and urban South African viewers in Cape Town report that they take rural-set Nigerian movies to represent the traditional life of a perceived pan-African countryside (Becker, 2013; Dipio, 2014). Perhaps the South African countryside is too close and too known, for it is the Nigerian countryside that anthropologist Heike Becker has found is the key attraction of Nollywood movies for urban South Africans. An urban viewer with whom she spoke explained, 'I see them as a way of how I, or my culture, are connected to the rest of Africa' (Becker, 2013: 190), suggesting that viewers there see themselves as simultaneously connected to and distanced from Nollywood settings, and that their viewing serves as a reminder of both. Viewing Nollywood can be a politically motivated claim to African-ness in a modern age, with countryside-set movies connecting people to what they see as traditional lifestyles set in modern times, while urban titles can 'Africanise' viewers' everyday city-bound experiences of modernity (ibid.).[17] In other words, they allow viewers to engage in modernity with a foot planted firmly on African soil.

Even as Nollywood movies disseminate widely through the anglophone African diaspora, they are also dubbed into French by unauthorised resellers based in the francophone market. Nollywood is also circulated among viewers speaking non-European local languages. One way this is achieved is through screenings with a local MC simultaneously narrating and explaining the plot, the characters and even translating foods that are eaten into locally understandable equivalents (Krings, 2010; Pype, 2013; Dipio, 2014).[18] In Dar es Salaam, this narration is into Swahili (Krings, 2010). In Kinshasa, this is into kiKinois (Pype, 2013). In Uganda, it is into Luganda (Dipio, 2014). Narrator MCs gain fans of their own; audiences flock to screenings narrated and interpreted by specific famous MCs. In Uganda, Dipio reports, these MCs (or VJs, as they are called in Uganda) record their narration of an English-language Nollywood movie and that narrated version is broadcast on local free-to-air television station, rights-free, with the narrator's voice drowning out the scripted dialogue and going off on tangents during slower segments (2014). In any case, narrators can localise this foreign content, connecting, for instance, a destructive fire in a Nollywood movie to one that recently destroyed a local market, affecting the lives of many in the marketplace video hall audience (ibid.). This form of circulation, Nigerian content interpreted into local languages and watched in public (or in private, if screened on local television in this way), has contributed to another life of Nollywood as a Nigerian cultural export: Nollywood's sibling industries.

Nollywood's Siblings

Nollywood is only the most famous and prolific of the growing video film industries that, in part, trace their roots to Kenneth Nnebue's business model. These industries, many claiming their own –wood moniker, are mostly in sub-Saharan Africa. What holds them together is the similarity in their business model and, usually, stylistic conventions to Nollywood, derived from the successful, often unauthorised, circulation of Nollywood through their territory. Though Nollywood came first, two close geographic neighbours based on physical video circulation can be considered twins – more than just siblings: Ghana's movie industry, based in Accra (sometimes called Ghollywood), and the Kano-based video production of the Hausa ethnic group in northern Nigeria (known sometimes as Kannywood).[19] Both Ghanaian and Hausa movies emerged around the same time as did Nollywood, out of similar political economic and technological contexts (see Garritano, 2008), but it can be argued that both were inspired by Nnebue's business model in their use of physical marketplace VHS circulation networks. The similarities between these video industries in name, style and industrial structure should not be overstated. Nollywood movies are quite different from even the Hausa movies coming out of Kano in the north. Movies from northern Nigeria tend to deal with romantic themes and stories often are neatly tied up with a happy ending. Southern Nigerian movies, however, are much more likely to centre on corruption, betrayal, criminal activity, or witchcraft. African film scholar Adamu attributes this focus in the north in part to northern Nigeria's tradition of Bollywood fandom and the conservative values that, in his reading of it, mark Hindu and Muslim societies more than they do Christian ones (2011). Despite Kannywood and Nollywood sharing the same nation-state, Nollywood's closest relation may be the Ghanaian movie industry. Ghanaian and Nigerian videos share not only many similarities in style, and links in business (see Garritano, 2013), but also it is not uncommon for stars of both industries to travel back and forth between the two to supplement the roster of productions on which they are working.

Following Ghanaian and northern Nigerian industries, the past decade has seen the rise of production booms in places that had previously been major sites of Nollywood consumption. Tanzania's Bongowood in Dar es Salaam and Kenya's Riverwood in Nairobi are the most visible and sustainably functioning of these newer sibling industries, inspired not just by the style of Nollywood's popular content, but also, more importantly, by the demonstrably sustainable economic model of Nollywood, the industry. Other countries featuring Nollywood-esque local content include Burkina Faso, Uganda and the Democratic Republic of the Congo. Perhaps the most interesting sister industry to Nollywood is 'Vollywood', a little-known small video industry made for and by the sizable ethnically Indian population living in South Africa, dealing with cultural and family issues set in South Africa's Indian communities (Mistry and Ellapen, 2013). This enclave in South Africa has chosen to create movies that resemble Nigerian movies more than they resemble movies from India. This is likely in large part because of the accessibility and simplicity of the Nollywood model. Budgets, scripts and expectations are all smaller, while distribution is much simpler, making barriers to entry much lower. All the same, the adoption of Nollywood as a model for Vollywood, as well as for the other industries mentioned above, speaks not only to the accessibility of its business model, but also to the appeal of the intersections of the traditional and the modern in its content.

Besides Nollywood serving as their aesthetic and industrial inspiration, the nature of these industries' relationships to Nollywood is up for debate. Are they simply inspired by Nollywood? Or are they essentially Nigerian movies made by local producers in the local language, with some adjustments for local cultural specificities? Anthropologist Matthias Krings has argued for the latter, outlining the connection between 'Bongowood' (Tanzanian) movies and the translation of Nigerian Nollywood movies into Swahili. He has looked at two forms of translation of Nollywood movies in Dar es Salaam – the MC-narrated screenings discussed above and photo-novels outlining the plot of Nollywood movies in Swahili text superimposed on freeze frames from the movie – as intermediary steps between consuming Nollywood movies and Tanzanian entrepreneurs producing 'Bongowood' movies in Tanzania (2010). In this way, these Swahili movies, made by Tanzanian directors with Tanzanian talent, could be considered a Tanzanian *translation* of Nigerian productions as opposed to a Tanzanian cultural production in their own right, and Krings argues as such (ibid.). Tanzanian movie-makers would likely not appreciate this reading of their work, however, as they take great care to delimit visible Nigerian cultural influence in their productions (Böhme, 2013) and the movies have achieved great success in their own right in the Tanzanian marketplace. Nollywood as a cultural archetype has pervaded African cultures in other ways as well. In Kinshasa, for instance, economic capital of the Democratic Republic of the Congo and another hub of MC-narrated Nollywood screenings, one of the most popular theatre troupes in the city, Cinarc, is noted for the similarity between their televised performances and Nollywood movies (Pype, 2013).

The flipside of this is the 'Nollywood' movies made by Nigerian expatriates in the USA[20] and Europe[21] for expatriate and diaspora audiences. Written, produced and distributed outside of Nigeria (though sometimes featuring a visiting Nigeria-based actor to legitimise them), the producers of these movies vehemently believe themselves to be part of the Nollywood industry. They refer to themselves as Nollywood directors and, in the case of the USA, they have named their independent guild the Film-makers Association of Nigeria – USA (FAN-USA), underlining their desire to be considered a part of Nollywood as opposed to a separate industry; the organisation does not, as the name would suggest, represent film-makers in Nigeria and, despite the USA hyphenation, there is no branch of this guild that is not in the USA. These foreign productions of Nollywood movies retain Nollywood aesthetics and are keyed in to Nigerian-ness and African-ness as themes, but are recognisably shot outside Nigeria. As such, they are not very popular in Nigeria and less popular than Nigerian Nollywood movies even with diaspora audiences, who generally watch Nollywood to feel some connection to Nigeria, West Africa, or Africa in general. Nollywood's continental siblings, however, have begun to enjoy some screening potential on pan-African satellite television channels, and Ghanaian and Hausa movies in particular also circulate widely in the diaspora.

While US and European Nollywood movie industries have their own drivers relating to the experience of dislocation and migration, the trend of Nollywood-esque movie production within sub-Saharan Africa has been steered by a number of forces experienced on a continental level, although the political and economic conditions that gave rise to Nollywood were first realised in Nigeria. The confluence of new inexpensive media technologies, the privatisation of state economies and the weakening of the nation-state and its national broadcasters, all trends associated with globalisation, have contributed to all of the African video industries (Garritano, 2008). Perhaps more than anything, however, we can cite the demand for local content: a main driver of Nollywood's growth was the near insatiable appetite for not just home, but also domestic (or regional, or African) entertainment. Although Hollywood and Bollywood films dominated much of Nigerian movie culture, this was a matter of accident rather than design, as no attempts were made to develop content particularly attractive to Nigerian moviewatchers, a large potential audience (after all, Nigerians make up a fifth of sub-Saharan Africa's total population). As Hollywood and Bollywood ignored the African market, space was created for a cultural product that felt locally relevant – and this space and potential was large in a country of 170 million people. Once Nollywood demonstrated the functioning of its industrial model, cultural groupings (via language, nation, ethnicity, or some combination thereof) with smaller potential audiences could see how to achieve Nollywood's goals themselves. In this way, we can see Nollywood's business model as an export as popular as its movies. Uneven connections to the global order spurred a demand for a local response, which came in both style (melodramas simultaneously recalling the traditional and the modern) and in business model; we can see the influence of both of these in other burgeoning movie industries in sub-Saharan Africa.

CONCLUSION

If Nollywood content reflects some of the global appeal of melodrama-infused content like soap operas, it is also reflective of the specific cultural appeal of West African and Nigerian life; this specificity appeals to a diversity of audiences who may feel at least a cultural affinity (see Straubhaar, 1991) to these specific details. On the one hand, Nollywood movies follow a telenovela-esque televisual form that has proved to be popular across cultures worldwide. (As Haynes points out (2000), they combine the narrative structures of story-telling traditions with a brand of imagery imported in the form of international advertising and television, in the sense of Martín-Barbero's theorising about telenovelas. Martín-Barbero (1995) places the popularity of telenovelas as rising, in part, from the way in which they blend the length and meandering qualities of traditional story-telling with the sorts of images (advertising, television, film, etc.) that mark 'modern' society and global culture.) On the other hand, they are also culturally specific. The presence of Nigeria in these movies is inextricably linked to the consumption of them. From danfo[22] and okada[23]-filled city streets to tiled up-market homes and wealthy women donning expensive Nigerian gowns and headwraps to depictions of modern village life, Nigeria is presented as a dynamic and current place. The themes presented, too, are particularly relevant to Nigerian culture – in the regular plot emphasis on black magic as a powerful and driving force in society, but also in the attention to religious mores and moralism. Stylistic elements, such as the desirability of larger women, adherence to traditional gender roles and the importance of religion, also reflect Nigerian cultural norms. While these elements, themes and depictions are certainly not unique to Nigeria, they reflect Nigerian lifestyles in particularly familiar ways, and in ways that appeal to Nigerian viewers and to viewers in other places seeking connections to Nigerian-ness, West African-ness, or even just African-ness in general.

It is this same familiarity and specific cultural appeal that drove the Yoruba theatre explosion earlier in the twentieth century, as discussed in the previous chapter. When Yoruba theatre troupes emerged, part of their appeal to mass popular audiences was connected to heightened desire at the time for cultural content connected to Yoruba heritage (Barber, 1987). At the same time, Yoruba theatre was also appealing in its employment of imported stylistic conventions, already familiar and appealing to many in the port city of Lagos (ibid.). In this way, we can see Yoruba theatre and Nollywood movies sharing a similar role in West African cultural production: between the global and local, between the modern and traditional, a popular art (see ibid.; Haynes, 2000). The vibrant and exuberant explosion of Nollywood mirrors well the explosion of Yoruba theatre by the 1970s not only in content, but also in industrial form, the key focus of this book. In the history of both, we can see new entrepreneurs launching new productions, stealing ideas and talent from one another and scraping a living together from the enthusiasm of an audience hungry for home-grown entertainment. While Yoruba video production wound up feeding into the Nollywood boom that has now captured much of the world's imagination, Yoruba theatre troupes themselves faded in popularity and their primacy and dynamism never fully returned. There are many parallels between the rise and subsequent heyday of Yoruba theatre troupes from the 1940s to the early 1980s: both cultural movements capitalised on audience demand for home-grown entertainment reflecting local cultural values, and both had some international recognition and success. Both were particularly dynamic in their adaptation of new technological and cultural forms and both were particularly creative in the flexibility of the new organisational forms that arose to structure the industries. Yoruba travelling theatre's decline came along with the advent of new (video) technologies (which pushed live performance aside) and with economic collapse in Nigeria. It is not yet clear whether similar elements could derail the Nigerian video movement. However, if we can think of Nollywood to some extent as an extension of Yoruba theatre troupes, with both being an expression of Nigerian popular culture, then we can also see a *permanent* space in Nigerian popular culture for such entertainment, and we can see Nollywood as being one face – the current face – of a shape-shifting movement of Nigerian popular arts.

Also worth noting is the 'travelling' nature of Nigerian travelling theatre. Travelling through circuits of the Yoruba-speaking world – and, later, even shifting formats to appeal also to non-Yoruba West Africa – the actors and directors of Yoruba theatre physically traversed the same networks that physical copies of Nollywood movies would later traverse. Theatre pioneer Hubert Ogunde's shift to including English language and western instrumentation in his productions in order to appeal to and conquer markets outside of purely Yoruba networks is also a precursor to Nollywood's adoption of the same. We can see the circulation of Nollywood movies both inside and outside Nigeria as part of similar networks, and we can see the circulation of Nollywood's business model spurring sibling industries throughout sub-Saharan Africa and the diaspora in a similar way. Both travelling Yoruba theatre and Nollywood movies, then, can be thought of as Nigerian popular arts inscribing their own networks of circulation and mobility on an international level, and spurring related African creative production in their wake.

NOTES

1. It won five Africa Movie Academy Awards (AMAA) in 2010 – the most prestigious awards ceremony for the industry, and was nominated in five more categories.
2. She acquires HIV in the first movie. However, in a sequel, she learns she does not have the virus after all.
3. 419 is the Nigerian penal code for fraud ('obtaining property by false pretences'). Nigeria is known throughout the world for one iteration of these: the email scam from, for instance, a purported Nigerian prince or former political figure, temporarily separated from their vast fortune, aimed at tricking the recipient into paying significant sums of money in advance of hypothetical future gains by freeing up a non-existent offshore account. The so-called Nigerian 419 scam, while known globally, is particularly prevalent and problematic inside Nigeria, and is certainly aimed at fellow Nigerians at least as much and likely much more than it is aimed at foreigners. Houses throughout Lagos, for instance, read on the outside 'This house is not for sale, beware 419' to protect against the practice of scammers 'selling' the house for cash with false documents while the rightful owners are on holiday.
4. For Nigeria, the designated training centre would have been the West African training hub that was opened in Accra (Ghana) in 1949, while Nigeria itself was home to the West African branch of the Colonial Film Unit.
5. Okome (1995) traces this specifically back to the 1963 appointment of Jean-Rene Debrix as the director of the Bureau du Cinema. Debrix had a vision of narrative cinema developing in France's former colonies.
6. Such as the benefit that the support of francophone cinema would have on French

cinema and the propagation of artistic production in the French language. See Armes (2006) for a more thorough critique of this.
7. Scholarly enquiry into African film is rich and furthers the goals of the cinematic productions themselves in drawing together the united political goals of celluloid film production across sub-Saharan Africa. This project has been advanced in a number of influential books, from Olivier Barlet's *African Cinemas: Decolonizing the Gaze* (2000) to Lindiwe Dovey's *African Film and Literature: Adapting Violence to the Screen* (2009); the relations of scholarly thought on African cinema to Nollywood have been explored in the book *Viewing African Cinema in the Twenty-First Century: Art Films and the Nollywood Video Revolution*, edited by Mahir Saul and Ralph Austen (2010).
8. Since Nollywood's emergence, however, significant work has been done on integrating these emerging video industries into the study of African cinema. A recent edited collection, *Viewing African Cinema in the Twenty-First Century* (Saul and Austen, 2010), deals with this project in great detail, integrating the study of 'art' films with 'video films' in a number of essays. Editor Jonathan Haynes also discusses the disconnect between the study of Nigerian video films and the tradition of scholarly enquiry into African film, suggesting that, while quite worthwhile, African film scholarship focuses on a few auteurs whose work is 'especially keyed to the political and other concerns of Western (or Western-based or Western-affiliated) academics', ignoring the realities of popular entertainment for most African citizens (2000), a critique of African film scholarship that closely echoes critiques of art-house African film productions.
9. See Jeff Himpele's book, *Circuits of Culture: Media Politics and Indigenous Identity in the Andes*, for more on this distinction via Himpele's study of media networks in Bolivia. Transitioning to self-made networks is what Himpele refers to as 'indigenizing the circuits of culture' (2008).
10. As Haynes put it, 'the Nigerian video films throw into startling relief how much the African cinema that reaches European or American shores is mediated in ways that make it comprehensible to foreign audiences' (2000: 5).
11. That said, Birgit Meyer is among those scholars challenging the binary between African cinema and African video content, through her work on the Ghanaian video industry, pointing out some synergy in the aims of both projects in content, particularly their treatment of tradition and heritage (2010).
12. See Obiechina (1990) for more on the long-reaching implications of oral traditions across the arts in Africa.
13. At the same time, unlike soap operas, each Nollywood part aims for closure as opposed to a cliffhanger ending. Adejunmobi suggests that each resolution offers another place to reaffirm commonly held moral and social values (2015).

14. This includes movies released in the USA, Hollywood's domestic market: the majority of new movies released annually in the USA are STV.
15. Like Nollywood, STV has seeped into an interchangeable video–television–online trifecta.
16. There are less than 10 million Akan speakers, while the major Nigerian languages – Yoruba, Igbo and Hausa – have more than twice that each.
17. Becker describes this as 'portrayal of supposedly "African" cultural practices within a familiar material "Western" world in what many regarded as a major challenge: to engage in global forms of modernity in terms of consumption and knowledge – the mall and the Internet – in ways that will not compel them to abandon our culture' (2013: 193).
18. Waliaula notes that, even without an official narrator, group viewing in video parlours and the like is often accompanied by narration: the narration of the loudest and most entertaining of the viewing audience, leading the ongoing side commentary and translation (2014).
19. Because of this, they have also inspired the most scholarship thus far. Birgit Meyer has been prolific at theorising about connections between Ghanaian video content and religious traditions in Ghana (see 1999, 2007, 2010, among others), while Carmela Garritano (2008, 2013) has worked on the political economic roots of Ghana's industry, tying the development of Ghanaian video production to the same globalising forces that further disenfranchised many poor Ghanaians. And Abdalla Uba Adamu (see 2007, 2011) has been at the forefront of theorising about Hausa video content, particularly in terms of connections between Hausa videos and the Bollywood movies that have been so popular in northern Nigeria, while Brian Larkin (2000, 2008) has done widely respected and influential work on the media architectures that have supported and guided Hausa videos.
20. See Haynes, 2013; Hoffmann, 2013.
21. See Samyn, 2013.
22. Privately run overcrowded minibuses that serve as Lagos's primary form of public transportation.
23. The local name for motorbikes.

4

Organising Nollywood: Government Policy and Guilds

On one hot summer day, a number of luminaries in Nigeria's arts industries met for a panel discussion at the National Theatre in Lagos's Surulere neighbourhood. Organised by Jahman Anikulapo, the Sunday editor of Lagos's premiere newspaper, *The Guardian*, this annual panel, known as the Art Stampede, has met for over fifty years and encompasses everything from Nollywood video to fine arts. After a number of hours speaking on directions the arts industries should take, one panellist demanded the microphone during the question and answer period. 'The government can't solve everything,' she cried. 'Artists are custodians of their own art! The government is there only to put in place structures.' Some applauded, but at the same time a cry went up in the audience as hands shot up across the room. Three audience members sitting near me at the back called out repeatedly in unison, 'But where is the structure, but where is the structure?'

This injection of passionate feeling was in response to director Francis Onwochei's comment detailing his view that government must step up to the plate and regulate Nollywood further. The issue of government oversight is significant. Many suggest that Nollywood was originally able to spring up precisely because of the lack of such oversight. It seems questionable that government intervention after the fact will transform the industry and achieve some sort of optimal efficiency. It seems more likely, at this point, that any policy would benefit either the state itself or the specific major players within the cultural and political capital lobby who support such policy – and probably both. This is the context against which the Art Stampede panellist expressed the view that it is a mistake look to what she defined as a paternalistic government to protect the industry when she believed the power is really in her own lap and that of her colleagues. She dismissed looking to the government to solve all problems when, she asserted, it is hardly capable of solving any.

Nollywood, as mentioned previously, is an industry that was born and emerged without any overarching external effort guiding it, particularly not any state-governed arts development initiatives. While states worldwide attempt to support growth in their cultural industries through policy, the early years of

Nollywood's growth occurred without the oversight – or, it would seem, even the acknowledgment – of most of Nigeria's government agencies, including the agency charged with promoting film industry growth (the Nigerian Film Commission, or NFC). In more recent years, Nigeria's government agencies have begun numerous, often half-hearted attempts to regulate, structure and otherwise interact with the now-successful movie industry; schemes to do so vastly outnumber those ever implemented.

This chapter will serve as an examination of efforts to govern an industry largely viewed as unregulated. After a review of the three governmental agencies with a charge to interact with Nollywood, we will look at four case studies of attempts to restructure or govern the industry. The first two are governmental initiatives. One was partially successful: an attempt by the Nigerian Film and Video Censors Board (NFVCB) to produce an oligopoly in distribution was implemented but didn't achieve the desired results. The other was clearly a failure: a bill to license film workers that never made it out of the Federal Assembly. These weren't chosen as the two most important initiatives, but rather as examples of the motivations of and challenges for those advocating for government involvement. The next two case studies are self-governing initiatives, managed by guilds. The case study that works is the one that rose with the industry: the use of guilds as a substitute for courts in solving labour disputes. The other initiative, an attempt by one guild to reconfigure distribution, ended in failure because of the strength of another guild. Taken as a whole, these case studies highlight the power of self-governance, as well as the political will of those already in power in the industry. All of these initiatives can best be understood when considering the nature of the Nigerian state and its goals. As such, before delving into the specifics of past and present movie policy and industry oversight in Nigeria, we must first examine the specifics of Nigeria, the state.

THE NIGERIAN STATE

Nigeria is a vast nation marked by its ethnic and geographic diversity and enormous heterogeneous population (one in five people in sub-Saharan Africa is Nigerian). The area we now know as the state of Nigeria is the product of relatively arbitrary borders drawn by colonialists and encompasses hundreds of ethnic groups and languages. The divisions between the Hausa-dominated north and the Yoruba- and Igbo-dominated south[1] are particularly pronounced, as they were separate entities even under British colonial rule, and developed separately at different paces. Nigeria's wealth, natural resources (vast oil reserves) and skyscrapers cluster in the more Christian south, while farms and underemployment stretch out across the more Muslim north. The recent sectarian violence that has gripped parts of Nigeria in the form of Boko Haram, the Islamist terrorist group, has been concentrated in the extreme northeast of the country, about as far from Lagos as one could be and still be in Nigeria, both physically and culturally (though the south has its own issues with violence in the form of local militants in the oil-rich Niger Delta region wishing to reclaim land and oil wealth from foreign, corporate and federal domestic interests through violence).

Nigeria gained independence from the UK in 1960 and declared itself an independent republic in 1963. The new nation's first forays into self-leadership quickly led to ethnic and regional tension over the make-up of that leadership and Nigeria's first years as a republic quickly transitioned into more than three decades of military control. Nigeria was ruled by a succession of military regimes achieving power through repeated coups d'état from 1966–99.[2] Some of these military governments were better or worse than others, but, as a whole, political power in Nigeria in these thirty-three years was something taken by force and thought to be employed mainly for the enrichment of those in power and their cronies. Towards the latter years of military rule, the Nigerian government became known not only as corrupt and ineffectual, but also specifically as a 'predatory state' (Lewis, 1996). Ibrahim Babanginda, notorious military dictator from 1985–93, seemed to have one goal in his governance: maintaining power by personally enriching those who could keep him there. This included extensive state engagement in illegal activities such as international money laundering and smuggling, reckless diversion of public resources to the private parties keeping him in power, abandonment of currency controls and a variety of other actions that signalled overt disinterest in the good of the Nigerian state in preference for the good of the Babanginda hold on power (ibid.). This particularly predatory approach to governance continued with Sani Abacha, president from 1993 until his death in 1998, and the subsequent advent of civilian rule (Lewis, 2007).

While the death of Abacha marked the dusk of Nigeria's classification as a predatory state (ibid.), the legacies of this attitude towards governance have persisted. While the civilian governments since 1999 have put into place reforms aimed at enhancing public good and conditions for private investment – and some local governments, particularly that of the most recent Lagos state governor Babatunde Fashola,[3] have improved quality of life dramatically – federal institutions have remained weak and some of the nation's new leaders have found it difficult to break free from the allure of patronage and collusive relationships with those private parties in control of the nation's dominant source of foreign exchange: oil. The oil wealth, and its concentration in the hands of a few, has led many scholars to argue that the average Nigerian may be worse off than if there were to have been no oil in the country at all (Osaghe, 1998; Peel,

2009). The election of opposition presidential candidate Muhammadu Buhari in 2015 has caused some to herald a reformist era with the potential to wean the country off its decades-old pattern of federal corruption and graft (*The Economist*, 2015). Others, remembering Buhari's previous reign as Nigeria's military dictator from 1983–5, are less optimistic.

It is in this context that we can best understand policy initiatives and governmental involvement by the Nigerian state. As we examine this involvement in Nollywood's structure and functioning, it is important to keep in mind the motivation behind it. I posit that there are three main drivers for the Nigerian government's interest, as it often ignores entire industries completely. The first motivation is self-enrichment or self-preservation: the more formalised and documented Nollywood is, the easier it will be for the state to profit from this money-making industry it had little hand in raising. This is what many Nollywood players grouse about and explains a significant part of the resistance to state participation. The second motivation is that, while governance may be partially corrupt, the government often pursues signs of external legitimacy. The success of Nigeria's movie industry on the world stage and the participation of Nigeria in international agreements, such as intellectual property rights accords, serves to legitimise the state in the eyes of its own bureaucrats and from the world perspective. The last motivation is a genuine desire to target weaknesses in an industry with high development potential, inspired by a desire to better the nation. All three of these motivations may be at work simultaneously; it is important to remember different government actors are behind each. Many policy suggestions arise from a sincere desire to benefit the country and the industry. However, it is likely that any actually implemented policy in Nigeria will be the product of two if not all three of these motivations, favoured by different key actors.

GOVERNMENT AGENCIES

Three government agencies currently carry a specific charge to interact with Nollywood: the Nigerian Film and Video Censors Board (NFVCB, formally inaugurated in 1993); the Nigerian Film Corporation (NFC, formally established in 1979); and the Nigerian Copyright Commission (NCC, formally inaugurated in 1989). All three have roots that stretch back further than the beginning of the video boom of the early 1990s, but the NFVCB was the only agency that had a relationship with the industry in its formative years. That relationship was not meant to be organisational or supportive and it had one goal: censorship. The NFVCB is the only agency that has been thought to hold any power in the industry, and the only agency to have succeeded in instituting policy that has had any significant structural effect in the industry, though, in recent years, this agency has also fallen behind.

NFVCB and Censorship

The NFVCB has its roots in colonial Nigeria. The first censorship board was established in Nigeria during colonial rule, in a 1933 Ordinance that also created a scheme in which only licensed venues could screen films (Okome, 1995).[4] This Ordinance went through a number of changes over the years, but was kept through independence, retaining much from its original form in its 1963 (independence era) revision. The films being censored in the early years of the post-colonial independent Republic of Nigeria were primarily state-funded educational and documentary films as these were the core of domestic production and foreign films were exempt from review (ibid.).[5]

In 1993, in the first full year or so of the video boom, the federal government inaugurated the NFVCB with the 1993 Act No. 85; the NFVCB began operating at full force in 1994. This Act formalised the requirements that any *video* sold in Nigeria must be reviewed by the NFVCB before it could be released to the public. The NFVCB immediately became a virtually unavoidable part of the movie production process in Nigeria.

Nigeria is, generally speaking, a socially conservative and religious nation. Explicit sexual content and depictions of bad behaviour without negative consequence are frowned upon by censors and the public alike. While the NFVCB can ask for certain movies to be re-edited, most movies do pass, perhaps due to self-censorship and market pressures. Recent upheaval in the industry surrounding the NFVCB-implemented New Distribution Framework, discussed later in this chapter, as well as the departure of a particularly productive director of the agency, has meant that the power of the agency has waned significantly, and some consider it to be a shell of its former self. With the exception of the past few years, however, the agency has stood as the core point of contact between the federal government and Nollywood movie-makers.

The power and reach the NFVCB achieved may seem quite surprising, as it stands in stark contrast to the informality and extra-legal qualities of much of the industry and the ineffectuality of most of Nigeria's government agencies – a contrast that seems particularly stark when one imagines the obligation that early Nollywood entrepreneurs felt in bringing their videos to the newly inaugurated NFVCB. It would appear that the drive of the Nigerian government to control the content distributed to its people proved much stronger than its drive to regulate the cultural industries in any other way, which speaks to the self-preservation motivation described earlier in this chapter.

This may not be as paradoxical as it seems: coming out of the colonial era, Nigerian governmental structures reflected the strategies and structures and, as a result, the priorities of its British colonisers. In the colonial era, film policy consisted mostly of directing what content – educational, usually – would be distributed in the country. This is reflected in the current housing of two of the agencies most closely associated with guiding the video industry – the NFVCB and the NFC (a developmental, as opposed to regulatory, agency) – in the Ministry of Information, as opposed to a Ministry of Culture. And, in 1993, the age of military dictatorship and Nigeria as a predatory state, self-preservation functions, such as that of censorship, could hardly have seemed more vital to the state. To put it in basic terms, there was already a drive for and culture of censorship functioning in Nigeria at the birth of Nollywood, and the government agency in charge of censorship was simultaneously powerful and flexible enough to adapt to the birth of new technologies and new industries. As we are about to see, the other governmental agency with a charge to direct the movie industry – the NFC – had neither of these two qualities, was never powerful or strong in the first place, was slow to adapt to change and is still struggling to find its role and relevance in a video age.

NFC and Development

In 1979, the Nigerian Film Corporation Decree established a governmental agency meant to support a domestic film industry: the NFC. This came about seven years after the 1972 Nigerian Enterprises Promotion Decree (also known as the Indigenisation Act), which was also meant to support local film production by setting up impediments to the distribution and exhibition of foreign films and trying to limit foreign ownership of cinema houses (Okome, 1995).[6] The ambitious charges of the newly formed NFC included the promotion of domestic film production through financial and other incentives; state-sponsored film production facilities and post-production facilities (the latter was particularly important when none existed in the country); financial and other incentives for the development of more cinema houses; training facilities; and the acquisition and distribution of domestic films deemed important. As ambitious as this Decree was, aside from establishing the NFC, still existent today, it did little else (Ukadike, 1994). One can easily posit that the Nigerian government's initial motivation in setting up the NFC laid in legitimacy-seeking. In attempting to join the ranks of major players on the world stage, the existence of arts development programmes could only serve to further legitimate the workings of the state. Additionally, the creation of new state agencies creates a new spate of coveted jobs that can be doled out to supporters.

Underfunded and disorganised, the NFC has struggled with relevancy since its inception. At the advent of the video industry in the 1990s, the NFC had still not instituted training facilities, production or post-production facilities, or any significant financial incentives for cinema construction or film projects. Its main achievement has been in creating an archive of important Nigerian films and the administration of a film school in Jos that is well-regarded but has little connection to the video industry centred hundreds of miles away from its rather remote location. The most visible actions of the NFC today and those on which it spends much of its budget are its participation in international film festivals, to which it sends some of its representatives (and sometimes some higher-profile Nollywood producers) on all-expenses-paid international trips to places from Cannes to Israel. This is not to deride the NFC: it has found itself with a limited budget and no longer any clear view of what its mission should be in supporting the development of a domestic movie industry that has already developed on its own. It has found it quite difficult to insert itself after the fact to support an industry that is largely wary of unwanted government interference. Consequently, it has been busying itself with other useful but far from vital tasks in the meantime, such as archiving the industry's history: tasks that serve the industry well, yet are not required for any significant level of industry function.

NCC and Copyright

The Nigerian Copyright Commission, although inaugurated five years earlier than the NFVCB, is still a much newer entity than either of the other two agencies. The 1988 Copyright Law[7] first recognised Nigeria's creative productions as copyright-able and allowed for the establishment of a governmental agency to oversee the administration of this copyright. In August 1989, Nigeria's federal government established the Nigerian Copyright Council, which was upgraded into the Nigerian Copyright Commission in 1996. This Copyright Law was the first time international-style copyright had been recognised and administrated by the Nigerian government and, as such, when the video boom began in the early 1990s, the NCC was still just trying to get its footing.

Copyright in Nigeria looks to be quite straightforward on paper, yet it is not really functional in practice. Nigeria became a signatory to the Berne Convention in 1993,[8] a baseline international copyright convention that today provides the foundation to most nations' copyright law. The motivation for the Nigerian state signing this convention and, at least nominally, providing for a governmental agency to administer it was almost certainly legitimacy-seeking. There is no motivation to provide resources to actually support its implementation, but being a signatory to this international agreement legitimises Nigeria as a participant in global standards while taking virtually nothing away from the government's power, especially when the law is rarely utilised.

The Berne Convention, internationally applicable, holds that copyright is considered to be automatic and not dependent on registration with any authorities. By law, the rights-holder is she or he who supplied the resources to make the film (i.e. the financier), unless there is a contract that says otherwise. If there are no documents and multiple people lay claim, then, hypothetically, both parties would be obliged to prove that they were the executive producer, or the main resource provider. While this may be true, few in Nollywood outside of the NCC are aware of this legal standard. It is rarely enforced and, in many cases, such proof would be quite difficult to provide. Few reliable records of transactions are produced in Nollywood as executive producers try to escape the scrutiny of the government, outside investors and their own business partners. And, in a society of informal employment, virtually no contracts are produced. Similarly, money often flows in from multiple places – many of which may be black market dealers with an aversion to the legal system – and proving who was in charge overall is almost always fraught with difficulty in the case of a dispute. However, what really prevents such cases from ever making their way through a formalised legal process is the lack of faith in and disgust with the bureaucracy of the court system, among the creative workers and even some lawyers at the NCC itself.

The court process tends to be frustrating to all parties. There are, for example, no specialised copyright judges, but this is far from the root of the problem, which stems from the inefficiency and bureaucracy of most court battles. Cases invariably drag out and, if a judge retires or gets transferred (a common enough occurrence), one has to start afresh in a new courtroom. Similarly dragging out the process, the inevitable appeals process will commonly take four to six years (NCC lawyer 1, 2009). As a result, NCC lawyer 1, employed by the NCC, admits 'real resolution of issues is a real issue' (2009). He notes he has been involved in some NCC prosecutions of certain optical disc replication plants for the past five years and sees no resolution imminent, expecting to work on the cases for years to come. Also, those subject to criminal prosecution for copyright violations are often allowed to continue operating as their case works its way through the system. NCC lawyer 1 complains that one of the biggest problems in the few prosecutions of copyright that occur (in the movie industry, it's been close to zero, and most prosecutions have occurred in the book-publishing industry) is the tendency for rights-holders to settle out of court and then refuse to testify in criminal proceedings: basically, a refusal to engage in the formalised court system and, in some cases, using the threat of a lengthy judicial process as a weapon in extortionist efforts (*The Economist*, 2015).

As it stands now, there are two paths by which to pursue a copyright claim in the courts system. The first is as a criminal offence. The NCC serves as the prosecutor in this kind of case. The second is as a civil case, in which the rights-holder pursues damages lost when their copyright was breached. In this sort of case, the plaintiff is in charge of securing private prosecution and can sue for damages. NCC lawyer 1 estimates that Nigerian attorneys will charge at least

1 million naira (around $5,500) for their provisional fees and, thereafter, will charge fees every time a court appearance is made (2009). For an industry like Nollywood, with such slim profit margins and low budgets, civil prosecution is rare, while criminal prosecution through the NCC is little known and little trusted.

During my visit to the NCC offices in the National Secretariat in Abuja, I could sense the frustration of the employees. Highly educated, intelligent and very knowledgeable in copyright law, they have a job they view as important with few resources to achieve their assigned goals and, as such, little respect or faith from those they are charged with protecting. The lawyer with whom I spoke the longest was a young and quiet bespectacled man of unimposing stature, whose face became more animated the more he discussed the intricacies of international copyright law. He and his colleagues seemed thrilled to have a chance to explain how copyright law should work in the country – indeed, happy to have a visitor at all. They provided me with reams of background material on Nigerian copyright law, including some widely circulated reports they had ghost-written for major international organisations – receiving no credit or fame for the analyses themselves.

My positive and cooperative experience with the lawyers of the NCC was not echoed by any of the rights-holders that I interviewed, whether they were representatives of US corporate interests or small-scale Nollywood producers. Falling among the large group of movie-makers disillusioned with the NCC, independent director and producer Peace Anyiam-Fiberesima angrily alleged, 'the NCC is lying if they say film-makers are not motivated to prosecute', saying that this is, in part, why prosecution has been rare (2009). She alleges that the NCC has caught illegal distributors in the past and not prosecuted them due to the personal connections of said unauthorised distributors. Taking a different tack, Emmanuel Isikaku, former president of the main marketers and distributors guild (FVPMAN), claims the reason his members will generally not prosecute or testify in NCC cases is because of fear of violence from unauthorised distributors (2009). 'Most of the pirates are deadly,' he answers calmly with a smile on his face. 'They can go to any lengths to track you down' (ibid.). His sincerity here is questionable, as many have accused members of his organisation of engaging in such unauthorised distribution in some of their business dealings; Isikaku, a calm man confident in his position, is extremely unlikely to be a victim of such violence, making one question his suggestion that it is a deterrent to appearing for the NCC prosecution.

When I interviewed the US Consulate employee in charge of copyright in Lagos, she wasted no time in dismissing the NCC as purposefully unhelpful. When we discussed a mutual acquaintance, a Nigerian private sector copyright lawyer who had recently joined the NCC, she referred to him as someone who had 'gone over to the dark side', insinuating that the NCC was a permanent impediment rather than a resource in her occasional efforts to protect US copyright interests. In my time at the NCC, however, I got no sense that the NCC lawyers had any different interests from those representing rights-holders; they just have very few resources.

Indeed, one of the biggest problems the NCC faces is that it lacks resources in almost every way. While the agency was meant, from its 1988 inception, to administer copyright law, it also was authorised in 1992 to enforce copyright law and appoint inspectors, an unusual task for a commission mostly made up of lawyers (most functional global copyright enforcement is the purview of police and other enforcement-oriented agencies, separate from the primary regulator). This change in law, however, was not matched by an increase in funding or staffing. Any seizures or raids must be undertaken by the police, who are themselves underfunded and unlikely to carry out any such raids from which they cannot be sure to profit. Foreign governments will occasionally fund raids, but only to protect their own nation's intellectual property. In this way, we can see that, while the employees of the NCC may have legitimate motivations in their work, truly intending to clamp down on copyright violations, they are hampered by the underfunding of enforcement mechanisms and lack of political motivation to provide more resources. After all, the existence of the NCC suffices to legitimate the state's intent; there is little self-preservation motivation for the state to actually enforce copyright.

While the NFC and NCC struggle with relevance and efficacy, the NFVCB has engaged in significant efforts to change the structure of the industry, as will be discussed in greater detail later in this chapter. However, these efforts thus far have had an impact more paralysing than anything else. Overall, with the exception of censorship, Nigeria's government agencies struggle to regulate or structure the video industry. An interesting sidenote is the heavy regulation of the Nigerian television industry. Perhaps this discrepancy is, in part, because a television station could be central in fomenting a coup, and the government has particular self-preservative interest in regulating such outlets, just as the NFVCB has more political will behind it than the NFC or NCC. Perhaps the structure of television, with fewer, more visible companies to keep track of, makes regulation easier. Perhaps closest of all to the heart of the matter is evolution: unlike television, the video industry rose up without regulation; government intervention after the fact has been challenging.

GOVERNMENT INTERVENTIONS

The optimal level of government involvement in the industry is a point of contention. Emeka Mba, Director General of the NFVCB from 2005–12 (and subsequent and current director of the Nigerian Broadcasting Commission, or NBC), says he believes, in theory, in 'light touch regulation', aimed only at helping the industry establish institutional strength and accountable distribution structures (2009). Yet there is good cause to mistrust government involvement in any endeavour in Nigeria, as government agencies have a reputation for self-interest as opposed to service. This mistrust is particularly true for those operating in the murky area between legality and extra-legality, for those who see the strengths in the current system coming from their efforts and particularly for those already profiting from the current system. As Isikaku notes, 'My people saw opportunity in Nollywood. Most wouldn't invest in Nollywood but we were the only ones who would. How, now, do you build on top of what is already in existence?' (2009).

However, it is not just the marketers who rail against governmental involvement. Anyiam-Fiberesima suggests that securing reliable electricity, security and water for the country should trump any film-related project, saying 'If the government can't sort out basic infrastructure needs of my nation, how can they improve on something made out of the tenacity and ingenuity of the people?' (2009). She also notes that billions of naira a year are spent on the three agencies that are meant to support the film industry (the NCC, the NFC and the NFVCB), and asks '[W]hat are they doing with it?'; she suggests that any more money spent on these agencies would not lead to any change in the industry (2009).

While marketers like Isikaku, president of the marketers' guild, may resent government interference after two decades of self-wrought growth, and producers like Anyiam-Fiberesima may express scepticism at the ability of the Nigerian government to effectively change anything, there are many in the industry that totally disagree and actively demand greater government involvement in structuring Nollywood; this is an area of contentious debate. At any given moment in Nollywood, there are usually at least one or two potential or even recently approved government initiatives in the works. Some are serious and have a degree of political will behind them, such as the NFVCB's attempt to reconfigure distribution during former director Emeka Mba's tenure, or the well-financed film-making fund announced to great fanfare by former president Goodluck Jonathan in his last year in office. Others are more moves by high-profile industry players seeking to initiate and perpetuate clientelist relationships, institutionalising their power and connecting them to those powerful in the government. What draws them all together has thus far been their inability to realise their professed goals. I take as case studies here one initiative of each type: the NFVCB's New Distribution Framework as an example of the more serious initiative and a failed proposal for a Motion Picture Practitioners Council (known as MOPICON) as an example of the latter.

'New Distribution Framework'

Despite the many calls for more government regulation, only one real regulatory 'reform' has been made in the history of the entire industry: that in distribution. In April 2006, Mba, then Director General of the NFVCB, accepted a proposal[9] to completely overhaul and 'formalise' the physical video distribution system within Nigeria. The policy was approved in February 2007; it took about two years, until December 2008, before implementation reached a point at which changes were seen in the industry. In subsequent years, however, the framework has been implemented only partially and for this reason many blamed it for a marked slow-down in production, as producers and marketers scrambled to understand what the new landscape looked like.

At its most basic, the framework stipulates that only those who register with the NFVCB may distribute videos in Nigeria. The framework institutes three levels of distribution licences: national, regional and local,[10] which are supposed to correspond with each firms' distribution capacity. Only one firm can get distribution rights per territory. Hence, any copies of a film found for sale in that territory should be able to trace their legitimacy or lack thereof back to one licensed distributor, and each retail outlet should be clearly labelled in a way that makes clear its legitimacy and accountability.[11]

I spoke with Mba during the early stages of the plan's roll-out. Visiting the NFVCB headquarters in Abuja was a departure from other government offices I visited. Unlike my trip to the NCC, via barren halls of the maze-like concrete compound that houses the forgotten bureaucrats of the National Secretariat, I found that the NFVCB has its own building complex in a residential neighbourhood; the offices buzzed with activity and apparent efficiency. After speaking with employees at the NFVCB headquarters, I met with Mba the next day at an up-market contemporary café, the sort of place that wouldn't be out of place in Brooklyn; the sort of place that is much more accessible in calm planned Abuja than in chaotic and crowded Lagos. In person, Mba is both open – in the sense that he answers each question asked of him fully, completely and seriously from an objective standpoint, with no attempts to obfuscate or aggrandise – and simultaneously reserved – in the sense that he offers no more information than that which is directly asked of him. His meeting with me came via a favour called in by a high-ranking government official; I doubt I would have had the opportunity to hear his perspective otherwise.

Mba came to the NFVCB from a successful career in industry, most notably as the Director of Nigerian Regulatory Affairs for South African satellite television giant MultiChoice, leaving the private sector to do work he felt was important. In this process, he switched from advocating for international (based in South Africa) corporate interests in Nigerian media policy to a regulator of

Nigerian media policy in an area with no major corporate players. He is very aware of the realities of Nollywood, the industry – particularly the dominance of the marketers due to their dispersed, opaque power. While the Nigerian government can directly negotiate with, regulate and tax a corporate giant like Mba's former employer, MultiChoice, Nollywood is much less penetrable due to the difficulty of negotiating with the power held by a collective of small enterprises.

Mba was quite clear in our discussion about the goals of his plan: the framework is unquestionably meant to jumpstart new entrants into the distribution system that come from outside the entrenched marketer networks, while simultaneously weakening marketer opacity, anonymity and cohesion in distribution. A key goal is for a few of these new firms, untainted by the strategies and extra-legal tendencies of the marketers, perhaps even graduates of business school, to rise to become one of a small oligopoly of dominant national distributors. With a small number of large players in charge of all distribution instead of a vast network of small-scale flexible enterprises, Mba's NFVCB hoped to achieve more control over distribution for itself and other government agencies, as well as prime the industry for external investment (Mba, 2009). After all, a large distributor will be much more visible and much more accountable than any individual firm in the small network of micro-firms making up the current distribution networks.[12]

This move by the NFVCB would appear to have both legitimate and self-enrichment motivations. Greater transparency in distribution and a move towards a small oligopoly of distributors would contribute towards efforts for the industry to benefit from formal international networks of financing and distribution, via the production of reliable formal sales estimates and sales reports. The move also would allow Nollywood to be co-opted by the state, allowing the state to tax and profit from Nollywood's sales in a way it is currently unable to do.

However, the NFVCB's stated vision of the future hasn't quite gone as planned. For one thing, anyone with clout and a bit of money has found it easy to register as a national distributor despite their questionable eligibility to do so, especially in the less populated corners of the country. In the planned model, national distributors take one of two forms: a chain that owns all of its facilities (the Board's preferred outcome), or a network of alliances with smaller distributors. The problem with this, in practice, has been the lack of entrepreneurs wanting to register as smaller-scale distributors. In some cases, the fee to the Board was deemed worth paying simply for the status of being able to call oneself a 'national distributor'.

Complicating this goal even further, after a lengthy period of antagonism between the NFVCB and the Igbo marketers' guild, FVPMAN, most FVPMAN

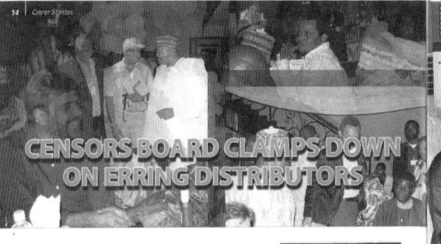

In a single 2009 publication, the NFVCB employed two tactics to register distributors: on one page they promoted voluntary registration and, on another, they publicised punitive measures against hold-outs

members registered with the NFVCB and, subsequently, continued to do business in exactly the same way as before. In the initial stages of implementation, FVPMAN, feeling (with some cause) that the new framework was aimed at evicting them summarily from the market, sued the NFVCB, both collectively and individually (through about fifty cases, most of which were dropped or settled out of court). These cases alleged that the NFVCB does not have the powers to license them, and that the new regulations are unjust. Subsequently, the NFVCB experimented with wielding its power in the only way it really can: refusing certification for any titles submitted by FVPMAN hold-outs (Bud, 2014). Eventually, most agreed to sign up, although in name only. With this great influx of new registrants to the NFVCB, Mba believed that some black market distributors had been able to register, but he posited that this is a good thing, as 'these registrees do not realise that they are more accountable now' (2009).

For this too is a goal of the distribution framework: to reduce unauthorised distribution and create accountability and statistics that make the entire industry more 'professional' on an international level, a motivation that is both legitimate and legitimacy-seeking. Obiora Chukwumba, Mba's deputy during his tenure, noted at the time, 'Our main goal is to create transparency, and to generate reliable statistics ... we want to create an environment for infrastructure, security, reliability, structure, accountability' (2009). Continuing in the same vein, Mba added, 'Unless you bring a level of formalisation into the business, you will never be able to get financing from banks, and you will never be able to grow' (2009). The industry consultant and author of the framework, Yinka Ogundaisi, says that the goal of this new framework is not just to secure profits for Nigerian producers but, even more so, extension of the markets: 'better distribution enables better funding. This is so there will be some kind of sanity in the system' (2009).

Isikaku, former head of FVPMAN, of course had a very different perception of this drive, one he says reflects the feelings of his members. 'Perhaps these larger companies can grow naturally from the more successful smaller companies,' he said, 'but the government shouldn't be muscling out those who already successfully created a profitable business out of nothing' (2009). He also suggests, as have many others, that the NFVCB's 'true' motives may be self-preservation: garnering additional income through licensing and registration fees. 'The government may want to help, but they also want to make money,' Isikaku noted (ibid.). Isikaku says that not much changed in the wake of the new framework and he warns that implementation was slow precisely because the NFVCB did not consult with the marketers throughout their design and implementation of the framework. In other words, any state efforts will be severely hampered by those that hold power in the industry – the marketers – if decisions are made without the marketers' involvement. Isikaku's remark can be read both as a threat and statement of simple fact. While many in the industry have claimed that the New Distribution Framework led to a slow-down in new production, both Mba and Isikaku, at least publicly, deny that anyone has permanently left the distribution business due to the new framework.

One might wonder why, if the original marketers were making things work, anything should change. 'It seems like they are thriving,' said Mba, 'but they're thriving in chaos' (2009). When everything is as informal as it is, Mba said, business suffers, as financing and distribution can never join global networks and never 'rise above' what they now are. As it stands now, the framework has never worked as originally intended (largely because the marketers collectively joined and continued doing business just as before), but it has created a large number of contentious battles within the industry, a slow-down in production and, some allege, a permanent rift between the NFVCB and the industry that limited the power of the agency as a whole. Once Mba left the NFVCB in 2012, the political will behind the framework waned.

As a whole, however, the new NFVCB distribution framework can be seen as reflecting all three motivations of the Nigerian state. Those running the agency may be motivated by legitimate as well as legitimacy-seeking impulses, while part of the force driving the framework forward is also the potential for future returns to the state from increased control and transparency – and even returns from the new registration fees levied for distributors of various levels. NFVCB officials readily admit that the ideal future for them would involve a few small oligopolistic distributors – much easier to coerce into transparency (and taxation) and much easier to control than the impossible-to-pin-down, constantly shifting network of small opaque distributors currently held together by relationships of trust and personal connections under the broad rubric of the FVPMAN. Without the support of FVPMAN, however, the NFVCB's new framework and alternative guild could not be said to be functioning to structure the actual industry, an industry in which few things happen without the support of the marketers. In fact, it would seem that the only thing that would serve to limit their power would be the rise of another form of distribution that bypasses them: theatrical, online, or satellite television. All three have potential but none have yet risen to dominate domestic distribution in the way that physical domestic sales have.

MOPICON

If the New Distribution Framework has failed in its goals at summonsing a small oligopoly of dominant corporate distributors from the sea of opaque small-scale marketers, at least the framework was implemented. This was a testament both to the historical power of the Nigerian censorship authority and the force of personality of its director, Mba. Despite the number of Nollywood players with ideas of changing the industry through government intervention, most such initiatives are never implemented at all. One such effort to change industry structure was MOPICON, an initiative sent as a bill through the Federal Assembly a few years ago. While unimportant in and of itself, it reflects the fate of many attempts to externally structure the industry.

Much less dramatic in its ambitions than the distribution framework, the MOPICON initiative also sought to formalise part of the informal industry. The proposal of MOPICON was the creation of a new government-mandated council governing the industry. The main function of this council would have been the requirement of a licence in order to work in the movie industry in a creative capacity. In other words, any aspiring director, producer, actor, or other creative talent would have to obtain a licence (the requirements of which would be decided by the leadership of the appropriate guild) in order to legally work on a movie production.

It is difficult to conceive of a scheme that could be more opposed to the spirit from which Nollywood was born than one formalising even the ability to work on a movie that makes its way to the mass marketplace. The main function this requirement would seem to serve would be to protect the already established movie-makers from competition from newcomers – perhaps fittingly, as it was the brainchild of one of the old guard of Nollywood, director and producer Mahmood Ali-Balogun (the bill's primary author and proponent). The old guard is where it found most of its support. While many supported this initiative, many others protested against it, claiming it would decimate the industry by legitimising an elite and depriving the industry of the creativity that fresh talent can bring. As Chukwumba, of the NFVCB, remarked, 'this is one of the gravest mistakes anyone in the industry can make. You cannot legislate creativity. You can't set up a government agency to tell you who can be a film-maker' (2009). Of course, it must be noted, his government agency, the NFVCB, does wish to dictate who can be a distributor.

At the same time, we can see the motivation for those supporting the bill and for those in the government to push it through, related to one another in a clientelist relationship. Those already dominant in the industry see the government as a prime place to look for the institutionalisation of their power, and those in the government may see supporting those already in power in the industry as an excellent opportunity to co-opt the industry, gaining revenue as well as loyalty from its already powerful players. The fact that implementation of such a council would likely decimate creativity and the existing (informal) structure of the industry would not be important to those lawmakers interested in self-preservation.

In both the New Distribution Framework and the MOPICON initiative, we see what we could expect from common sense alone: those who would stand to profit from the regulations are among the loudest supporters of governmental involvement. Yet we also see in both initiatives the problems inherent in structuring a self-organised networked industry. In the NFVCB framework, those already running the industry (the marketers) have the power to stop it from functioning. Any attempt to sweep them from power will beget chaos and a vacuum, at least for a time and possibly forever. In the advent of MOPICON, we can see that governmental intervention can often be based on the will of the self-interested and can serve to rob a self-made industry of its lifeblood. In both efforts, the government was trying to disrupt two self-made processes: informal distribution and informal employment. If the efforts succeeded as planned (which they did not), both were likely to disrupt the functioning of the entire industry.

In both initiatives, as well, the state is incentivised to act, at least in part, for self-preservation reasons: the prospect of greater control over an industry that mostly escapes regulation and taxation (with the exception of censorship). This is not the only motivation for this greater level of control, however; the more control the government has over its increasingly high-profile movie industry, the greater the government's legitimacy on the world stage. And even more important are the genuine drivers of governmental intervention. Perhaps less applicable in the MOPICON initiative, we can see at least the NFVCB legitimately trying to provide a functional formalised structure for Nollywood, an informal industry that is, in some ways, hampered by its informality (even as it is served in other ways by that same informality). Lack of accountability and transparency in distribution indeed delimit the industry's potential to benefit from international networks of funding and distribution. At the same time, the forced formalisation of an industry that draws its very strength from informality is likely to be more destructive than constructive.

GUILDS

Yet without much effective state governance, Nollywood is not in chaos. It is self-regulated, self-organised and, largely, self-governed. Some of this stems from entrenched relationships of trust and reputation. But the industry is more structured than simply a network of trust-based relationships. There are elected representatives and organisations for even the most opaque parts of the industry: the guilds. Nollywood's guilds serve many of the functions that legal solutions could also serve, such as contract or dispute mediation, although their ability to do this effectively is hampered at times by their informality (i.e. inability to pursue grievances past internal review through the court system). Guilds can also attempt large-scale structural changes, but, as we will see, this is fraught with difficulty.

It should not be all that surprising that formal guilds have proved so popular in Nollywood. Nigerian society is full of organisations and leadership positions. It is not uncommon for people to spend their little spare time going from meeting to meeting: church governance groups, church special interest groups, groups of those originally from the same village, groups of those that speak the same ethnic language, groups of those that live in the same neighbourhood. It seems that anyone who is anyone (and many who are, in effect, nobodies) holds or has held a leadership position in some organisation or another. In a state where political ascendency is thought to be directly related to financial reward, ascendency to leadership in any organisation is afforded a great degree of respect and importance, and leaders of even the smallest of these organisations are usually addressed by their title in public.

The Guild System

Before the video boom, there was already a tradition of guilds in place in the arts. The two dominant guilds that fed into the video boom were the Independent Television Producers Association of Nigeria (ITPAN), which represented producers working for the NTA, and the National Association of Nigerian Theatre Arts Practitioners (NANTAP), which represented those working in the theatre arts (i.e. stage productions, mostly including Yoruba drama troupes). As the video boom brought about new kinds of creative workers, new guilds rose up to represent them. NANTAP fed into the Nigerian Actors Guild (which later morphed into today's Actors Guild of Nigeria) and ITPAN fed into today's Association of Movie Producers (AMP). Gradually, other professions in the industry formed their own guilds. It is not uncommon for current producers to be members or in leadership roles in both ITPAN and AMP: there is much overlap but no redundancy.

Today guilds represent almost every aspect of the industry from marketers to the make-up artists. They tend to meet monthly. Despite the separate nature of the movie industries in the north and the south, the guilds are national, with branches in multiple zones – for example, Kano, Onitsha and Lagos. There may be multiple guilds per profession as they fragment via ethnic ties, but there usually tends to be one guild in which power is cemented. For instance, FVPMAN is the Igbo distributors guild, but there are also guilds for Yoruba distributors of Yoruba movies and Hausa distributors of Hausa movies. FVPMAN's control over the more popular English-language production renders it the key distributors' guild, however. The leaders of the guild are elected by all national members. While they abide by a democratic system, elections can be quite contentious. In one recent summer, an antagonistic battle between the then-incumbent of the AMP, Paul Obazele, and a prominent challenger, Teco Benson, erupted into violence. Benson's supporters asserted that incumbent Obazele hired street thugs to attack them and Benson himself.[13] What was particularly notable about this conflict was the attitude of those involved. When asked why they supported one candidate over the other, or what the difference in platforms was between the two contenders, people seemed unable to be specific. They cited mainly their deeper personal ties to one candidate over the other and what that candidate could do for them. The main criticism of the incumbent was cronyism and squandering of funds, but those supporting his challenger seemed to expect him to engage in similar activities for their benefit.[14] However, besides cronyism, one of the main functions of the guild in an everyday context is to solve disputes.

Guild as Contract Substitute

Official contracts drawn up with the help of lawyers are of little use in Nollywood. Business relationships built on informal 'memorandums of understanding' and, even more, trust, respect, clout and handshakes, form the basis of collaboration in Nollywood. Substituting for contracts can be considered one of the main functions of the guild system in Nigeria: the solving of disputes without resorting to legal methods.

Disputes run the gamut from actors finding their hotel to be of unacceptable quality to complex financial disputes regarding post-shoot compensation, but the process of redressing the dispute is supposed to be the same. If, for example, a producer and an actor have a dispute over payments or agreements to work, the guild of the party deemed to be in the wrong is supposed to discipline the offender or otherwise rectify the situation. Those (most people) without influence in the offender's guild can go to their own guild, whose representative will represent them in negotiations.

Yet the self-organised guild system as substitute for the government-organised contract system carries its own set of problems. For one thing, many creative workers believe the guild does nothing for them, and takes the part of the powerful in contract disputes. Additionally, despite the mission of the guild to protect its members, any informal grouping of non-famous creative workers will typically lead to grousing about working conditions on any number of sets, and the failure of their guild or anyone else to do anything about it. Complaints about working conditions can range from the necessity to be awake and available to shoot for twenty-four hours on end to being provided with only one meal in the course of a fourteen-hour shoot.

Despite the informality of employment, contracts in Nigeria do exist. They are rarely drawn up, however, due, in part, to legal costs and to their tertiary connection to the existent system. They are even more rarely drawn upon if they are violated, for the same reasons those without contracts find they cannot pursue their more powerful adversaries. For example, active Nollywood screenwriter Yinka Ogum told of wanting to pursue a broken contract through the appropriate framework open to him at the time – only to find that it was in his best interest to swallow his losses and move on, as those who had wronged him were more powerful. He had a contract with a group of executive producers after he had pitched his idea and treatment of a potential movie to them. After blatantly stealing his idea and offering no payment, the producers then called him, saying, in colourful language, 'We know you have us by the balls right now and we ask that you don't squeeze,' strongly suggesting it was in his best interests not to do so (2009). 'It is one thing for the law to be on your side on paper,' Ogum said, 'but if you're up against a multi-millionaire, what can you do?' (ibid.). What is particularly important about Ogum's story is to note that the various factors holding guilds back from truly policing all industry deals are the same as those that keep legal contracts from being pursued: relationships of rank and trust can be stronger than any method of governance. This is a tale that could also be told in contract-heavy places like Hollywood: even with rock-solid legal contracts, the perils of pursuing the wrongs of the more powerful are strong in any context. However, these issues are most significant in this informal environment and it is the guild system that seems to offer the most effective dispute resolution.

Guild as Alternative Distribution System

Guilds can serve not only as substitutes for legal relationships, but also in a similar role to government. It is particularly enlightening to look at guilds' attempts to alter the industry in much the same way as the NFVCB, with its New Distribution Framework. The keyword here, however, is attempt. While some of the guilds are made up of those that *do* structure the industry (most notably FVPMAN, the main marketers' guild[15]), as we will see in the case study of the failed initiative of Film-makers Cooperative of Nigeria (FCON), those not already in entrenched positions of market control find it difficult to alter the system on their own, particularly if distribution remains based on physical exchange.

FCON was a cooperative of producers (primarily those who thought of themselves as the respected artistic elite, now perhaps embodied in the New Nollywood corner of the industry) aiming to completely reconceptualise and reform the structure of the industry to become one in which producers and creative talent had control over financing and distribution of their products. The idea was that this would allow the elite creatives to bypass the marketers. Led by two well-regarded producers, including Peace Anyiam-Fiberesima, FCON set up an alternative movie market in Surulere, an area that, while still in central Lagos, is miles away from the dizzying crowded markets in which marketers ply their trade.

This initiative was ill-fated. One of the main problems was the dearth of products offered for sale at the collective. The existent marketers would not allow their movies to be sold at the very visible FCON market, and these constituted the majority of Nollywood's popular output. Additionally, unauthorised reproductions of movies released by the Cooperative could also be found for sale by street hawkers, even just outside the Surulere market location. For these reasons, few shoppers felt motivated to make a trip there just to buy a small selection of movies.

This initiative was not the only way FCON tried to break the marketers' cartel; Anyiam-Fiberesima and colleagues also attempted to break free of the existent distribution and funding structures. They established an entertainment desk at a premier Nigerian Bank (the United Bank of Africa, or UBA) that was authorised to fund up to $50,000 per movie. This did not go to plan either, with the majority of film-makers unable to provide the paperwork required by UBA, most specifically showing a financial plan for the production that included distribution and sales (Anyiam-Fiberesima, 2009). With FCON's distribution outlet, Anyiam-Fiberesima said, there was a chance of this happening, but with FCON dead, any chance of guaranteeing distribution had also died, at least until non-physical distribution models such as online distribution became dominant and widespread. As such, FCON cannot be said to have had success in either restructuring distribution or restructuring financing, despite its members being more acceptable (being well educated and well spoken) to national and international funding and distribution bodies than the generally less-educated entrepreneurs that make up the marketers. It is worth noting that there has been some further bank investment since this time but never on a scale that could affect the industry as a whole; a small handful of resourceful and connected producers have been able to realise some bank investment opportunities, but with little accompanying long-term change in industrial structure.

CONCLUSION

In a state marked by corruption and self-interested government, we can best understand policies made by the state in the context of the benefits they offer to the decision-makers. We can certainly see the motivations of the state in the three main governmental agencies currently interacting with Nollywood: the

NFVCB, the NCC and the NFC. Both the NCC and the NFC have proved ineffectual thus far in their efforts to affect the industry. The existence of both serves legitimising functions for the Nigerian state. And, if functional, both could also serve the industry. As the Nigerian state seeks external legitimacy on the world stage, the existence of the NCC signals to the international community that Nigeria is engaged in supporting international agreements (involving intellectual property rights), and the existence of the NFC signals that it is developed enough to actively support national artistic output. Neither of these agencies is supported by the sort of political will and budget that would let them actively pursue their charter, however. The NFVCB is the only one of the three agencies interacting with Nollywood that has been successful in its corner of industry governance: censorship. The success the NFVCB enjoyed for many years stemmed in large part from the importance of information control in a society marked by political instability and a history of military coups, and by a government concerned with self-preservation above all else. This emphasis is nothing new; the NFVCB's success could also be attributed to the tradition of censorship in Nigeria stretching back as far as the colonial era, with the strength of subsequent censorship institutions due to path dependence. While we can see all three posited motivations at work in supporting these governmental agencies, it is clear that self-preservation is the strongest driver.

We can see a similar story when examining the two case studies of government initiatives that attempted to intervene in the way industry functions. The NFVCB-sponsored New Distribution Framework was also driven by each of the three aforementioned motivations. Its stated goals (greater transparency in distribution and the emergence of a small number of oligopolistic distributors) are genuinely believed by industry actors to be likely to advance Nollywood as an industry; such a move would also help to legitimate Nigeria on the world stage. Yet, not coincidentally, greater transparency and the emergence of a few larger distributors would also benefit the state directly, affording it more control over the industry, as well as more chance to tax it. MOPICON, the failed effort to formalise and mandate guild membership, was even more tilted towards this third motivation. While posited by its drafters to legitimately help the industry and to enable Nollywood to 'join the rest of the world' through formalisation and regulation, the move would, above all, serve to ingrain clientelist relationships between Nollywood heavyweights and politicians, at potential benefit to both parties.

It is far from clear that bank and foreign investment and the fall of the marketers would 'help' the industry, as the goals of the industry are not universal, varying depending on one's position. It is certainly possible that toppling the marketers who built the industry would serve to destroy the industry, rather than help it. However, for those whose goals *are* to see the marketers fall and for the industry to become more corporate and more formal, with larger budgets and higher accountability, government efforts so far have been short-sighted. Recent government attempts to force existent distributors to restructure their business (New Distribution Framework), or to create a film fund that benefits the small number who successfully navigate the application process (former president Goodluck Jonathan's recent Nollywood Intervention Fund) have not toppled the marketers. The latter's forays into Nollywood in his final year in office even included a reported Nigeria Bank of Industry $11.4 million investment into an effort by veteran producer Gabriel Okoye (known as Gabosky) to replicate Alaba's national distribution network with a network controlled by his new company, G-Media Productions, a 'privately owned national distribution system' (Bud, 2014). While it is too soon to say for sure, past experience with external efforts to restructure physical distribution would suggest that is highly unlikely that this investment of formal money will bring about any major change in the Alaba-led informal distribution system – and that this endeavour's success is so unlikely as to be virtually guaranteed to fail.

The only thing that could bring about this controversial goal would be a mass shift in domestic distribution *format*, such that marketers could not maintain dominance. This could mean the mass construction of theatres on a national level, accompanied by the even more challenging (re)construction of a theatre-going culture from cities to villages. It could mean significantly raising the prices paid for movies by satellite or terrestrial television channels so that they could fully support movie production, though this is unlikely to ever make economic sense on its own. Or, it could be the advent of online distribution, a distribution channel not widely available in Nigeria due to issues with bandwidth capacity and data charges (explored further in the next chapter). If government action is to 'transform' Nollywood without the marketers, it will not only need to include cinema construction, but also significantly increased funding of police forces to patrol streets at night, as well as solar-powered streetlights,[16] two developments that could contribute to people feeling comfortable, once again, with leaving the house in the evenings for entertainment. Or, the government could encourage more submarine internet cables and last-mile connectivity, raising national bandwidth capacity, along with reforming mobile networks and domestic ISPs or encouraging more competition among them to bring data prices down. This would best be paired with an effort to strengthen electricity generation and distribution. This ensemble of policy suggestions – streetlights, police, electricity, national bandwidth capacity and reforming domestic ISPs and telecoms – would not only enable cinematic or online distribution, but also have the extra 'side effect' of reducing costs for the majority of Nigeria's industries and significantly bettering the lives of the majority of Nigeria's citizens. These basic infrastructural needs have been politically unimportant for so long that even minor improvement in each would likely transform the entire national economy (see *The Economist*, 2015). And, until such a shift happens, the marketers remain in control.

It would seem that attempts to restructure the industry through direct government intervention are ultimately unlikely to push the industry forward and more likely to seriously derail it, even if those controlling the industry actually allowed these efforts to be fully implemented. The major role for government would be indirect: strengthening infrastructure on a national level, an action that would benefit many more than just the movie industry. While the Nigerian government has attempted to touch the industry in many ways, few of these efforts have worked thus far, and no planned efforts seem likely to succeed either. After all, it is difficult for policy to touch the invisible, an industry structure operating in the opaque world of vast networks of small distributors.

The policy implication here is that governance will fail unless it comes from those already in control and has the political will of those already running the industry. Guild networks already serve many of the same functions as written contracts, for instance, and guilds have the potential to regulate many other things. Overarching structural change in the industry which evicts the marketers and their quasi-legal business dealings from their current position of power is highly unlikely if the industry continues to function concurrently via physical copy sales. And other distribution formats – cinema, online, or television – have a long way to go before they can command budgets the way the marketers' distribution networks can. In an industry marked by dispersed power, governance is likely to come from the industry's own existent sources of strength. In an industry founded on self-organisation, guilds have the potential to organise solutions that the government cannot, despite their frequent replication of the very power relationships that cause problems in the first place. And, despite the strength of the other guilds of the industry, it is the Igbo marketers' guild that wields by far the most power, leaving it at the top of the heap. In an industry based on a self-grown networked structure, it is likely that the most effective form of governance will be self-governance, led by dispersed networks of self-grown guilds. While their will to change as opposed to self-enrich may not be as robust as it could be, it would appear that the self-formed unregulated guilds offer the most effective path towards governance in Nollywood.

NOTES

1. Despite their high profile, the three dominant ethnic groups only constitute about two-thirds of the population between them.

2. With the exception of a brief civilian government from 1979–83.
3. Fashola was in office from 2007–15. His efforts may well be continued by his successor, Akinwunmi Ambode, especially as Ambode is a member of the same reformist party as the widely well-regarded and effective Fashola, the All Progressives Congress. However, as this book is being prepared in the first few months of Ambode's tenure, it is too early to say for sure.
4. 'Cinematographic Ordinance 20: An Ordinance for the Better Regulation and Control of Cinematograph and Similar Exhibition and Purpose Connected There'.
5. Not a sizable class at first, film importation soared in the 1970s and 80s, particularly during the oil boom of the late 1970s; by 1982, 80 per cent of domestic cinema screens were airing foreign films, which didn't go through the NFVCB (Okome, 1995).
6. At the time, most were held and run by Lebanese owners, who form one of the more powerful of the small enclaves of foreigners who have risen to the top of a number of industries in Nigeria.
7. Decree No. 47 of December 1988.
8. Just five years after the USA signed.
9. Written largely by industry consultant and producer Yinka Ogundaisi, also interviewed for this project.
10. Local was originally broken down into three categories: state, 'local government authority' (similar to county) and local retail point (now called community retailers). No one was motivated to register as any of the smaller-sized distributors and, as a result, the three smallest classifications were condensed into one.
11. Each retail outlet must visibly display their official authorisation code outside and any street- level vendor must have a sign showing their licence number, or that of their licensed supplier. In rural areas, where playing machines are scarce, licences are available for 'community viewing centres', which are essentially anywhere with a power supply and a television – a viewing space that seems to defy efforts at full documentation by nature. Rentals shops, too, are a part of the new framework. They are meant to pay 20,000 naira ($133) for five rental copies and the rights to rent them out. In a country where films can be bought in the markets for 150 naira ($1) and on the streets for less than 300 naira ($2), this does appear to be an uphill battle, particularly when there are not any significant enforcement efforts.
12. Of course, this goal has not gone unnoticed by the marketers. FVPMAN, the marketers' guild, has protested against this vigorously.
13. While I didn't see the physical incident, I did see the majority of those involved both the day before and the day after the alleged altercation and can attest that some injuries to Benson's crew were inflicted by someone, at the very least, though I cannot say by whom.

14. For instance, Bruce Idigbogu is a martial artist, large in size and frequently found pumping iron at the National Stadium gym, where I interviewed him. Known popularly as 'Natty Bruce', he is also an aspiring producer; in the summer of 2009, a near zero-budget movie he'd shot was being edited by King Asu, the editor and office manager to Teco Benson, the challenger to the presidency of the AMP. When asked whom he was supporting for the presidency, Natty Bruce was quite clear about the direct relationship between his support for Benson and the editing assistance Benson was providing for him. He also was quite clear about the likely relationship between his physical prowess and intimidating appearance and Benson's overtures towards him, including him as a member of his inner circle during his drive for the presidency. He appeared to be bothered by none of this and seemed to consider it par for the course in his efforts to succeed as a producer.
15. There are other guilds representing other ethnic groups involved in distribution, but, as most marketers are Igbo, FVPMAN is the distributors' guild that represents the majority of the industry.
16. Electric-powered streetlights seem futile in a nation with a constantly faltering electricity supply. The few streetlights in Lagos are solar-powered.

5
Nollywood's Global Circuits

At a gathering of Nigerian movie producers and actors, along with international academics, at Georgia Tech in Atlanta,[1] I was seated at lunch next to the two women who had brought the Nigerian catering. In their early twenties and as fashionably dressed and made up as any Nollywood star, the two young women, proprietors of their own successful Nigerian food catering business in Atlanta, were noticeably nervous and giggly. A well-known Nollywood actor was seated just a few tables away, and they were hoping to be able to speak with him and get a photo – as soon as they plucked up courage. Both had lived outside Nigeria for the vast majority of their lives, but had intimate knowledge of the Nollywood gossip machine and release schedule. They spoke over lunch of their favourite websites to stream Nollywood movies and the Atlanta shops where they purchase US-packaged Nollywood DVDs. Thousands of miles from Lagos, in Atlanta, Georgia, these Nollywood fans living in the Nigerian diaspora seemed to be as plugged in to current Nollywood as women the same age living in Lagos would be. (And, in some ways, one could say they are more literally 'plugged in', as they have reliable electricity and internet connections, and access to credit cards for easy mobile payments.)

Despite the focus in previous chapters on the loci of Nollywood's *exclusion* from dominant global networks, Nollywood does have many international and global connections. Mostly forged by hand, by individual entrepreneurs, these largely informal connections, taken as a whole, constitute alternative networks that run counter to and under the radar of the dominant global linkages. Urban theorist AbdouMaliq Simone, in his 2001 work on African and 'Fourth World' cities in the global order, touches on this. Envisioning the African city as a place of intermittent points of contact with the global order that never manage to pull the city forward as a whole, Simone also describes the flipside of these uneven connections. Not only do African urban residents use the city as an opportunity to engage globally, those who live in these cities have also created new circuits within Africa as well as throughout the developing world. In his analysis, Simone cites Mumbai, Dubai, Bangkok, Taipei, Kuala Lumpur and Jeddah as examples of important city nodes in the alternative global networks that matter to urban

Africa. These cities are linked together with African nodes in circuits of trade that function as alternative to (and in) the dominant global order. The hallmark of these circuits, Simone says, is informality and unofficial (i.e. semi-legal and illegal) export and trade. This particular informality enables individuals to act on a global level based on self-built resources.

Media anthropologist Brian Larkin builds on Simone's conceptualisation of the uneven role of networks in African cities – particularly those same alternative informal networks. Basing his research in Kano, the largest city in Muslim and Hausa northern Nigeria, Larkin's work explores the alternative paths of distribution that mark Nigerian commerce, particularly in media, as global 'pirate' networks fill in for official networks of distribution, linking Nigerians to 'a vast array of world media at a speed they could never imagine, hooking them up to the accelerated circuit of global media flows' (2008: 224–5). Larkin argues that the informal (though often meticulously structured) alternative networks of piracy fuel global connections in places disconnected from official global flows.

Geographers Marston *et al*. (2007) are also drawn to the concept of networks as the ideal spatial conceptualisation with which we can think about the position of an industry like Nollywood in a globalising world. They point to the conceptual exemption of a network from 'scalar imaginaries' (46), allowing a flatness in our imagination of Nollywood's place in the world order. In other words, the concept of networks allows us to leave behind the local versus global dichotomy that structures much thinking about globalisation. Instead, we can view Nollywood's networks in their entirety, without needing to compare them in scale to, for instance, Hollywood's networks.

Nollywood's global connections are not just via these informal networks, however. As Nollywood has risen in profile, formal global capital has been itching to find a way to invest in the industry. Investment in physical Nigerian distribution is difficult as sales are almost entirely made up of undocumented transactions for physical copies of content performed in cash transactions based in open-air markets. Investment in diaspora distribution, however, is a different story. The popularity of satellite television and internet distribution in non-Nigerian markets (particularly ex-African diaspora markets) has allowed for both corporate and investment firm capital to be targeted at diaspora circulation. These investments are marked by an uneasy relationship between the logics of Nollywood in Nigeria and the opportunities Nollywood content presents in the diaspora. While informal and unauthorised distribution still proliferates in Nollywood's international distribution and formal Nollywood circulation has benefited from this unauthorised circulation, the attempts at formal investment in domestic Nollywood highlight the points of disjuncture in the interaction of these systems. This chapter explores these intersections, and the frustrating experiences formal foreign capital has had in trying to penetrate Nigeria's domestic informal industrial structure. First, however, let's look at the alternative informal networks Nollywood has drawn on a global level.

LAGOS AS AN ALTERNATIVE MEDIA CAPITAL

Simone's general descriptions of individuals connecting worldwide through informal global networks in African cities are concretised in the realities of trade in daily Lagos life. As discussed in Chapter 2, Alaba, the sprawling open-air market on Lagos's outskirts that serves as the nerve centre for electronics sales (and resales) for all of southern Nigeria – and, in many sectors, even all of West Africa – can be seen as a microcosm of business practices and industrial structure in Nigeria. A warren of small business owners essentially creating both their inventory (often third and fourth hand, cobbled together, or remaindered goods rejected from other markets) and their market (often those unable to obtain or afford first-hand merchandise) from scratch, the electronics and VCD traders of Alaba are not only connected nationally across Nigeria, but globally as well.

In their 2001 treatise on Lagos, architect Rem Koolhaas and his colleagues investigate the global networks that spill out of Alaba's tin-roofed stalls. In their assessment, if Alaba can be considered the hub of this West African electronics network, then Taipei, Moscow, Singapore, Mexico City, Sao Paolo and Dubai are key nodes. 'Scouts' are sent to scour these sister cities on what Koolhaas *et al.* term 'market-funded missions of capitalist reconnaissance' (2001: 709), trading in remaindered and previously used stock sourced globally. Each of the cities mentioned, while themselves significantly connected to dominant global networks, are alternative nodes in this worldwide linkage of antiquated, broken and remaindered electronic technologies or, as Mattelart put it, the 'underground networks of cultural globalization' (2009).

Far from an anomaly, the alternative global circuits created by Alaban entrepreneurs (many of whom may also be Nollywood's major marketers, i.e. distributors/executive producers) are the hallmarks of much business in the 'Fourth World'. When excluded from dominant or official global networks, alternatives will be created in the spaces left unpaved. A simplistic way of looking at these connections would be to call them 'periphery-to-periphery', a term that has traditionally been meaningful in studies of international communication and business to describe trade between nations in the developing world that exists without interactions with more developed economies. It is more apt to describe them simply as alternative networks – circuits with fewer distinctions between black market, grey market and white market, or between formal and informal than dominant global networks. After all, within many of Nigeria's and urban Africa's global networks of trade, we can find Dubai, for example, at the core, or at least as a major hub. And Lagos is, at the very least, at the core of alternative networks of movie production and distribution in Nigeria, in West Africa and, perhaps, even in sub-Saharan Africa as a whole, depending on your perspective. While Lagos may be a peripheral node in the dominant formal global cultural industry system (if it even makes an appearance at all),[2] in these alternative networks it is both central and integral to the functioning of the entire system.

In this way, we can also take Lagos to be an alternative media capital. Michael Curtin (2003) proposes that logics of media flows can no longer be mapped onto a geography based on the shape of the nation-state; instead, he proposes an understanding of media as a product of global 'media capitals', hubs of media production that can be understood best at the city level, proffering Hong Kong as a key example. I argue for the exploration of a different typology of media capital, one that will be of increasing importance in a globalising world: one that exists with few to no connections to major media multinational corporations (MNCs) and little ability to connect to them, given its entirely different industrial structure, based on informality and links to alternative networks. The formality of an industry allows it to integrate economically into dominant global cultural industry networks. It is my argument that such integration renders it a part of that same network, whether it is based in what has traditionally been referred to as the global North or the global South. Industries like Nollywood, whose structure is largely discrete from integration into those same networks, represent a different and alternative media capital formation – central to alternative networks and near invisible to dominant ones, and governed by some very different industrial logics. Before discussing Nollywood in this light, however, let us first address the myriad global connections marking the industry in production and distribution.

GLOBAL PRODUCTION INPUTS

Production in Nollywood is not very global in nature. With the exception of the many collaborations and exchanges with the nearby Ghanaian movie industry, Nollywood movies tend to be home-grown affairs, borne of Nigerian funds, run by Nigerian producers and using Nigerian talent (again, with the exception of frequent exchanges with the Ghanaian movie industry). Yet Nollywood is not entirely insular; global forces do have some presence in Nollywood production processes.

In terms of funding, Nollywood movies almost never receive foreign aid, a source of pride for many producers, yet some resourceful Nigerian directors have found themselves eligible for such funding. Directors wishing to fund movies while breaking out of the control of the marketers have, at times, pursued such resources, although this is a rarity. Director Francis Onwochei, for instance, produced a movie in 2008 for mass Nollywood release (*Claws of the Lion*). The movie's plot has a strong HIV prevention theme.[3] As a result, it was eligible for and received money from the French Ministry of Foreign Affairs for its production. The ability to tell a story free of marketers and the stresses of self-funding was, perhaps, the driving force behind seeking this funding rather than a specific attempt to educate viewers on the perils of HIV, but Onwochei sees little problem with including the latter message in his story if it helps garner finance (2009). As a counterpoint, Emmanuel Isikaku, president of the marketers' guild, expresses distaste for even this level of support. 'In Kenya,' he says, 'you write proposals on proposals and the agency wants it to be about AIDS. We tell our own stories and we don't give a damn if you[4] appreciate it or not' (2009). It is in Isikaku's interest, of course, to encourage continued dominance of the marketers' virtual cartel in movie production. Holding centralised power in the alternative networks of Nollywood production, the marketers have no desire to challenge French or other foreign forces for control of content and production.

Domestically, the Nigerian Foreign Ministry has begun to utilise the international star power of Nollywood actors in their own cultural diplomacy efforts. They have sponsored everything from a Nollywood North American Film Festival in Mississagua, Ontario, to inviting Nollywood actors to partake in parades and cultural events held at Nigerian consulates worldwide in an effort to effect synergies with Nollywood's widespread appeal (Olukanni, 2009). Former president Goodluck Jonathan made marked efforts to promote the popularity of the industry's stars. For the most part, though, these are side missions and afterthoughts. After all, the bulk of the cultural diplomacy of Nollywood occurs simply in the actors and movies popularising Nigerian styles of dress, speaking and living throughout African and African diaspora communities. It is a potent national 'soft power' (see Nye, 2004), produced regardless of the efforts of Nigeria's government. Nigerian cultural influence has extended far and wide through black market networks of distribution and informal links to the diaspora, the importance of which cannot be overemphasised. As a result of the prolific nature of Nigerian arts, as well as the significant emigration of Nigerians both within and outside Africa (dating back to a long tradition of far-flung trading), Nigerian culture and manner of dress has become popular throughout sub-Saharan Africa and even the non-West-African African diaspora. Billions of dollars are sent back 'home' annually in remittances from expatriates, who simultaneously spread Nigerian culture in their adopted homes. While much of Nigeria's global image revolves around the negative, such as 419 scams and drug trafficking, the centrality of Nollywood to various global mediascapes serves to promote a different image of Nigeria: a normalisation of Nigerian dress, customs, music and mannerisms. In the face of this soft power, active efforts by the Nigerian Foreign Ministry are not taken very seriously. Governmental requests for cooperation made to famous Nollywood practitioners are resented by many in the industry who feel they are neglected until the government wants or needs something from them.

Nollywood also has international links in some of its training programmes. While many directors have set up training schools (of varying degrees of professionalism), those most serious about the endeavour have arranged partnerships with foreign institutions, partnerships that at lest lend their schools influence on paper. In a few rare instances, those active in Nollywood have gone to the USA or the UK to seek training from schools there; for example, Stephanie Okereke, a popular Nollywood actress, attended the New York Film Academy (NYFA). While there, she created a film, in which she starred, featuring a number of aspiring American actors; she subsequently released it in Nigeria to much fanfare. NYFA has, since then, sought to set up more formal classes for Nollywood practitioners (for profit, of course), thus drawing others to New York to follow in Okereke's footsteps. However, no matter how many enrol in such international schools, it remains highly unlikely that foreign education will become a major influence in the industry in terms of artistic or business model inspiration. For one thing, NYFA is a technical, as opposed to an art, school. And Okereke has suggested that she, herself, described to astounded classmates and instructors the techniques to make a low-budget movie at breakneck speed, as opposed to the converse. If anything, exchanges like this could contribute to technical knowledge acquisition on an industrial level.

Nollywood practitioners also often receive internationally sponsored training in a less formal way. The Sony store in Lagos's Victoria Island offers occasional workshops for Nollywood's cinematographers, teaching prospective clients how to use Sony's new equipment. The store is more than just a supplier of equipment and knowledge about equipment to the industry; it represents the most notable, consistent presence in production inputs of a major global corporation making direct profits from the industry, involved for motives other than altruism or cultural diplomacy or exchange. The store opened around the year 2000 and sells to both the movie and the television industries. Ruth Shashore, sales representative at the store, estimated that Sony has 80 per cent market share in new equipment for Nollywood (2009), though, like most statistics offered about the industry, that should be taken with healthy scepticism, as there are no reliable ways to even initially gather, much less verify such figures. That said, Sony is widely seen as dominating the industry, with JVC and Panasonic present but lagging behind. As the industry has matured, demand for new (as opposed to used and repaired) equipment has grown.

While equipment purchased in Nigeria is more expensive than the same purchased in Europe, due to import duties and the costs of shipping, the Sony store is popular for a number of reasons. For one, the store offers Nollywood practitioners the opportunity to order products without having to deal themselves with shipping, as package delivery in Lagos is often fraught with difficulty. Shashore reports that the store usually orders this equipment from a Sony central office in Singapore, although it sometimes goes through other Asian or European offices instead (ibid.). Besides delivery, the Sony store also offers service and warranties. These are not available when cinematographers buy equipment cheaper via their or friends' trips abroad to locations with a place in the dominant global equipment sales circuit such as London and Dubai – places without the inflated prices for import that mark international electronics (and many other) imports in Nigeria. While acquiring equipment through such informal shopping trips is popular, cinematographers that work frequently will accept the expense of the Lagos Sony store equipment in return for the reliability that formal exchange with the representatives of a multinational corporation can offer.

Shashore notes that the drive to obtain market share and sell more to Nollywood comes from the store owners' own entrepreneurial instincts, rather than directives from foreign Sony offices (ibid.). So, while this store is an example of MNC participation in the Nollywood value chain, the identification of this opportunity – this gap that could be filled by MNC involvement – came from within Nigeria, by Nigeria-based entrepreneurs. (It should be noted, however, that the Sony store is not an example of home-grown Nigerian entrepreneurship. The shop was actually founded and is managed by entrepreneurs of South Asian descent, one of the more visible ethnic groups realising individual entrepreneurial opportunities in Lagos. The extent to which profits stay in Nigeria is unclear.)

All equipment used in Nollywood is not new, of course. Nollywood movie sets also often incorporate at least some second-hand equipment (generators, for instance, tend to look consistently weathered) that probably began its lifecycle abroad. The electronics markets of Lagos, like the markets of other places excluded from MNCs' global distribution networks, are full of previously used electronics, imported in bulk, many in broken or distressed form (see Sundaram, 1999, and Parks, 2007, for more on such 'recycled modernity'). In places like Lagos's Alaba and 'Computer Village' markets, workers may piece together parts of broken equipment to create newly workable, saleable electronic goods. In this way, used equipment is sourced globally and then filtered through importers, repairmen and resellers.

Similarly, it is worth noting that software created by western companies is used for various stages in the production process, from scriptwriting to editing to the creation of special effects. This software is likely acquired through the black market for all but the most established of users, however, marking more alternative international networks. The hardware (computers and laptops) is, of course, also the product of MNCs, but computers in Nigeria are often purchased second-hand (or third-hand or fourth-hand and so on) from resellers at electronics markets – again, having arrived in Nigeria through alternative global networks of electronics distribution.

GLOBAL PHYSICAL DISTRIBUTION

While international inputs into production are mostly one-off and haphazard, with the exception of physical hardware and software, Nollywood's arms in international distribution spread out like a vast web – and much of this is an invisible web, due to its informality and opacity. Despite the advent of authorised television airings and authorised online viewing in the diaspora, much of Nollywood's global circulation still follows the logics of informality, opacity and small-scale enterprises that mark the domestic industry, as they flow through unauthorised or informal distribution networks of online, televised, or physical content. Trade of Nollywood content takes place within the alternative networks of the industry connecting Lagos to markets from Dar es Salaam to east London to St Lucia.

Nollywood movies are available all over the world, throughout the rest of sub-Saharan Africa and the African diaspora (including places many generations removed from Africa, such as heavily African Caribbean nations). Countries throughout Africa (and particularly the rest of West Africa) have complained about the proliferation of Nigerian movies, which are seen as riding roughshod over local cultural production. Markets from the Democratic Republic of the Congo (DRC) to Barbados to the Ivory Coast are overflowing with Nigerian productions, usually dubbed or narrated in non-English-speaking areas. In some countries, this influx of Nigerian content has not only influenced local culture, but has also spurred local production following the Nigerian style and business model, particularly in Kenya and Tanzania, but in a diversity of other countries as well, as discussed in Chapter 3.[5] The biggest markets are in the UK and the USA, countries with huge Nigerian expatriate populations, and the rest of sub-Saharan Africa, but countries with smaller whole numbers of African immigrants figure too, such as Spain, Italy, France, Malaysia, Germany and the Netherlands, as well as parts of the African Caribbean, such as St Lucia, Barbados and Haiti. Despite the wide and rapid global networks dedicated to distributing Nollywood movies, much of the money derived from foreign distribution does not circulate back into the pockets of those producing the movies.

Physical copies of Nollywood movies are a significant force in ex-Nigerian distribution, via VCD or DVD – depending on what is preferred in each market. The majority of international physical distribution is unlicensed and often consists of the seller burning unlicensed copies themselves. Distribution in sub-Saharan Africa often looks similar to distribution within Nigeria: open-air markets and small dedicated shops. Outside sub-Saharan Africa, movies are most usually available in shops dedicated to selling a number of products from the diaspora. The streets of certain east and south London neighbourhoods, in particular, are peppered with grocery shops and small restaurants catering to the large Nigerian population; each of these will likely offer some opportunity to purchase a Nollywood movie as a sideline of the business. However, dedicated movie shops catering to the diaspora also exist. In almost all cases, there is no export of large numbers of copies produced in Nigeria. Instead, resellers or regional distributors need only one copy from Nigerian sources to populate their shelves.

Despite the prevalence of unlicensed distribution, there are also licensed international distributors, particularly in North America and Europe. Grocery and video stores that prefer more consistent products, accompanied by official-looking posters and other marketing materials, will order directly from these regional distributors. In the USA, for instance, a few large distributors have surfaced, such as Executive Image and Sanga Entertainment.

Sanga Entertainment

One figure in this small world of legitimate international distribution is Rabiu Mohammed, who owns a distribution business named Sanga Entertainment (also known as African Movies Mall) based in a heavily Caribbean and African neighbourhood in the Bronx in New York City. His business can serve as a case study, a glimpse into the dynamics of Nollywood's international physical distribution through the window of legitimate international distributors. Mohammed had been involved in informally selling copies of Nollywood movies (Anyiam-Fiberesima, 2009) when he realised the opportunity to connect with Nollywood producers and offer legitimate authorised copies for sale, a business move which has led him to do a brisk business in the North American market in a number of ways. A number of producers have enduring relationships with Sanga wherein they give Mohammed a master copy and he buys the rights to reproduce this movie for a flat fee. This flat fee varies, but can be fairly low and, again, both Mohammed and the producers can often only make decent profits based on large catalogues of movies for sale as opposed to individual 'blockbuster' movies. Mohammed sometimes edits the footage, uploading the movie onto his computer to fix audio and glitches. As his market is mostly English-speaking, he has no need to insert subtitles or dubbing.[6]

The company has been doing business since 2000, selling not only to individual consumers, but also to store owners across North America and the Caribbean. While these owners don't necessarily care about legality, Mohammed's business remains popular, in his opinion, because it is a reliable source with consistently new content on offer. He believes that another element that sells his legitimate copies is the effort he puts into marketing, with posters he makes and circulates himself and professional-looking DVD packaging. 'They look like Hollywood,' he says (2009). The biggest markets for the movies are New York, the greater Washington, DC, area, Houston and Florida. The first three are hubs of Nigerian expatriates, while the last is a base for Haitians, a group that adores Nollywood nearly as much as the West African diaspora. Mohammed does not just distribute domestically in the USA; he uses his North American rights to the full, connecting also to the alternative networks that embroider together international Nollywood audiences, selling to Caribbean and Canadian vendors as well. Just as Sanga's business spreads across North America and the Caribbean through a network of small business and individual entrepreneurs, built on the basis of personal connections between Mohammed and Nollywood producers, so too go Nollywood's networks on a global level. Built on informality, Nollywood's networks run counter to global ones yet spread a Nigerian cultural product powerfully.[7]

However, despite the growing profile of companies like Sanga and the ability of producers like Emem Isong to garner a four-figure flat fee for territorial distribution rights, a large portion of international sales are unlicensed, with no profits going back to any of those making the movie. Many producers in Nollywood make no effort to sell their movies outside Nigeria or to combat sales of their movies by others globally. Such is the focus on known and visible 'piracy' *in* Nigeria that unauthorised copies *outside* the country are just not an issue for most producers.

High-profile New Nollywood producers like Isong connect to their international physical sales through building individual relationships with distributors like Sanga. Less well-connected independent producers and Alaba marketers may attempt to make some extra money from the international physical market through sales agents. These agents will have an established relationship with someone involved in sales in the destination country and that person will act as a representative for a significant cut of the proceeds. It is most common for Nollywood producers to have partnerships with Ghanaian sellers in Accra, as movie culture in Ghana and Nigeria has a number of overlaps and synergies (see Garritano, 2013). London and Johannesburg are two other major hubs in international distribution. In virtually all of these instances, connections with sales agents in these foreign markets are made informally and through personal connections and introductions, as well as chance meetings.

Each of these sales agents has multiple clients and they are not exclusively contracted with just one producer or distributor, but these relationships are rarely well organised or documented. It is difficult to verify that someone claiming to be a sales agent for a Nollywood producer is, in fact, engaged in an ongoing business relationship with that producer, either inside or outside Nigeria. False agents proliferate, though a signed agreement accompanied by a photocopy of the signer's ID or even a video of the seller signing documents has become a popular check on identity. And, of course, most sales outlets have no great incentive to buy en masse from sales agents, as they too can make copies of others' work while only paying for one copy (though the promise of consistent and timely product with accompanying marketing materials is a significant lure towards licensed distribution as long as wholesale prices are low).

UNAUTHORISED PHYSICAL DISTRIBUTION

Networks of unauthorised distribution are de rigueur in Nollywood's global distribution circuits, but the line between black market and formal market is blurred here too. Unauthorised resale agents, operating with the promise of near 100 per cent profits on Nollywood's inexpensive movies, can be incredibly rapid and pervasive and have spread productions much further than would have been the case if they were distributed via centralised top-down distribution networks. And these 'pirate' networks may add value to their merchandise. Some may, for instance, decide to create more 'professional'-looking packaging, in sturdier cases and with higher-quality artwork or better-written blurbs on the casing (this usually applies to markets in the USA and Europe, where such packaging is expected). In francophone countries, for another example, unauthorised parties often undertake an entire dubbing of the movie into French and subsequently sell their value-added version with no permission and no rights – yet the original producers would be unlikely to dub their movies into French for sales to francophone Africa anyway, so this is only economically feasible as an export due to the economic logics of black market distribution. In this way, Nollywood product is altered to be culturally specific to the destination country by the local contacts in each country, who are incentivised by 100 per cent profits (in the case of unauthorised distributors) or even near 100 per cent profits (in the case of many sales agents) on the low-cost merchandise – with little formally standing between an individual sale and profit.

In an illustration of the multiple layers of black, white and grey markets that Nollywood negotiates to reach the diaspora in physical form, Nollywood scholar Alessandro Jedlowski investigated the serpentine path by which a Nollywood movie, dubbed in French, arrived at the open-air market in Naples, where he purchased it.

The video was shot in Lagos around 2005. Probably only a few weeks later, a pirated copy was acquired by a television studio in Abidjan and dubbed [into French] by professional artists. The Ivorian producer based in Italy managed to access a copy of the dubbed version and replicated it, working in partnership with an Italian digital media company. The film was then sold in Italy, Switzerland, France, Belgium, and Germany. One of the 'original' pirated copies ended up in the hands of some other entrepreneur, presumably Senegalese, who pirated it once again and put it on the market in Naples. This was the version I finally bought. (2013b: 33)

Jedlowski was able to trace this because his copy luckily came imprinted with the current contact details of the Italy-based Ivorian producer, who was then able to present his best estimation of the movie's path. This type of path is usually much more difficult to trace, if not impossible, and reflects the complex interplay of legality, illegality, market identification and value addition to these movies. As Jedlowski points out, each path on this circuit entailed a 'reinvention or rebranding' (ibid.) of the original, and each distributor, authorised or unauthorised, has left a trace of his or her market behind.

Copyright is often difficult in Nollywood's global circuits, even where every effort is made to do things in a formal manner. Sanga Entertainment's competitive advantage lies with the exclusive contracts Mohammed has with movie producers. However, it is extremely difficult to prosecute those violating his rights to the title. On the one hand, there is a group of pro bono lawyers with whom Mohammed has a relationship that will pursue violations in US courts; he has also pressured local police into carrying out at least one raid on those 'pirating' titles to which he holds licences. On the other hand, most violators are small shops, often grocery stores, selling only three to five copies of any given title; it often seems hardly worth the time and effort of prosecution when little money will be gleaned from the defendants.

Additionally, there are problems connecting legal standards (or disregard thereof) in Nigeria with standards that would be a given in the USA. For instance, one problem is with chain of title issues. While producers usually employ local music they have permission to use, some use foreign music.[8] Although Mohammed's suppliers claim to have purchased the rights, he certainly cannot pay the copyright fees to music produced by global entertainment companies and, as he receives the sound all on one track, he can't replace the music in his post-post-production editing – which means that some films simply cannot be legally distributed in the USA.

Mohammed has become a mostly formalised outlet in the USA for movies produced via informal means. Engaging with US copyright protections, for better and for worse, Sanga Entertainment is a mostly formal cog in an informal alternative machine. Still, operating out of a small warehouse in the south Bronx and via a modest website, and with no formal investors, even Sanga is still quite distant from the media MNC capital that supports dominant global networks.

GLOBAL ONLINE DISTRIBUTION

The flipside of this is the significant presence of formal money and formal interest in Nollywood's global satellite television and online distribution. The latter offers a particularly compelling case study in the intersection of the formal and the informal. Internet-based distribution – mostly streaming services – are particularly and increasingly popular with Nollywood's audiences in places where fans are likely to have the ability to easily stream full-length movies without data or power interruption (i.e. outside Nigeria and much of sub-Saharan Africa). This has attracted investment in the diaspora market, and some of that investment has also gone to try to break into the domestic market.

As international technology investors attempt to diversify their portfolios, some have eyed sub-Saharan Africa as the next smart investment opportunity. The idea is that, as internet connections and smartphones have limited penetration in most countries on the continent thus far, this is the ideal time to stake out a claim to significant market share in the future African 'technoscape', expected to expand rapidly once infrastructure becomes more robust. London-born Nigerian entrepreneur Jason Njoku is at the helm of iROKOtv, a streaming service dubbed in some popular international media coverage as the 'Netflix of Nollywood'. iROKO[9] was able to get very significant – $21 million so far – investment in the form of venture capital from technology-focused hedge funds, most notably US-based Tiger Global Management and Swedish investment firm Kinnevik, in return for their partial ownership of his company.

While the intention of iROKOtv and its global investors is to position itself for future dominance of the Nigerian online market once the infrastructure for video streaming becomes more widespread, iROKO currently does much better in the diaspora market: according to their own metrics, viewers outside of sub-Saharan Africa constitute the vast majority of iROKOtv's viewers; it is the most popular source for streaming content among online diaspora audiences. The conquering of the diaspora market is not iROKO's goal, however. Njoku's company moved their headquarters from London to Lagos, where they purchase the global online rights to Nigerian movies and guide their push to dominate distribution in the domestic Nigerian market, their stated long-term goal, but one which is, as yet, still quite distant. These movies are then delivered via iROKO's stand-alone online platform; the company makes money through paid subscriptions. This is a change from their initial business model that looked to advertising sales for their free content. This free streaming content initially was

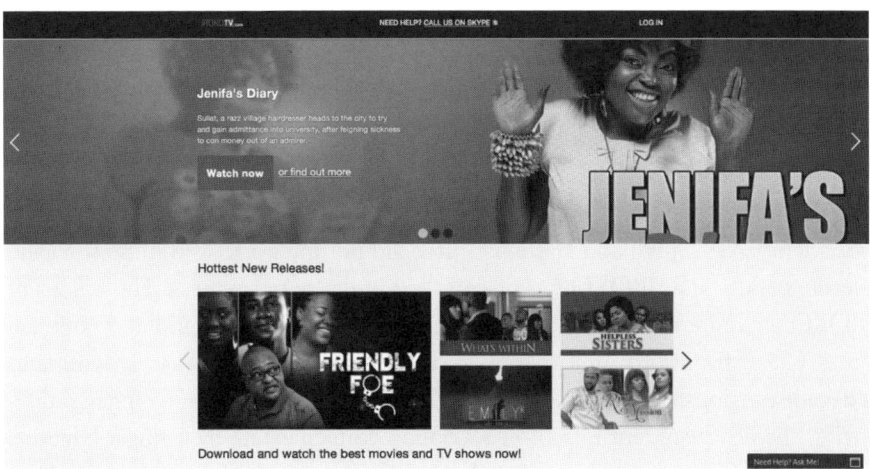

iROKOtv's international website landing page in 2015

delivered solely through YouTube, an American Google subsidiary, until Njoku branched out and built his own platform. iROKO also partners with other American content delivery giants, including iTunes, Amazon and Vimeo.

For readers who have read this book in order, from the beginning through to this page, this should seem remarkable, perhaps even a shock. An American hedge fund, a Swedish investment firm, multi-million-dollar investments, partnerships with YouTube (and, by extension, Google), iTunes, Amazon and Vimeo: this is not the infrastructure of investment and partnerships that marks the rest of Nollywood. In fact, this is the very sort of investment that we could say seems antithetical to Nollywood's industrial structure. How have these global corporate giants and heavyweight investment firms been comfortable enough to invest in or partner with a Nollywood internet-based distribution company, while there has been no such investment in the financing of production or distribution of physical copies of Nollywood? The answer is simple. With iROKO's initial tracking of their views and ad sales through corporate entities like YouTube, investors can feel assured that distribution can be accurately and formally documented, allowing profits to be tracked, double-checked and distributed to investors. And it doesn't hurt that investors can now visit iROKO's sleek MBA-filled office in a central neighbourhood in Manhattan,[10] an environment that likely makes venture capitalists feel much more at home than would a backroom office in Alaba or, as with Sanga, the south Bronx. iROKO offers a platform that distributes Nollywood to international audiences (their advertiser factsheet lists the top countries as the USA, Canada, the UK, Italy, Spain, Germany, France, Malaysia, Nigeria and Ghana) without needing access to the marketers' closely guarded domestic open-air distribution networks. iROKO also offers transparency in their sales figures, profits, viewing numbers, business strategies and ongoing objective analyses of their current successes and failures, available on the frequently updated blog of founder and CEO Njoku.

The Development of iROKOtv

Founders Jason Njoku and Bastian Gotter did not intend to found the so-called Netflix of Africa, as iROKOtv is often called in the popular press. The origins of iROKO are quite recent: in 2010, the year the two founded an ill-fated Nigerian music CD distribution portal online. The two had been classmates and roommates a decade previously at the University of Manchester: Njoku, an outgoing nightlife-loving chemistry student raised on a London council estate by a single Nigerian mother, and Gotter, a more reserved French-German management student. After graduation, Gotter became an oil trader, while Njoku doggedly pursued a steady stream of failed entrepreneurial projects, sometimes enlisting Gotter's business acumen in the process. When the two discovered that their Nigerian music CD distribution website (a main project at the time for Njoku and a side project for Gotter) had failed to sell virtually any CDs, they decided to shift their focus. Njoku noted that his mother watched Nollywood movies insatiably, and learned that licences for online viewing could be purchased for as little as $100–$500 at the time. After negotiations with YouTube-Germany,[11] Njoku and Gotter shifted their business in late 2010 to be an ad-fuelled free YouTube channel called NollywoodLove; $200,000 in angel investments (mostly from Gotter's savings from his oil-trading career) went, in part, towards a catalogue of 200 movies by January 2011. Straight away, the advertising aggregator networks they used to serve ads to NollywoodLove turned out to be generating encouraging profits.

Small companies making money from ad space for free content on YouTube are fairly common. What happened next for NollywoodLove was not. By August 2011, eight months later, this small YouTube channel had millions of dollars in its bank account, and the money was not from selling advertising. Instead of pursuing growing revenues, iROKO went down the path of tech start-up funding and expansion, with various rounds of venture capital. Their first major investor was Tiger Capital, which invested $3 million as part of iROKO's Series A financing round that finished in August 2011. This money immediately went towards exiting YouTube: on 1 December 2011, iROKOtv launched as a stand-alone platform, with iROKOplus, a premium subscription service, launching in the middle of the next year.

By 2014, subsequent financing rounds brought them to a remarkable total sum of $21 million raised, including further investments from Tiger as well as significant capital from Swedish investment firm Kinnevik and US-based Rise

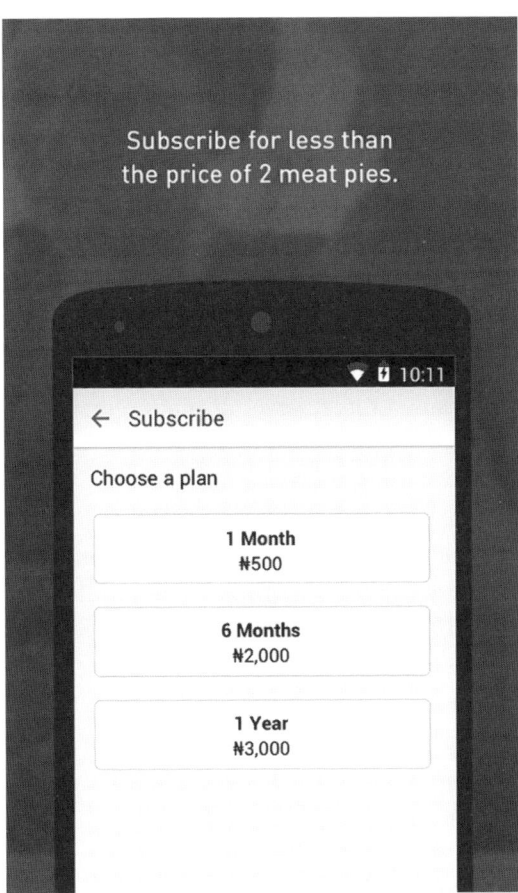

iROKOtv has experimented with various pricing models in the Nigerian market, most recently targeting mobile viewers

Capital. iROKO used this funding to shift its focus from the diaspora to Nigeria (starting first with just Lagos) and the rest of sub-Saharan Africa.[12] Their first step was to switch to a full subscription-based service. While ad sales had worked well in western markets where prices for advertising were high, the inexpensive rates for advertising to Nigerian consumers, coupled with an absence of ad-serving-networks targeting Nigerian consumers,[13] meant this model would simply not support the prices that iROKO was committed to paying for movies, and a subscription service was the only way to monetise content effectively in the Nigerian context.

The online subscription services were targeted at the Nigerian market with features that make them marketable there. Subscriptions started at $9 per month and scaled to $30 per year, essentially $2.50 a month. They have experimented with allowing downloads, attractive to viewers experiencing interruptions in their internet connection, as the full download can occur over lengthy periods of time and needs less consistency than streaming video. They've also worked on reducing file sizes so movies are less than 150MB in data download, as users pay exorbitant rates in Nigeria for data. In the summer of 2015, they made yet another cut in prices, moving their Nigerian business from an online to a purely mobile model. Still, however, it will be quite some time before online or mobile viewing becomes widespread among audiences in Nigeria. Extremely expensive data plans and limited broadband speeds are just two of the problems facing iROKO in creating an online viewership. Despite the massive attention being paid to capturing Nigerian audiences, the vast majority of iROKO's revenue still comes from markets outside Nigeria (Njoku, 2015c). Currently, the diaspora business is where iROKO's success lies; it is only able to invest in competing within Nigeria because of its reserves of venture capital.

iROKO in Nigeria: Problems

The case study of iROKOtv is compelling here because it takes a company schooled in the ways of and fed by the milk (venture capital) of Silicon Valley and transplants it into an environment that could hardly be more hostile in its infrastructure and business culture. iROKO now bases its business in Nigeria – Njoku himself relocated to Lagos from London[14] and now has two entire buildings' worth of offices there – and has had to deal with the challenges presented by the Lagos business environment. This environment is not just more challenging than Silicon Valley, London, or New York, but also significantly more challenging than in the major cities of southern Africa or East Africa. Njoku commented on this in multiple blogposts, in which he described the ease and comparatively inexpensive cost of business in Kigali, Dar es Salaam, Kampala and Johannesburg in comparison to Lagos.[15] Not only is infrastructure distinctly challenging there, but iROKO also must now do business in the realm of the marketers, a massive opaque network of business owners allergic to the contracts, copyright, transparency and quantification (current and projected revenues, users, clicks, etc.) which fuel Silicon Valley.

In his blog, Njoku outlines the myriad issues that emerged in Nigeria after the company moved there from London, things he didn't initially anticipate from his British-raised vantage-point. For instance, means of payment in Nigeria hampered the capacity to sign up new subscribers – the majority of iROKO's global subscribers use credit or debit cards, but these are unknown to the majority of Nigerians. Mobile payment services,[16] a system that duplicates credit card capabilities in payment, have widely proliferated in southern and East Africa, but have made little headway in Nigeria. Nigerian ISPs[17] are also an issue and, according to Njoku, are far and away the biggest impediment to penetrating the market (2015a). Data downloads cost consumers $12 for 500MB. This has meant that, even though a subscription is affordable, and even though iROKO has compressed movie download sizes to 150MB, people pay significant amounts to download just one movie. Though iROKO has tried to implement creative solutions to pricing, payment and streaming problems, it has yet to find a way to disrupt the exorbitant data pricing charged by Nigerian ISPs. This means that iROKO in Nigeria is more popular – or even just possible – with wealthy households and those using the internet connections provided at work. iROKO's viewing data suggests the latter is most significant, as the busiest viewing hours are from 11 a.m. to 4 p.m. within Nigeria – prime business hours (Njoku, 2014c).

iROKO experienced significant problems with its own Lagos internet contracts. Initially paying a local ISP standard Lagos business prices of $3,000 per month for 2–3MB upload and download speeds while trying to upload over 100GB a day's worth of content in iROKO's early days, Njoku found it was cheaper and easier to load up external hard-drives with 500GB of content and fly with them himself to London to upload content using British ISP speeds and rates (2013e). The company finally found a solution that ended the need for physical aeroplane-carry-on-bag-transport of internet-bound data via a deal with a new Nigerian company called MainOne. MainOne has built and operates its own private 7,000 kilometre (4,350 mile) submarine cable that runs along the coast of West Africa carrying data at 1.92TB per second from London, where the cable begins, to Lagos, with landings in Seixal (Portugal), Casablanca, Dakar, Abidjan and Accra along the way. As part of its 'last-mile' infrastructure, it built a 160 foot (49 metre) tower outside iROKO's office complex that links to the Lagos landing station via point-to-point microwave technologies and provides 15MB upload and download speeds ('burstable' to 30MB), obviating the need to deal with regular Nigerian ISPs. Njoku estimates that this service costs them $70,000–$100,000 per year, but it is more reliable, faster and cheaper than attempting the same uploads using local ISPs.

Unfortunately, the average consumer still must go through the Nigerian ISP pricing structure; neither iROKO nor MainOne has plans to construct public towers throughout Lagos. As Njoku put it, 'When I look at how easy it was to connect [our] London, NYC and JoBurg offices (wired and no need for 160ft towers), I really appreciate how brutal it is doing business in Lagos and Nigeria' (2013e). Consider the number of generators and the level of consumption of generator fuel needed to run such a business in Lagos – added to the aforementioned difficulties with internet procurement via a personal tower connecting to a private cable – and one can see the challenges for a formal internet-based company doing business in Nigeria. Marketers might look on in bemusement from the single generator-run stall from which they manage their tiny corner of Nollywood.

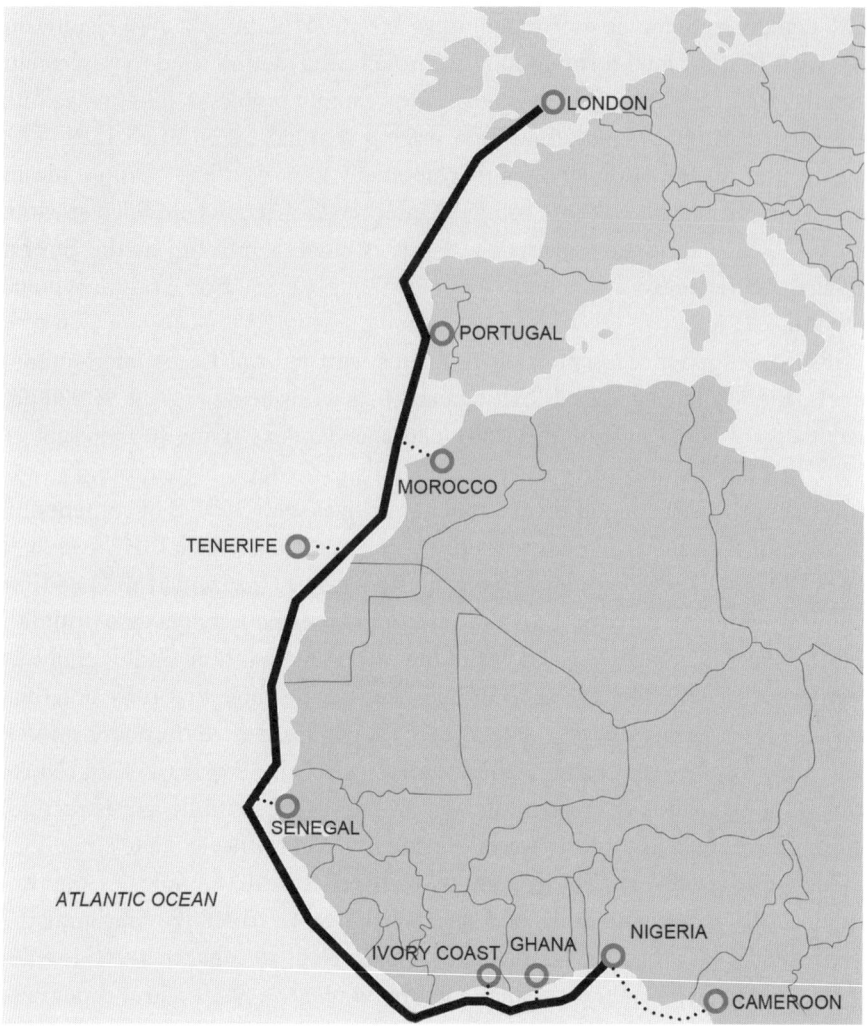

MainOne's private submarine cable brings high-speed bandwidth from London, down along the coast of West Africa, to Lagos

iROKO in Nigeria: Fixes

iROKO has received remarkable levels of investment. This money is not meant to produce movies, but rather to build an entirely new distribution and formal documentation structure. To be sure, much of the $21 million that iROKO has raised has gone on labour costs of converting VCD content for upload, bandwidth, hosting, building its own online platform, editing out copyrighted songs and other standard issues. But the money has also gone towards completely restructuring the industry so that a formal business such as iROKO can enter into deals with the informal sector. iROKO's formal outputs (traceable and corporate-partnered online distribution) are predicated on a formalisation of inputs – certification and sale of copyright to Nollywood's intellectual property. With personal relationships, such as those Mohammed and Njoku alike enjoy with producers like Isong, this is easy. But building a huge catalogue of titles means entering into agreements with people who are not friends and, at times, with people who are not even necessarily trustworthy. The danger of false agents is always present. Nigerian movie production functions in a space not governed by official documents. There is effectively no legal prosecution of broken contracts or violated copyright in Nollywood, as the legal infrastructure to support such actions is not functional (see Chapter 4 for more on this); a number of different movie workers may even legitimately believe that they own copyright on a particular title.

To combat – or conquer – the informal (word of mouth) documentation of rights ownership that marks Nollywood, iROKO's Lagos office has put huge effort into verifying copyright in this context. Locating its headquarters in Lagos has allowed buyers to have a permanent place in the industry, and its intimate knowledge of the market allows it to be more confident in its business contacts. iROKO's buyers ask rights-sellers to bring in ID and documents 'proving' their copyright, and employees videotape the entire transaction, including an oral statement of the contract's terms as a record, with both parties present. Njoku describes his strategy:

> People say contracts are worthless in Nigeria. No problem. Get them to pledge to the contract details on camera. Try fighting that in court! People could close the deal with you, turn around and sell the content again to someone else. Brilliant; for the first year we paid producers over three instalments, over the course of the multi-year contract. In Nigeria especially, if someone owes you money, they have allocated and planned for how they are going to spend that money as soon as the deal is signed. If you pay them in instalments, they are seriously motivated to keep to the deal terms to ensure they get what they've already spent in their heads. By that time, iROKO had closed deals with most of their peers making screwing us more difficult. (2013c)

Njoku may be a little over-confident here: iROKO still must establish with whom they are supposed to be negotiating. The presence of a video certainly won't make the Nigerian justice system or copyright enforcement system become efficient or timely. However, it might serve as leverage in an out-of-court settlement and disincentivise false agents from selling rights that belong to friends or colleagues. The combination of iROKO's dominance of the online rights market (one doesn't want to be boycotted by the highest-paying and largest buyer on the market) and the investment it has put into ensuring that its buyers recognise a diversity of sellers has lent it much leverage here.

Another strategy iROKO has used in rights acquisition is orchestrating a drastic intentional rise in the price of licences for Nollywood content. When the company began, it was able to buy licences for $100–$500 and put content on the NollywoodLove YouTube channel as soon as it could digitise it. Five years later, iROKO rates for combined online and airline licences are $3,000 minimum and can potentially go up to $22,000 (ibid.), though below $10,000 is a more common range. Far from a victim of rising costs, Njoku was its architect. As he explains, 'I increased the price thousands of percentiles in absence of any competition because a) I thought the content was much more valuable than $100–$500 … and b) it seriously discouraged any fast followers' (ibid.). In other words, Njoku sought to disrupt Nollywood distribution by outbidding his competitors and identifying iROKO to producers as the most serious contender in the industry. As it stands today, he reports that it buys only approximately 12 per cent of the available content, with decisions based on ratings by the army of Lagos iROKO employees who spend all day watching recent movies and rating them for quality and appeal (Njoku, 2015a). The high prices he pays means even Alaba's staunchest marketers hope their latest titles make the cut and garner the extra income (ibid.). iROKO buys online and airline rights packaged together for popular titles, increasing the whole amount it can offer to producers, while dominating the modest domestic and international airline market by streamlining content acquisition, and simultaneously branding itself as the foremost distributor of quality Nollywood content to the up-market clientele that utilises air travel.

Yet, for all of these innovative solutions fitting formal into informal, iROKO is still far from the Netflix of Africa, at least not the 2016 iteration of Netflix. iROKO is known globally as the go-to Nollywood online subscription service, among those that *do* consume Nollywood content online. It is known internationally in the technology sector for the level of venture capital it has raised from high-profile sources and its prominence in a challenging market. It is known continentally in business circles for being one of the best-funded technology start-ups in Nigeria. And it's known in Nollywood, the industry, as the go-to buyer of online licences, a buyer to whom all vie to sell. These are all enviable ways to be known. As for now, however, VCDs still dominate the large domestic market and the vast majority of Nollywood content is not put out by the few producers known as 'New Nollywood'. 'Nollywood, the industry' is still, at its core, the Alaba marketers' industry. What would it take for iROKO to be 'successful' at the level its funders and founders would like? In his somewhat envious assessment of a Finnish tech start-up's recent good fortune, Njoku blogged:

> Could a similar company explode like that in Nigeria and/or Africa? It finally dawned on me that would be largely impossible. [This company] benefits from the hidden hand of infrastructure being largely solved. Large and sophisticated user base? Check. Credible payments? Check. Undisrupted internet which ensures continual game play? Check. Affluent consumers? Check. Time? Check. This environment doesn't exist in Nigeria. So that type of torrid revenue growth is impossible. (2013d)

The infrastructure that would need to be in place would hypothetically include not just reliable electricity, but fast and reliable internet, reasonable ISP contracts,[18] reliable payment systems and a user base comfortable with accessing entertainment content online.

Alaba and iROKO

When iROKO moved from YouTube to its own web platform, and when it began to move from an ad-based to a subscription-based revenue model, free YouTube airings were certainly not left behind. The model pursued by NollywoodLove has lived on, and there are thousands of full-length movies available for free on YouTube via channels of varying legality, usually accompanied by advertising. And iROKO is not the only full-service online provider. There are other stand-alone websites on which viewers pay for credits to watch a number of movies, with actual payment sometimes as low as 50 cents per streamed title.

Some of the free Nollywood YouTube channels[19] are actually collectives of five to ten Alaba marketers, banded together to pool their content into one shared YouTube channel, monetised at modest levels by deals with ad-networks to serve targeted ads with their free content. In some cases, these channels are managed by former iROKO employees; Njoku predictably describes their offerings as 'Primarily taking their older content or anything iROKO didn't [want to] buy and throwing it online [for free] to monetise as best they can. Admirable I guess, they (and many others) think they are hurting me. In fact they are mostly hurting themselves' (Njoku, 2013a).

Indeed, Njoku sees his business model as literally at war with Alaba's. He describes their competition in warlike terms, accusing them of orchestrating the unauthorised posting of New Nollywood blockbusters on YouTube on non-ad-served channels as part of a strategy to retain their power, having their free content compete with the content iROKO has put behind a paywall. Some of these may be the same marketers he does business with, paying them for their content, while they pirate other content he owns the rights to. He sees his company and its multi-million dollar investments as tasked with routing these small market-based businesses from their persistent position of control. **'The Alaba way will fade,'** Njoku declares on his blog (bold in the original). 'The digital migration has begun. They have chosen to not live in the new world so will be forced to die in their old one' (2015b). The 'digital migration', however, has begun very, very slowly. We can look at the persistence of VCD technologies, even as other developing markets have moved to DVDs, and the slow introduction of mobile payment systems in Nigeria, as perhaps representative of the likely slow pace of the advent of online consumption of Nollywood among the Nigerian public on a scale that would indicate that iROKO and formality have, indeed, routed Alaba and informality.

GLOBAL TELEVISION DISTRIBUTION

Besides iROKO, the other major buyer of Nollywood licences is also fuelled by formal global money: Africa Magic. Originally one channel, launched in 2003, Africa Magic is now a package of co-branded channels that air Nollywood movies twenty-four hours a day for sub-Saharan African satellite television subscribers. There are now around nine[20] Africa Magic channels,[21] each with a different focus, showing Nollywood content, Nigerian soaps and other non-Nigerian African-made content in the Nollywood style concurrently. Africa Magic is part of a suite of channels linked by the M-Net entertainment content brand. These M-Net channels, including Africa Magic, are carried exclusively by DSTV, the dominant satellite television provider in sub-Saharan Africa. DSTV and M-Net (so, by extension, the Africa Magic channels) are both fully owned by South African media company MultiChoice, in turn owned by South African media giant Naspers. Naspers is a major MNC with global business interests across the world, including significant media holdings in Latin America, Europe, South Asia, East Asia, Southeast Asia and sub-Saharan Africa. MultiChoice has been the leader in satellite television in sub-Saharan Africa for years and it is not surprising that it identified a demand for Nollywood content in the channels it simultaneously serves to Nigeria and the rest of Africa.

MultiChoice has only around 4 million subscribers in Nigeria out of the 170 million population, but it is seen and known by many, many more. In a recent study, 80 per cent of Nigerian respondents reported watching Africa Magic often or very often, despite the low level of subscription, and they reported a high degree of preference for titles that had been acquired by Africa Magic as a stamp of quality (Ekwuazi, 2014). This discrepancy – only 4 million subscribers yet 80 per cent brand loyalty – can be explained by domestic viewing patterns. For one, it is very common to watch Africa Magic at a neighbour's or friend's house; some fund their subscription via small charges to their neighbours to watch at night. It is also common to watch Africa Magic in public spaces, such as a stall at the market or a beer parlour. It has been reported that, in 'high-density low-income' neighbourhoods, a video parlour may pay the subscription fees and then splice their cables to send their paid programming to private screens in the surrounding area for reduced rates (ibid.).

Africa Magic pays prices for Nollywood movies that are comparable to iROKO, though usually a little bit lower, and popular movies will sell to both. Satellite added to online and airline rights sales offer options to New Nollywood producers seeking greater control over their own titles' destiny outside of the marketers' sphere. One prominent New Nollywood producer I interviewed (Isong) offered a break-down of what she might expect to garner for a hypothetical popular movie in multiple windows apart from physical domestic sales (2014). She could get $3,000–$10,000 in regional DVD distribution rights from an international physical distributor like Mohammed; iROKO could pay $10,000 for combined online and possible airline rights; and Africa Magic could offer $4,000–$8,000 (ibid.).[22] This is certainly significant in the context of Nollywood's low budgets. However, the reality in Nollywood is the same as in most creative industries worldwide: to make money, a movie must be a success in the core domestic market. The bulk of a movie's gross comes from domestic sales – physical copies and, in the case of New Nollywood's bigger-budget fare, perhaps some significant cinema receipts as well. Isong's figures are higher than that of the average movie's profits, and she utilises Africa Magic and iROKO, the top-paying and more selective buyers of such content. The average producer is not consistently able to realise profits from all of these potential avenues of distribution.

While Africa Magic is the most prominent buyer of authorised television screening licences, Nollywood movies are available via many different online and television outlets. In Nigeria and throughout sub-Saharan Africa, there are many opportunities to view Nollywood movies on television. Africa Magic is popular among satellite subscribers, but the African televisual-scape features a multitude of pay and terrestrial channels that also screen Nollywood. For instance, in Uganda, Dominica Dipio has listed every place Ugandans might watch Nollywood movies: while Africa Magic screens English-language Nollywood 24/7 on satellite television, viewers can also daily watch three or more Nollywood movies in English on free-to-air channels Nation TV, a Ugandan station, or Citizen TV, a Kenyan station that can be watched in Uganda (2014). Furthermore, Ugandan free-to-air channels Star and Bukedde air Nollywood movies with translation, usually by VJ narrators, into Luganda, the primary local language (ibid.). The ubiquity of these prepaid and free viewing opportunities has caused some consternation in recent years that it will undermine the public's desire or willingness to pay for access to individual movies at all: in Uganda, daily audiences in video halls have certainly declined (ibid.). Outside sub-Saharan Africa, there are multiple satellite channels featuring Nollywood as well, targeting North American or European audiences, with London being the largest hub for these.

Despite the formality one might expect in rights acquisition by a highly visible satellite channel, the distribution of Nollywood movies on television channels – even government-run channels – is no guarantee that producers have been paid for this content. An increasing differentiation in Nollywood content by quality, coupled with iROKO's raising of licence fees, has contributed to Africa Magic raising the fees it pays for licences and beefing up its efforts to make sure the fees are going to the right parties. Outside Africa Magic, however, acquisition of movie content has continued to be a minimally documented and sometimes blatantly unauthorised process. While few admit publicly to such procurement, in her work on Nollywood in Kinshasa (in the DRC), anthropologist Katrien Pype noted clearly pirated copies of foreign (American and Nigerian) films in the offices of television station directors, awaiting broadcast on DRC's national airwaves (2013). In other cases, channels might be infringing unintentionally, so *someone* is getting at least a little money for supplying Nollywood movies – and that person is offering to sign over the broadcast rights in return – although probably not the person who originally produced or made the movie. It is easy to approach the buying desk at a television channel with a portfolio of Nollywood movies; verifying the identities of sales agents is complex, with much counterfeit documentation circulating. Due to their physical presence in Lagos and their fame among producers, entities like Africa Magic and iROKOtv have more to lose if their business practices are questioned; thus they make great efforts and expend significant resources to pursue valid rights with authorised parties. Smaller television stations, even those serving developed markets, may have neither the resources nor the presence in Lagos to pursue this level of assuredness, unless they source their content from Africa Magic themselves.

CONCLUSION

The tale of Nollywood in the preceding chapters – Nollywood's domestic development, functioning, appeal and organisation – has taken informality and opacity as a running theme. Most of Nollywood's global networks are similarly informal and opaque. From the core of the industry, we can see alternative global networks of production inputs and distribution circuits spinning out from Lagos, an alternative media capital, at the hands of the networks of small-scale Nigerian entrepreneurs known as marketers. However, we can also hear a knocking at the door: the knocking of global capital in the form of two well-financed companies, iROKOtv and MultiChoice's Africa Magic, itching to make inroads with Nigerian audiences while making their current profits mostly by selling Nigerian content to foreign audiences of African descent.

iROKO, in particular, offers a compelling window into the myriad challenges presented to global capital by the Lagosian market. From local ISPs to subscriber payments to contract enforcement, business in Nigeria has been fraught with difficulty. It has produced creative solutions for the Nigerian context and has emerged as the foremost online Nollywood subscription service, as well as a prominent and coveted buyer of Nollywood content. Yet it is still operating on the periphery as opposed to the core of the industry. The prices paid by iROKO, though significant, don't cover the movies' budgets. Even with the other international distribution licences that can be sold (television and international physical rights), Nollywood movies still need physical distribution in Nigeria to make a profit. And this still mostly means recourse to marketer-run networks of Nigeria's open-air markets.[23]

If the infrastructure supporting online content grows in Nigeria to the extent that hard copies are a thing of the past, this will certainly offer a window for others to gain control of Nollywood, and iROKO seems to be in a very good position in that regard. But one might consider what it is that would be controlled by these new parties? Would it be Nollywood? Who would produce these titles? Would iROKO, a company begun in the UK, a company fed on corporate partnerships and significant investments from the USA and Sweden, be the ideal party to hold the power to commission the majority of Nigerian production through its consolidated dominance of the distribution market? Would a new set of Nollywood producers rise? What would their vision of Nollywood be? If we take the most aspirational of New Nollywood directors as the likely answer, we can see that this could mean higher-budget movies primed for access to international film festivals. Yet the core of Nollywood fanship has been built much in the way soap opera and STV fanship has: 'old' Nollywood's interchangeable formulaic, juicy, melodramatic storylines, told via scripts and performances that are indebted to soap opera and live theatre more than to art cinema – and we can see this content as speaking especially clearly to mass audiences (Adejunmobi, 2007).

Outside this highly documented, transparent and globally linked corner of the industry, Nollywood's other global connections are much more opaque and harder to trace. Outside these authorised online and satellite television portals, Nollywood productions *are* sold in the global marketplace: in the unofficial corners of it. On the underbelly of the global network of the entertainment industry is another global network, with very different nodes and hubs. In London, the centre will be Peckham or Essex, as opposed to the central London BBC headquarters and film production houses. Instead of Los Angeles, there might be ungentrified areas of Brooklyn; there might be Accra, Onitsha, Beirut, Johannesburg. In this alternate network, documentation is unreliable or non-existent, and lines between authorised and unauthorised distribution overlap and blur.

Much of the global trade in Nollywood's inputs and exports is via circuits marked by informality and unofficial trade, circuits that enable disconnected individuals to act on a global level. The realities of this trade reflect theorising done, most notably by Simone (2001), on the African city's role in the global order: disembedded, but peppered by opportunities for connections to global networks on an informal and individual level. Alternative networks, as also explored by Larkin (2008), are created in this way – via one-off personal connections and informal globalisation – and, in this way, a city like Lagos, disembedded from dominant global networks, becomes an important hub in alternative ones.

Nollywood's production inputs are particularly reflective of this fractured connection to the global order. Any input in the industry supply chain is mediated through some disjuncture with the official global economy. Sony (and other international) equipment, editing software, lights, generators and computers are all originally sourced from MNCs – and some are even purchased first hand through an official retail outlet *in* Nigeria. This connection (epitomised here by the Victoria Island Sony store) is a key place of connection between Nollywood production and official global networks, but all such inputs into the industry supply chain reflect connections to official global networks, even if mediated through multiple previous owners, 'tropicalisation' in a dusty marketplace, black market networks, a significant mark-up on official global prices, or a lengthy journey with a hard-won visa to purchase new from a duty-free electronics shop in a far-flung location such as Dubai or London.

Distribution, however, has many faces. Authorised television and online outlets constitute only part of Nollywood's global distribution. Available anywhere there are Africans living, Nollywood has achieved global physical distribution without any top-down architecture devoted to it. While much of this distribution is 'pirate', or unofficial, sending no money back to support production, it is still successful in its ability to spread Nollywood as a cultural product – and it enriches many along the way. From foreign sales agents to Nigerian aggregators to terrestrial television in sub-Saharan Africa to small African grocery stores and open-air market stalls, there are few checks on ownership and rights. This is a result of the fundamentally informal system as well as economic imperatives:

without a large aggregated catalogue of titles, there is little profit to be had thus far in international sales for most producers. The motivation is stronger for someone making 100 per cent profit on aggregated stock (often a 'pirate') than for those sharing percentages or paying for rights

Despite Nollywood's general disconnect from dominant global cultural industries networks, the industry is, in fact, connected globally via a mostly alternative system. This reflects the capacity of Nollywood's producers and distributors for innovation – and the disconnect between the industry and the agreements upon which mainstream global networks in the creative industries are based: enforced copyright and respected legal contracts. Yet there are places where Nollywood is also connected to the global economy in direct, official and formal ways, such as the efforts of Sony's equipment sales team on Victoria Island. These salespeople are directly plugged in to the dominant networks of creative industry technology supplies, and they enable Sony, an internationally networked global Japan-based MNC, to profit. Sony's presence in production inputs is comparable to iROKO and M-Net's presence in distribution channels, perhaps marking the beginning of global MNC investment and integration into Nollywood – although this is by no means certain, and is not foreseeable within the immediate future. The foreign equipment sales entrepreneurs in Lagos and formal distributors whose revenue is mostly based in the diaspora may, instead, be indicative of the ability of these formal global companies to profit from – and, in many ways, support (e.g. workshops, reliable equipment supply, commissioning movies, raising prices for rights) – emerging creative industries, even though their reach is strictly limited.

NOTES

1. A conference on distribution organised by Dr Michael Best of the Georgia Institute of Technology.
2. See, for instance, the extremely limited intentional and legal distribution of Hollywood films there, only taking place in Lagos's major multiplex theatres in wealthy neighbourhoods, and brokered by South African interests.
3. In the movie, a group of seemingly respectable young women decide to sleep with older men for financial gain, eventually leading to negative consequences like HIV transmission, unwanted unwed pregnancy, death and shocking revelations of inappropriate fatherhood.
4. This comment, I suspect, was specifically directed at me, a white researcher from the USA.
5. See Krings (2010) and Böhme (2013) for more on the connections between Tanzania's burgeoning movie industry and Nollywood. Other 'sibling' industries, as mentioned in Chapter 3, are based in the Democratic Republic of Congo,

Burkina Faso, the Indian community of South Africa and various expatriate communities in North America and Europe.
6. The movies he sells that were originally produced in Hausa or Yoruba come to him with English subtitles already inserted.
7. See Athique (2008) for an alternative case of the informal global networks of Bollywood.
8. This is a much greater problem for Ghanaian movies than Nigerian.
9. It is officially pronounced 'ee-roh-koh', after the African tree; Nigerian viewers call it this. However, founder Njoku pronounces it 'eye-roh-koh' when talking to people outside of Africa to make sure they spell it properly, with an 'i', something he feels is more important as a businessman. He says the former is technically correct but both are acceptable and he consistently uses the latter in filmed interviews.
10. While iROKO began in London, that office is now closed. Headquarters are now in Lagos; its ex-African office is now in New York instead of the UK. It moved this office from London to New York due to its many relationships with American funders.
11. They began with German YouTube because Gotter had connections there.
12. In July 2014, it announced an expansion into the East African market, opening an office in Rwanda targeted not only at Rwanda, but also Uganda, Kenya, Burundi and Tanzania.
13. iROKO would need to sell ad space directly to advertisers instead of being able to rely on aggregators such as those that serve ads to YouTube viewers in western markets.
14. Though, even more recently, he has shifted his family to New York.
15. 'When you build a business in Lagos, one sometimes forgets (I am obviously guilty on all accounts) that the challenges and issues are typically abnormal ones. Lack of electricity and poor infrastructure. Kigali, Dar es Salaam and Kampala were modernised compared to anything I came across in Lagos. Predatory government agencies, lack of security and terrible healthcare? Not the norm' (Njoku, 2014a).
16. Banking and money transmission via mobile phone credits.
17. Internet service providers (ISPs) are the companies from whom consumers contract internet access, paying for particular speeds or data plans at the rates the company offers. Given the costs of construction of the 'last-mile' (connections from their networks to their customers' buildings and devices) infrastructure necessary to deliver access, most buildings throughout the world will have a limited selection of accessible ISPs, if, indeed, there is a choice at all.
18. In an interview with me, Njoku said this was the element he would most want to change: that the best hope to better iROKO's chances would be reducing charges for data by Nigerian ISPs (2015a).

19. Njoku estimates that there are about fifty of these collective marketers' channels.
20. Channel titles and foci shift frequently.
21. At the time of writing, this consists of Africa Magic Epic (epic movies), Showcase (new movies), Urban (a mix of movies and television shows set in cities), Family (movies about families as opposed to movies targeted at children as this name suggests in the West), World (mixes programming from multiple African nations and regions) and Yoruba-, Igbo-, Hausa- and Swahili-language channels for movies shot in each of those languages, though new channels are formed and others may be shuttered at any time.
22. Though less popular movies will garner much less – even as low as $600.
23. The exception is the small handful of high-profile New Nollywood titles that have gained significant cinematic returns, but reaching the villages or any audience outside the well heeled in large cities requires recourse to marketer networks as well.

Conclusion

In the last chapter of his book on the geography of Hollywood the industry, economic geographer Allen J. Scott addresses the future of the global movie industry, wondering if burgeoning production centres (he identifies London, Paris, Mumbai and Manila as front-runners) could overtake Hollywood (2005). What he perhaps *should* be asking is not what could overtake Hollywood, but whether Hollywood will 'take over' these industries: not overlaying them to make way for US-made content, but incorporating them into its umbrella of global business relations while maintaining their cultural specificity. Integration into dominant global industry networks may 'standardise' production (and it will certainly 'standardise' financing, legalising and distributing a movie), but it also serves to draw a map of the world as a networked society, one with multiple hubs, constantly being redrawn. Cultural industries may emerge outside this system and they, like Nollywood, may attract formalisation efforts (of varying efficacy) from those who wish to penetrate this network. For now, Nollywood stands as a representative not just of cultural diversity of global cultural industries, but also of their economic diversity. In a blindspot of global Hollywood, an industry from which it is largely absent in terms of official representation (due, in part, to the uncertainties involved in the informal distribution networks of the 'Fourth World'), we can see a cultural industry that dominates the small screens of an entire continent – and that continent's diaspora – and that continues to draw strength from the very elements that make the environment inhospitable to global Hollywood: informality, quasi-legality and opacity.

Nollywood is, from one perspective, central: specifically, when viewed from sub-Saharan Africa. In sub-Saharan African networks of cultural product distribution, Nollywood movies are both dominant and ubiquitous: practically unavoidable in networks of popular culture in the region and related diaspora circuits. From another perspective, Nollywood is peripheral in the extreme. In the context of global Hollywood, Nollywood, Nigeria and, indeed, most of sub-Saharan Africa are barely considerations. Nollywood, as an object of study, offers a window through which to examine the rise of a cultural industry, peripheral to dominant networks but central to alternative networks. The informal nature of these networks both gives the industry its very specific strength and delimits its potential for co-option by dominant global cultural industry networks.

THEMES

This book has looked at Nollywood's birth and growth, as well as its current functioning, its appeal, legacy and audience, the governing bodies that do (and do not) structure it and its global connections. A few major themes emerged throughout the course of this analysis. One is the specific implications of the location of Nollywood, in what can be called the 'urban global periphery'. We have seen that the growth of Nollywood as an object of study is inseparable from the environment from which it emerged: an exemplar of the rapidly growing hyper-modern African mega-city, able to be considered both part of a disenfranchised 'Fourth World' and globally connected via its own networks. This growth, marked by informality and the strength of black and grey market networks, is an exemplar of the different challenges and opportunities that confront creative industries in this context. The extremely fragmented incorporation of Lagos into dominant global networks is reflected in its products, and the potential of industries born there to rise and grow in fundamental ways is that much more fraught with difficulty. Despite these challenges, Nollywood has not only grown but also found a way to thrive. As such, we have seen that the creative milieu may prosper at the periphery – not necessarily the urban periphery, but the global periphery: the non-spatially bounded 'Fourth World', which exists in the gaps between connections to the dominant global order, as in Simone's work on African cities (2001).

In analysing the structure of Nollywood, the dominant theme is of the intersection of informality and power, and creative responses to challenges in the industry's business model. Flexibility, opacity and informality mark this trade on the flipside of formal global networks. While much Nollywood equipment, for instance, is purchased from corporations like Sony, most exchanges are informal and undertaken without storefronts. The only places in which we can see formal money invested are distribution networks with current revenue streams keyed to the diaspora – satellite television and online distribution – and the major players there have found doing business in Lagos ridden with challenges every step of the way. Trust and informal ties link the industry, but that does not mean the industry is haphazard; these ties also structure it quite rigidly, as the marketers demonstrate by their collective grip on industry power. In that vein, another important theme that emerges in this analysis of Nollywood is how, in the place of government-shaped structure, a system of self-organisation can step in: guilds, trust and informal links. When the instincts of the state are primarily self-preservation, it cannot be relied upon to guide the industry. Instead, we see self-organisation as a key element in the industry: specifically, the strong guilds and, particularly, the guild in which power is most centralised, that of the marketers. In the face of the formalisation and corporatisation of global media industries, Nollywood stands as a counter-model: networks of small informal enterprises that self-organise and keep out formal capital via their industrial structure.

And this informality is conscious and active. I remind readers that my focus on informality here is not meant to exoticise, but rather to investigate the conscious adherence to this system in order to block power moves by government and external investors. The marketers' lack of documentation is intentional, meant to retain power locally. Major external actors, such as Emeka Mba, former head of the NFVCB during its distribution initiative, and Jason Njoku, head of a well-funded online distribution service, have both been perfectly clear regarding the intentions of their efforts to formalise and document Nollywood. Both explicitly state that this formalisation is meant to rout the marketers from their position of power, and to give their organisations (the NFVCB and an ambitious, foreign-funded start-up company, respectively) the means to control the industry and make it more manageable and palatable to outside investors. In interviews, marketers themselves were also perfectly aware of this intention, and the means by which these interlopers have attempted to reach their goals. It would be naive to believe that the marketers – considered shrewd businessmen by all who encounter them – engage in informality and lack of documentation blindly, perhaps too stubborn to 'achieve' the formality that the industry 'needs'. It would be foolish to ignore their very conscious alignment with and adherence to these business practices as an active strategy to resist incursions of formal parties wishing to dethrone them. While popular press articles deem them blind or short-sighted, the marketers are, in fact, cultivating a distinct vision in which Nollywood remains independent and in their hands.

We have seen also that Nollywood is, indeed, connected globally, but largely separate from official dominant networks. Instead, its global connections tend to be alternative, informal, opaque and unofficial. These are, in some ways, a boon, spreading Nollywood content much further and more quickly than authorised connections could travel and, in some cases, even creating new value-added content (as in the case of unauthorised francophone dubbing when the original creator would never undertake such an endeavour on their own). The foil to these informal alternative global connections is the forces of formal global capital, which stand in the wings, searching for a way in via the only openings they can find: the online or satellite screenings of content produced by an industry still based primarily on informal exchange of physical copies in open-air market places.

ANALYTICAL IMPLICATIONS

The implications of these analyses are far-reaching when considered in the context of debates surrounding the global flows of cultural products. The (now somewhat dated) cultural imperialism argument (and the many other arguments that it has spawned) is predicated on the notion that global cultural flows are both unidirectional, from North to South, and oppressive. Contra-flow (Thussu, 2006), offered as a counter-model, judges industries based on the physical location of the nation-state in which they are housed, and cues us to examine South–North and South–South flows. This theory does not, however, incorporate into its argument the shifting level of integration of many contra-flow 'example' industries (telenovelas, Al-Jazeera, Bollywood, etc.) into dominant global networks via their ownership structures, co-production agreements and other investment relationships. It is the argument of this book that Nollywood can be considered emblematic of an industry that truly stands 'contra' to dominant global cultural industry networks: an industry with extremely limited incorporation into those dominant networks and an industry unlikely to be incorporated into them in any significant way in the near future.

The power of MNC-owned or MNC-invested cultural production is mitigated in a market where there is little guarantee of profit or (transparent) control over distribution. In a landscape like Nollywood, where few business relationships are codified and most transactions could be deemed informal, most cultural industry MNCs are not even incentivised to invest in distribution, much less production. In this way, there is ample space for cultural industries of a very different shape to arise. In the case of Nollywood, we can see how they can draw their strength from the very qualities that keep them peripheral to global cultural industry networks: the preponderance of informality and opacity in industrial structure.

Just as telenovelas, for example, can be considered to contribute to the cultural diversity of the global mediascape, so too can Nollywood movies. Before they are products of West Africa, Africa, or of the 'global South', they are, first, the cultural output of southern Nigeria, and they reflect the characteristics *of* southern Nigeria in a number of specific and clearly identifiable ways. And these southern Nigerian productions flow in many directions: both within sub-Saharan Africa, sometimes referred to as 'minor transnational flows' (Adejunmobi, 2007), and through the paths of the loosely defined African diaspora on a global level. Nollywood also flows in the form of business model and style, spawning sibling industries from the Indian diaspora in South Africa to the Nigerian diaspora in the USA to Swahili production in Tanzania. Yet flows of cultural content and business model are not the only thing to consider when examining the nature of an industry in relation to global networks: flows of financing, distribution and industrial ownership are just as important. Nollywood has very little collaboration and cross-investment with global MNC-dominated networks of global media products. The industrial structure of Nollywood is also complex and goes beyond a simple South–South or South–North conception. It is more accurate to say that Nollywood runs via globally interlinked networks; these do not run between dominant media capitals. They run between hubs in black market and grey market trade, between Alaba Market, Nollywood's nerve centre, and cities like Singapore, Accra and Johannesburg, and specific peripheral neighbourhoods of the mega-cities of the global North, like east and south London, and New York City's Brooklyn and south Bronx. These alternative global networks connect Lagos's Surulere, Idumota and Alaba, as well as Onitsha in Nigeria's Igboland in the southeast, with distribution outlets from Tanzania to Haiti to Italy. As of yet unincorporated into global cultural industry networks (and with few signs of any significant integration to come in the next few years), Nollywood serves as an example of media moving through alternative, hard-to-pin-down networks of popular culture, produced in and exhibiting industrial qualities of the global 'Fourth World' and globally interlinked. These qualities include informality and lack of firm demarcation between authorised and unauthorised trade, or between white markets, black markets and grey markets. These networks are mostly – though not entirely – discrete from dominant global networks and derive their strength from the spaces and gaps between connections to the dominant world order. In the context of debates on global media flows, we can see the global connections and popularity of Nollywood as an example of the multi-polarity of global networks and multi-dimensionality of flows in the cultural industries. And we can see Nollywood as an example of a specific sort of cultural industry – one which may become more important in a globalising and urbanising world: an industry born and continuing to function largely outside dominant global cultural industry networks.

How best can we conceive of an industry's place in global media flows? Is Nollywood a Nigerian cultural industry or specifically Lagosian? Rather than thinking of global media as travelling from nation to nation, Michael Curtin's theory of media capitals (2003) allows us to see certain global cities as key switching points in the flows of global media that traverse the spatial patterns of diasporas, cross-border ethnic or linguistic groups, the spaces between rural and urban populations and intra-corporate connectivity via partial ownership, partnerships and ongoing distribution deals. He looks at media capitals as not just hubs of media production, but also as meeting places and sites of translation, with both their shape and their status as a media capital always subject to change, subject to the forces of migration, travel and exchange (ibid.). The concept of media capitals is central to this study: this book is, in part, a cultural economic and geographic study of Lagos as a hub of media production, looking at questions of why and how media came to be concentrated on this very specific city, what the nature of this city is and how it can help us to better understand the nature of global media flows. As such, I argue for the exploration of a different typology of media capital: one that exists with few to no connections to major multinational media corporations (media MNCs) and little ability to connect to them, given their entirely different industrial structure, based on informality and alternative networks. In other words, an alternative media capital.

NOLLYWOOD AND THE FUTURE

Discourse on Nollywood, the industry, be it popular journalism or academic enquiry, frequently features the question: is this person or that initiative on the horizon going to formalise the industry? Are they going to change it forever to a form that encourages or enables formal investment and the growth in budgets that comes with it? The answer has been and, at this point, still is always no. Any analysis must be clear about that. No, they probably will not. Despite numerous initiatives, regulations and investments, the industry remains in the hands of the marketers and the physical VCD market. Any successful alternative initiatives in the system have been small and have done little to disrupt the continued domination of the market by marketer-controlled open-air VCD distribution. This doesn't mean they have no effect. iROKO's exponential increase in fees for online rights, for instance, has solidified its position in the industry and has had an expansive effect on potential revenue streams for independent producers, even as it has not toppled power relations in the industry. This also doesn't mean the answer will always be no. A day will probably come when entertainment content is *primarily* delivered through virtual networks in Lagos. That day, however, seems to be a long way away. A look at Nollywood in 2016 must acknowledge that, as long as physical distribution has reigned within Nigeria, formalisation efforts have only changed little corners of the industry, never the industry as a whole. And there is a lot of ground to travel between today and the day that the domestic market – Nigerian audiences – abandons the physical disc as the primary Nollywood medium.

The relentless efforts to formalise the industry and the relentless enthusiasm these efforts receive in the popular press and academia is worth examination. Yes, Hollywood began as an informal upstart industry in the USA's largely undeveloped southern West Coast; and, yes, it subsequently became more formal when New York money flowed towards it after initial successes. Yes, Bollywood has recently been increasingly corporatised and formalised, as Indian banking regulations in the late 1990s have made the sector more investable for formal money (Lorenzen and Taeube, 2008). Is this relevant to Nollywood? This book has thus far highlighted the ways in which the Lagosian context is far removed from these other examples, and I've worked to highlight the dubious justifications for comparing Nollywood to these industries, as it more closely resembles stand-alone STV and other televisual industries than theatrical release-oriented film industries. Nigeria's economy has been and continues to be majority informal and, in a post-predatory state, documentation for government or other bodies is still usually avidly avoided. The Nigerian government cannot, for example, with one fell swoop, make the entire industry investable by corporate and bank forces, as India did with Bollywood in 1998 by recategorising the industry (ibid.). Jason Njoku, the co-founder of iROKOtv (discussed as counter-point to informality at various points throughout this book), has noted the vast difference between business infrastructure in Nigeria, as compared to East Africa (specifically Kenya, Rwanda and Tanzania) and South Africa – marvelling at the unbelievable ease, quickness and low expense of trading in these places in contrast to Lagos (2014a). The Nigerian context is different. Lagos and Nigeria are distinctive in their level of hostility to formalisation, but they are not alone. We can think of this as the context of the 'Fourth World', of creative production via networks that are, by nature, difficult for global formal capital to touch.

The frequent narrative of Nollywood possibly being on the brink of formalisation brings up some interesting questions. Is formalisation better? For whom? How is the worth of a movie industry measured? Formalisation is surely better for the creative arm of the industry, such as the big-name directors that make up New Nollywood, just as it is better for those acquiring heavy government or bank investment, such as Gabosky's G-Media,[1] or international venture capital, such as iROKOtv. For these parties, formalisation is a requirement for the type of growth that would transform the industry with both bigger budgets and a smaller number of distributors. On the one hand, such a transformation could expand potential industry profits in a way that would benefit the above parties (the industry's creative arm who wish to dissociate themselves from marketers and produce bigger-budget titles and those investing in ownership of a hypothetical future formal distribution system). On the other hand, we must acknowledge that remaining opaque – *not* formalising – is a possibility and there are those that benefit from this as well. Remaining opaque maintains power in the hands of the industry's founders, the Alaba marketers, maintains budgets at an attainable level and renders the industry virtually untouchable to investment by the federal government, national banks and foreign capital of the venture or MNC variety. Remaining opaque keeps Nollywood's business model accessible to imitators as well, from Riverwood to Vollywood. (And, even if Nollywood formalises, informal Nollywood may live on in the start-up industries still relying on its original business model.) Reliance on the marketers' informal distribution limits the financial ability to realise an artistic vision, yet it also maintains control over artistic production in the hands of local small to medium-sized businesses. If we look at Nollywood as a fledgling film industry shot on video out of necessity and lack, we can see the appeal of large budgets realising greater and broader artistic visions, allowing the industry to potentially support film festival-style titles at some future point. If we look at Nollywood as a glittering star among STV industries (Tsika, 2015), however, we can see the size of budgets and inter-changeability of content as part of what drives the industry and makes it appealing and sustainable (Lobato, 2010). The question, then, is not just whether a wholly STV industry can transform into something more cinematic, but, if it could, why it should.

Online distribution has transformed media industries worldwide, but, despite efforts in Nigeria, it will be years before connectivity, bandwidth and data pricing allow online or mobile distribution to usurp physical distribution as a motor for the industry. New Nollywood and its proponents have, instead, pinned their hopes on cinema-building. Thus far, however, cinematic distribution has disrupted little, mostly serving as an option for a modest collection of New Nollywood titles. And, besides, it is not just cinemas that would need to be constructed; advocates would also need to (re)construct a cinemagoing culture outside Nigeria's biggest cities, among a diverse collection of viewers that have become accustomed to home entertainment. Since nothing has yet transformed the industry, what we have now is largely an opaque and informal industry still in the hands of those who started it: the 'man in the marketplace' (Isikaku, 2009), the 'Igbo distributors' (Bud, 2014), the 'Alaba pirates' (Njoku, 2013a). In other words, the marketers. This industry, however, is now accompanied by a smaller yet productive contingent, known as New Nollywood, that now has multiple formal distribution channels through which to sell its products (cinemas within and outside Nigeria and licences for air, satellite and online in Nigeria and the diaspora) and the potential to build something separate from the marketers. Perhaps the two can grow separately, in different directions.

I come at this project not as an expert in the strategies of media industry formalisation, but as an investigator of the possibilities of building a sustainable industry of creative production without government or other external architects, and an investigator of sustaining a creative industry that exists absent MNC or other global capital co-ownership or control. If we think of alternative media not as politically resistant in message but as politically resistant in form (see Adejunmobi, 2007), we can think of Nollywood as a shining example of such media, peripheral to global Hollywood's networks, but central in its own alternative networks. To be sure, many question how sustainable the marketers'

Nollywood really is, as it seems constantly to be in a state of industrial crisis, changing pricing and distribution strategies in wildly unnerving ways, suddenly shutting down production in reaction to external challenges, squeezing margins more and more until they are barely perceivable and continually being declared 'over' by competitors. But what *is* Nollywood? Jude Akudinobi (2015) suggests that the definition itself is constantly shifting: that the main constant in Nollywood is its flexibility, its ability to morph in the face of changing institutional, social and economic circumstances. We can see this both in the constant reworking of recently proven genre formulas and the constant reworking of the industry structure in response to perceived threats. The rapidity of response to current events (movies about Ebola released in the midst of the Ebola crisis in West Africa) mirrors the rapidity of response to 'pirate' ingenuity (the institution of brutally tiered pricing windows, in which intellectual property is wholesaled for 6 cents a disc after three weeks, and separation of movies into increasingly numerous parts to squeeze the margins of unauthorised distribution). Nollywood is, perhaps, best seen as a particularly flexible iteration of the Nigerian popular arts. In this way, like Yoruba theatre troupes and Nigerian soap operas, we can see Nollywood as a Nigerian popular cultural form melding the traditional and the modern, distributed via circuits and business models that currently make sense in the networks in which Lagos is a central hub, as opposed to a peripheral node (see Barber, 1987).

In a globalising world, we can see this not as a study of the possible futures *of* Nollywood, but also of Nollywood *as* the future: a future featuring a diversity of creative production being produced in the gaps between and the flipsides of dominant global networks. Even if the day comes, far in the future, when Nigerian movies are co-produced by, for instance, a Sony Studios Nigeria, helmed by a current New Nollywood director, distributed online by a Nigerian Netflix subsidiary called iROKO and screened via a network of corporate Silverbird[2] branded cinema screens in every other Nigerian village, there will still be cultural production that looks like the Nollywood described in this book, operating via the same logics of informality, wherever the gaps between connection to the Network Society then lie. As long as there remain gaps between connections to the Network Society, there will also be room for alternative media capitals and alternative circuits in international cultural industries. And for as long as an industry's power resides with the opaque and informal, integration into global Hollywood's networks will remain difficult and, hence, unlikely. For now, it seems likely that the majority of Nollywood, like Lagos, will remain central to alternative networks, with little integration into dominant global media industry networks.

NOTES

1. In connection with efforts by former president Goodluck Jonathan to influence the industry while he was in power, Nigeria's Bank of Investment, a government entity targeted at providing funds to emergent Nigerian industries, provided over $11 million to Gabosky to jumpstart a private distribution shake up (Bud, 2014). This initiative included the formation of a subsidiary called G-Media to attempt to replicate Alaba's infrastructure according to Gabosky's own design.
2. The South African cinema corporation that has built Nigeria's current small number of high-end cineplexes.

Bibliography

Adamu, A. U. (2007). Currying favour: eastern media influences and the Hausa video film. *Film International* 5, pp. 77–89.

Adamu, A. U. (2011). Transnational flows and local identities in Muslim northern Nigerian films: from *Dead Poets Society* through *Mohabbatein* to *So…* In H. Wasserman (ed.), *Popular Media, Democracy, and Development in Africa*. London: Routledge, pp. 223–35.

Adejunmobi, M. (2007). Nigerian video film as minor transnational practice. *Postcolonial Text* 3 (2), pp. 1–16.

Adejunmobi, M. (2013). Evolving Nollywood templates for minor transnational film. *Black Camera* 5 (2), pp. 74–94.

Adejunmobi, M. (2015). African film's televisual turn. *Cinema Journal* 54 (2), pp. 120–5.

Adenugba, O. (2008). Genres of the Nigerian film. *filminnigeria* 3 July. Retrieved from http://filminnaija.blogspot.co.uk/2008/07/genres-of-nigerian-film.html

Adesanya, A. (2000). From film to video. In J. Haynes (ed.), *Nigerian Video Films*. Athens: Ohio University Center for International Studies: Research in International Studies Africa Series No. 73, pp. 37–50.

Aft, R. (2008). Chain of title basics: owning your movie and avoiding problems. Paper presented at the WIPO National Seminar on Intellectual Property Rights for Professionals in the Film Industry, Lagos, 13–14 October. WIPO document WIPO/CR/NG/08/. Retrieved from http://www.nlipw.com/wp-content/uploads/WIPO-CR-NG-08-1-Chain_of_Title_Basics.pdf

Akudinobi, J. (2015). Nollywood: prisms and paradigms. *Cinema Journal* 54 (2), pp. 133–9.

Anikulapo, J. (2009). Personal communication with the author, 9 July.

Anyiam-Fiberesima, P. (2009). Personal communication with the author, 3 August.

Appadurai, A. (1996). *Modernity at Large: Cultural Dimensions of Globalization*. Minneapolis: University of Minnesota Press.

Armes, R. (2006). *African Filmmaking: North and South of the Sahara*. Bloomington: Indiana University Press.

Arsenault, A. and Castells, M. (2008). The structure and dynamics of multi-media business networks. *International Journal of Communication* 2, pp. 707–48.

Asu, K. (2009). Personal communication with the author, 20 July.

Athique, A. (2008). The global dynamics of Indian media piracy: export markets, playback media and the informal economy. *Media, Culture, & Society* 30, pp. 699–718.

Atlanta Fans 1 and 2. (2011). Personal communication with the author, 18 November.

Ayakoroma, B. (2014). *Trends in Nollywood: A Study of Selected Genres*. Ibadan, Oyo State: Kraft.

Barber, K. (1987). Popular arts in Africa. *African Studies Review* 30 (3), pp. 1–78.

Barber, K. (2000). *The Generation of Plays: Yoruba Popular Life in Theater*. Bloomington: Indiana University Press.

Barber, K., Collins, J. and Ricard, A. (1997). Three West African popular theater forms: a social history. In K. Barber, J. Collins and A. Ricard (eds), *West African Popular Theatre*. Bloomington: Indiana University Press, pp. 1–55.

Barlet, O. (2000) *African Cinemas: Decolonizing the Gaze*. London: Zed.

Becker, H. (2013). Nollywood in urban southern Africa: Nigerian video films and their audiences in Cape Town and Windhoek. In M. Krings and O. Okome (eds), *Global Nollywood: The Transnational Dimensions of an African Video Film Industry*. Bloomington: Indiana University Press, pp. 179–98.

Böhme, C. (2013). Bloody bricolages: traces of Nollywood in Tanzanian video films. In M. Krings and O. Okome (eds), *Global Nollywood: The Transnational Dimensions of an African Video Film Industry*. Bloomington: Indiana University Press, pp. 327–46.

Boyd, D. and Straubhaar, J. (1985). Developmental impact of the home video cassette recorder on Third World countries. *Journal of Broadcasting and Electronic Media* 29 (1), pp. 5–21.

Bruce, N. (2009). Personal communication with the author, 7 August.

Bryce, J. (2013). African movies in Barbados: proximate experiences of fear and desire. In M. Krings and O. Okome (eds), *Global Nollywood: The Transnational Dimensions of an African Video Film Industry*. Bloomington: Indiana University Press, pp. 223–44.

Bud, A. (2014). The end of Nollywood's guilded age? Marketers, the state and the struggle for distribution, *Critical African Studies* 6 (1), pp. 91–121.

Castells, M. (1998). *End of Millennium*. Maiden, MA: Blackwell.

Caves, R. (2002) *Creative Industries: Contracts Between Art and Commerce*. Cambridge, MA: Harvard University Press.

Chukwumba, O. (2009). Personal communication with the author, 29 July.

Clark, E. (1979). *Hubert Ogunde: The Making of Nigerian Theatre*. Oxford: Oxford University Press.

Curtin, M. (2003). Media capital: towards the study of spatial flows. *International Journal of Cultural Studies* 6 (2), pp. 202–28.

Diawara, M. (1987). Sub-Saharan African film production: technological paternalism. *Jump Cut* 32, pp. 61–5.

Dipio, D. (2014). Audience pleasure and Nollywood popularity in Uganda: an assessment. *Journal of African Cinemas* 6 (1), pp. 85–108.

Dovey, L. (2009). *African Film and Literature: Adapting Violence to the Screen*. New York: Columbia University Press.

The Economist. (2010). Lights, camera, Africa: movies are uniting a disparate continent and dividing it too. *The Economist*, 10 December. Retrieved from http://www.economist.com/node/17723124

The Economist. (2015). Opportunity knocks: Special Report Nigeria. *The Economist*, 20 June. Retrieved from http://www.economist.com/sites/default/files/20150620_sr_nigeria.pdf

Ejenoboor, U. (2009). Personal communication with the author, 8 July.

Ekwuazi, H. (2014). The perception/reception of DSTV/MultiChoice's Africa Magic channels by selected Nigerian audiences. *Journal of African Cinemas* 6 (1), pp. 21–48.

Florida, R. (2004). *The Rise of the Creative Class: And How It's Transforming Work, Leisure, and Everyday Life*. New York: Basic.

Foreign Ministry 1. (2009). Personal communication with the author, 30 July.

Foster, V. and Pushak, N. (2011). *Nigeria's Infrastructure: A Continental Perspective, Volume 1*. Policy Research Working Paper WPS 5686, Sustainable Development Project, Africa Region. World Bank, Washington, DC. http://dx.doi.org/10.1596%2F1813-9450-5686

Gabosky. (2009). Personal communication with the author, 20 July.

Gandy, M. (2005), Learning from Lagos. *New Left Review* 33, pp. 36–52.

Garritano, C. (2008). Contesting authenticities: the emergence of local video production in Ghana. *Critical Arts* 22 (1), pp. 21–48.

Garritano, C. (2013). *African Video Movies and Global Desires*. Athens: Ohio University Press.

Graham, S. and Marvin, S. (2001). *Splintering Urbanism: Networked Infrastructures, Technological Mobilities and the Urban Condition*. London: Routledge.

Haynes, J. (1995). Nigerian cinema: structural adjustments. *Research in African Literatures* 26 (3), pp. 97–119.

Haynes, J. (2000). Introduction. In J. Haynes (ed.) *Nigerian Video Films*. Athens: Ohio University Center for International Studies.

Haynes, J. (2007a). Nollywood: what is in a name? *Film International* 5 (4), pp. 106–8.

Haynes, J. (2007b). Nollywood in Lagos, Lagos in Nollywood films. *Africa Today* 54 (2), pp. 131–50.

Haynes, J. (2010). A literature review: Nigerian and Ghanaian videos. *Journal of African Cultural Studies* 22, pp. 105–20.

Haynes, J. (2013). New Nollywood: Kunle Afolayan. *Black Camera* 5 (2), pp. 53–73.

Haynes, J. and Okome, O. (2000). Evolving popular media: Nigerian video films. In J. Haynes (ed.), *Nigerian Video Films*. Athens: Ohio University Center for International Studies: Research in International Studies Africa Series No. 73, pp. 51–88.

Himpele, J. (2008). *Circuits of Culture: Media Politics and Indigenous Identity in the Andes*. Minneapolis: University of Minnesota Press.

Hoffmann, Claudia. (2013). Made in America: urban immigrant spaces in transnational Nollywood films. In M. Krings and O. Okome (eds), *Global Nollywood: The Transnational Dimensions of an African Video Film Industry*. Bloomington: Indiana University Press, pp. 121–38.

Igwe, A. (2009). Personal communication with the author, 4 August.

Isikaku, E. (2009). Personal communication with the author, 31 July.

Isong, E. (2011). Personal communication with the author, 18 November.

Isong, E. (2014). Personal communication with the author, 22 October.

Jedlowski, A. (2012). Small screen cinema: informality and remediation in Nollywood *Television and New Media* 13 (5), pp. 431–46.

Jedlowski, A. (2013a). Nigerian videos in the global arena: the postcolonial exotic revisited. *The Global South* 7 (1), pp. 157–78.

Jedlowski, A. (2013b). From Nollywood to Nollyworld: processes of transnationalization in the Nigerian video film industry. In M. Krings and O. Okome (eds), *Global Nollywood: The Transnational Dimensions of an African Video Film Industry*. Bloomington: Indiana University Press, pp. 25–45.

Kelani, T. (2009). Personal communication with the author, 12 July.

Koolhaas, R., Harvard Project on the City, Boeri, S., Kwinter, S. Tazi, N. and Obrist, H. U. (2001). *Mutations*. New York: ACTAR.

Krings, M. (2010). Nollywood goes east: the localization of Nigerian video films in Tanzania. In R. Austen and M. Saul (eds), *Viewing African Cinema in the Twenty-first Century: Art Films and the Nollywood Video Revolution*. Athens: Ohio University Press, pp. 74–94.

Krings, M. (2013). *Karishika* with Kiswahili flavor: a Nollywood movie retold by a Tanzanian video narrator. In M. Krings and O. Okome (eds), *Global Nollywood: The Transnational Dimensions of an African Video Film Industry*. Bloomington: Indiana University Press, pp. 306–26.

Larkin, B. (2000). Hausa dramas and the rise of video culture in Nigeria. In J. Haynes (ed.), *Nigerian Video Films*. Athens: Ohio University Press, pp. 209–41.

Larkin, B. (2003). Itineraries of Indian cinema: African videos, Bollywood, and global media. In E. Shohat and R. Stam (eds), *Multiculturalism, Postcoloniality, and Transnational Media*. New Brunswick: Rutgers University Press, pp. 170–92.

Larkin, B. (2004). Degraded images, distorted sounds: Nigerian video and the infrastructure of piracy. *Public Culture* 16 (2), pp. 289–314.

Larkin, B. (2008). *Signal and Noise: Media, Infrastructure and Urban Culture in Northern Nigeria*. Chapel Hill, NC: Duke University Press.

Lee, K. S. and Anas, A. (1989). *Impacts of Infrastructure Deficiencies on Nigerian Manufacturing: Private Alternatives and Policy Options.* Infrastructure and Urban Development Department Report No. 98, February. World Bank, Washington, DC. Retrieved from http://www-wds.worldbank.org/external/default/WDS ContentServer/IW3P/IB/1989/12/01/000009265_3960928133046/ Rendered/PDF/multi0page.pdf

Lewis, P. (1996). From prebendalism to predation: the political economy of decline in Nigeria. *Journal of Modern African Studies* 34 (1), pp. 79–103.

Lewis, P. (2007). *Growing Apart: Oil, Politics, and Economic Change in Indonesia and Nigeria*. Ann Arbor: University of Michigan Press.

Lobato, R. (2010). Creative industries and informal economies: lessons from Nollywood. *International Journal of Cultural Studies* 13, pp. 337–54.

Lobato, R. (2012). *Shadow Economies of Cinema: Mapping Informal Film Distribution*. London: BFI.

Lorenzen, M. and Taeube, F. A. (2008). Breakout from Bollywood? Internationalization of Indian film industry. *Danish Research Unit for Industrial Dynamics (DRUID) Working Paper No. 07-06.*

Marston, S. A., Woodward, K. and Jones, J. P. (2007). Flattening ontologies of globalization: the Nollywood case. *Globalizations* 4 (1), pp. 45–63.

Martín-Barbero, J. (1995). Memory and form in the Latin American soap opera. In R. C. Allen (ed.), *To Be Continued … Soap Operas Around the World*. London: Routledge, pp. 276–84.

Martins, I. (2009). Personal communication with the author, 20 July.

Mattelart, T. (2009). Audio-visual piracy: towards a study of the underground networks of cultural globalization. *Global Media and Communication* 5, pp. 308–26.

Mba, E. (2009). Personal communication with the author, 30 July.

Mboti, N. (2014). Nollywood's aporias part 1: gatemen. *Journal of African Cinemas* 6 (1), pp. 49–70.

McDonald, P. (2007). *Video and DVD Industries*. London: BFI.

Meyer, B. (1999). Popular Ghanaian cinema and 'African heritage'. *Africa Today* 46, pp. 93–114.

Meyer, B. (2007). Pentecostalism and neo-liberal capitalism: faith, prosperity and vision in African pentecostal-charismatic churches. *Journal for the Study of Religion* 20, pp. 5–28.

Meyer, B. (2010). Tradition and colour at its best: 'tradition' and 'heritage' in Ghanaian video-movies. *Journal of African Cultural Studies* 22, pp. 7–23.

Miller, J. (2010). Ugly Betty goes global: global networks of localized content in the telenovela industry. *Global Media and Communication* 6, pp. 198–217.

Mistry, J. and Ellapen, J. (2013). Nollywood's transportability: the politics and economics of video films as cultural products. In M. Krings and O. Okome (eds), *Global Nollywood: The Transnational Dimensions of an African Video Film Industry*. Bloomington: Indiana University Press, pp. 46–69.

Mohammed, R. (2009). Personal communication with the author, 18 December.

NBS (National Bureau of Statistics of Nigeria). (2012). *Annual Abstract of Statistics*, pp. 115–17. Retrieved from http://www.nigerianstat.gov.ng/nbslibrary/nbs-annual-abstract-of-statistics/nbs-annual-abstract-of-statistics

NBS (National Bureau of Statistics of Nigeria). (2015). *Nigerian Gross Domestic Product Report: Quarter 4, 2014*. Retrieved from http://www.nigerianstat.gov.ng/pages/download/272

NCC lawyers 1, 2 and 3. (2009). Personal communication with the author, 30 July.

Njoku, J. (2013a). Alabanomics: yesterday, today, and the future of Nollywood. *Just Me: Jason Njoku: Blog*, 13 December. Retrieved from http://www.jason.com.ng/post/70277008903/alabanomics-yesterday-today-and-the-future-of

Njoku, J. (2013b). Follow your users: profits might be lurking there. *Just Me: Jason Njoku: Blog*, 11 June. Retrieved from http://www.jason.com.ng/post/52708301079/follow-your-users-profits-might-be-lurking-there

Njoku, J. (2013c). The hard stuff … *Just Me: Jason Njoku: Blog*, 13 May. Retrieved from http://www.jason.com.ng/post/50330412880/the-hard-stuff

Njoku, J. (2013d). Building a $10 mn start-up in Africa: 2020. *Just Me: Jason Njoku: Blog*, 21 April. Retrieved from http://www.jason.com.ng/post/48518497988/building-a-100mn-startup-in-africa-2020

Njoku, J. (2013e). Nigerian internet: we have a long way to go. *Just Me: Jason Njoku: Blog*, 7 February. Retrieved from http://www.jason.com.ng/post/42497222464/nigerian-internet-we-have-a-long-long-way-to-go

Njoku, J. (2014a). IROKOtv East Africa: Kigali. *Just Me: Jason Njoku: Blog*, 24 July. Retrieved from http://www.jason.com.ng/post/92714471685/irokotv-east-africa-kigali

Njoku, J. (2014b). Embracing failure. *Just Me: Jason Njoku: Blog*, 3 March. Retrieved from http://www.jason.com.ng/post/78458883150/embracing-failure

Njoku, J. (2014c). A couple of interesting data points. *Just Me: Jason Njoku: Blog*, 7 March. Retrieved from http://www.jason.com.ng/post/78855803328/a-couple-of-interesting-data-points-peak

Njoku, J. (2015a). Personal communication with the author, 26 May.

Njoku, J. (2015b). 1 billion and creating the future. *Just Me: Jason Njoku: Blog*, 18 February. Retrieved from http://www.jason.com.ng/post/111369044100/1-billion-and-creating-the-future

Njoku, J. (2015c). Burning boats and bridges to win Lagos. *Just Me: Jason Njoku: Blog*, 15 January. Retrieved from http://www.jason.com.ng/post/108154973385/burning-boats-and-bridges-to-win-lagos

Nye, J. S. (2004). *Soft Power: The Means to Success in World Politics*. New York: Public Affairs Press.

Obaseki, D. P. (2008) Nigerian video as the 'child of television'. In P. Barrot (ed.), *Nollywood: The Video Phenomenon in Nigeria*. Bloomington: Indiana University Press, pp. 72–7.

Obiechina, E. (1990). *Language and Theme: Essays on African Literature*. Washington, DC: Howard University Press.

Ogum, Yinca. (2009). Personal communication with the author, 15 July.

Ogunleye, F. (2004). A report from the front: the Nigerian videofilm. *Quarterly Review of Film and Video* 21, pp. 79–88.

Oh, E. (2014). Nigeria's film industry: Nollywood looks to expand globally. *United States International Trade Commission Executive Briefings on Trade*, October. Retrieved from http://www.usitc.gov/publications/332/erick_oh_nigerias_film_industry.pdf

Okome, O. (1995). Film policy and the development of the African cinema. *Glendora Review: African Quarterly on the Arts* 1 (2), pp. 46–53.

Okome, O. (2010). Nollywood and its critics. In M. Saul and R. Austen (eds), *Viewing African Cinema in the Twenty-First Century: Art Films and the Nollywood Video Revolution*. Athens: Ohio University Press, pp. 26–41.

Olukanni, Bolanle. (2009). Personal communication with the author, 30 July.

Ondego, Ogova. (2008). Kenya and Nollywood: a state of dependence. In P. Barrot (ed.), *Nollywood: The Video Phenomenon in Nigeria*. Bloomington: Indiana University Press, pp. 114–20.

Onwochei, F. (2009). Personal communication with the author, 10 July.

Orakpo, C. Y. (2009). Personal communication with the author, 20 July.

Osaghe, E. (1998). *Crippled Giant: Nigeria since Independence*. Bloomington: Indiana University Press.

Packer, G. (2006, 13 November). The megacity: decoding the chaos of Lagos. *The New Yorker*. Retrieved from http://www.newyorker.com/magazine/2006/11/13/the-megacity

Parks, L. (2007). Falling apart: electronics salvaging, *Junkyard Wars*, and the global media economy. In C. Acland (ed.), *Residual Media*. Minneapolis: University of Minnesota Press.

Peel, M. (2009). *A Swamp Full of Dollars: Pipelines and Paramilitaries at Nigeria's Oil Frontier*. London: I.B.Tauris.

Pendakur, M. (2003). *Indian Popular Cinema: Industry Ideology and Consciousness*. New York: Hampton Press.

Power, D. and Hallencreutz, D. (2004). Profiting from creativity? The music industry in Stockholm, Sweden, and Kingston, Jamaica. In D. Power and A. J. Scott (eds), *Cultural Industries and the Production of Culture*. London: Routledge, pp. 224–42.

Producer 1. (2009). Personal communication with the author, 16 July.

Pype, K. (2013). Religion, migration, and media aesthetics: notes on the circulation and reception of Nigerian Films in Kinshasa. In M. Krings and O. Okome (eds), *Global Nollywood: The Transnational Dimensions of an African Video Film Industry*. Bloomington: Indiana University Press, pp. 199–222.

Rosenthal, E. (2012). Nigeria tested by rapid rise in population. *New York Times*, 14 April. Retrieved from http://www.nytimes.com/2012/04/15/world/africa/in-nigeria-a-preview-of-an-overcrowded-planet.html

Ryan, C. (2013). Nollywood and the limits of informality: a conversation with Tunde Kelani, Bond Emeruwa, and Emem Isong. *Black Camera* 5 (2), pp. 168–85.

Samyn, Sophie. (2013). Nollywood made in Europe. In M. Krings and O. Okome (eds), *Global Nollywood: The Transnational Dimensions of an African Video Film Industry*. Bloomington: Indiana University Press, pp. 100–20.

Saul, M. and Austen, R. (eds). (2010). *Viewing African Cinema in the Twenty-first Century: Art Films and the Nollywood Video Revolution*. Athens: Ohio University Press.

Scott, A. J. (2005). *On Hollywood: The Place, The Industry*. Princeton, NJ: Princeton University Press.

Screenwriter 1. (2009). Personal communication with the author, 15 July.

Shashore, R. (2009). Personal communication with the author, 23 July.

Simone, A. (2001). On the worlding of African cities. *African Studies Review* 44 (2), pp. 15–41.

Sinclair, J. (1999). *Latin American Television: A Global View*. Mahwah, NJ: Lawrence Erlbaum.

Slome, M. (1996). Cheick Oumar Sissoko. *Bomb 56.* Retrieved from http://bombmagazine.org/article/1962/cheick-oumar-sissoko

SmartMonkeyTV (2014). Kunle Afolayan on his latest thriller *October 1*, 11 October. Retrieved from http://www.smartmonkeytv.com/channel/emerging_media/kunle_afolayan_on_his_latest_film_october_1_an_eve_of_ independence_thriller

Straubhaar, J. D. (1991). Beyond media imperialism: asymmetrical interdependence and cultural proximity. *Critical Studies in Mass Communication* 8, pp. 39–59.

Sundaram, R. (1999). Recycling modernity: pirate electronic cultures in India. *Third Text* 47, pp. 59–65.

Thackaway, M. (2003). *Africa Shoots Back: Alternative Perspectives in Sub-Saharan Francophone African Film*. Oxford: James Currey.

Thussu, D. (2006). Introduction. In D. Thussu (ed.), *Media on the Move: Global Flow and Contra-flow*. London: Routledge, pp. 1–8.

Tsika, N. (2015). *Nollywood Stars: Media and Migration in West Africa and the Diaspora*. Bloomington: Indiana University Press.

Ukadike, F. (1994). *Black African Cinema*. Berkeley: University of California Press.

Waliaula, S. (2014). Active audiences of Nollywood video-films: an experience with a Bukusu audience community in Chwele market of western Kenya. *Journal of African Cinemas* 6 (1), pp. 71–83.

Wang, S. (2003). *Framing Piracy: Globalization and Film Distribution in Greater China*. Lanham, MD: Rowman & Littlefield.

Index

Page numbers in **bold** indicate detailed analysis; those in *italic* denote illustrations; n= endnote.

Abacha, Sani 95
Achebe, Chinua 71
Actors Guild of Nigeria 111
Adamu, Abdalla Uba 92*n*19
Adejunmobi, Moradewun 76, 78, 91*n*13
Adesanya, Afolabi 28*n*1
Adichie, Chimamanda Ngochi 71
Afolayan, Kunle 36, 37, 65
Africa Magic (television network) 48, 63, 142, 143, 145
  channels 149*n*21
  fees 144
African cinema
  colonial **71–3**, 97
  as distinct from Nollywood **71**
  Nollywood contribution 76, 86–8
  perception in Europe 74
  political nature 77
  post-colonial **73–6**
African Movie Academy Awards (AMAA) 90*n*1
African Movies Mall *see* Sanga Entertainment
Aiye (1979) 12
Ajani Ogun (1976) 12
Aje Ni Iya Mi (1991) 16
Alaba electronics market 6–7, 14, 18, 33, 57–8, 116, 122
  Chinese influence 10
  Competition with online distribution 41–2

infrastructure 35
layout 34
map *34*
as Nollywood hub 35, 154
size 34
Ali-Balogun, Mahmood 109
Ambode, Akinwunmi 118*n*3
American Idol 60*n*2
Anikulapo, Jahman 81, 93
anti-colonialism, West Africa 11
Anyiam-Fiberesima, Peace 101, 103, 114
Armes, Roy 74
Art Stampede 93
Association of Movie Producers (AMP) 111, 119*n*14
Asu, King 119*n*14
audience for Nollywood film
  domestic **81–3**
  international **83–5**;
  translation 84–5
Austen, Ralph 91*n*7

Babanginda, Ibrahim 13, 95
Bahati, Rashid 1
Balogun, Ola 12
Barber Karin 11, 77
Barlet, Olivier 91*n*7
Battle of Musanga (1996) 65
Becker, Heike 84, 92*n*17
Before the Light (2009) *68*
Benson, Teco 67, 112, 118*n*13, 119*n*14

Berne Convention 99
Best, Michael, Dr 147*n*1
Beyonce and Rhianna (2008) 69
black magic
  as plot point 62, 65–6
  widespread belief in 69
black market 6, 107, 130
  endemic in developing world 20
  software 126–7
  see also piracy
BlackBerry Babes (2011) *66*
BlackBerry Babes Reloaded (2012) 66–7
Boko Haram 94–5
Bollywood 3, 153
  development 27
  formalising of business model 27, 155–6
  neglect of African market 88
  popularity in Nigeria 80, 86
  suspect funding 27
Bongowood 86–7
  connection with Nollywood 147
British Overseas Film and Television Centre (BOFTC) 72
Brothers War (2013) 67
Bryce, Jane 84
Buhari, Muhammadu 96
Bullfrog in the Sun (1971) 75
Bureau du Cinéma 73, 90*n*5

Castells, Manuel 30
censorship 40, **97–8**, 115
Checkmate (soap opera) 18
Chukwumba, Obiora 107, 109
Claws of the Lion (2008) 124, 147*n*3
Colonial Film Units 71–3, 90*n*4
colour reversal stock (film type) 13
Consortum Audiovisual International (CAI) 73
copyright **99–102**, 139, 158
 in global circuits 131
Copyright Law 1988 99
Curtin, Michael 123, 154

Daybreak in Udi (1949) 71, 72
D'Banj 71
Debrix, Jean-Rene 90*n*5
development of African cinema **9–20**
diaspora (African)
 effect on international distribution 83
 as Nollywood audience 83–5, 120
 use of 'online viewing' 31
Dipio, Dominica 143
distribution **46–57**
 global DVD market 2, **127–32**
 informality 47, 146–7, 150–1
 licensing **47–8**
 links to electronics market 20
 online 39, 117, **132–42**
 television 117, **142–4**
 theatrical **46–7**, 117
 unauthorised 31, 53, **55–7**, 130
 video sales **49–55**
 see also piracy

Domitilla: The Story of a Prostitute (1996) 66
Dovey, Lindiwe 91*n*7

Edikan (2009) 43
editing *see* post-production
employment in Nigerian film industry **42–6**
 actors and actresses 43
 apprenticeships 42, 58
 payment 46
 quantity of work 40
 training 42
Executive Image 128

Fashola, Babatunde 24, 95, 118*n*3
Federal Assembly 94
The Figurine (2009) 37, 65
Film-makers Association of Nigeria – USA (FAN-USA) 87
Film-makers Cooperative of Nigeria (FCON) 113–14
financing in Nigerian cinema **38–9**, 77
 link with distribution 39
 overseas funding 123–4
Florida, Richard 20
'fourth world' **22–7**
 alternative global networks 151
 definition 23
 distribution networks 150
 resistance to formalisation 156
fraud 90*n*3
French Ministry of Foreign Affairs 124
future of Nigerian cinema **155–8**
FVPMAN (marketers guild) 45, 101, 107, 111–12, 113, 118*n*12
 efforts to regulate movies releases 52

G-Media 19, 116, 156
Gabosky (Gabriel Okoye) 18–19, 116, 156, 159*n*1
Gandy, Matthew 59
Garritano, Carmela 77–8, 82–3, 92*n*19
genre in Nigerian film 62, **65–9**
 comedy 68
 melodrama 80
 romance 67
 thrillers 67
Ghana, as Nollywood distribution centre 51
Ghanaian cinema *see* Ghollywood
Ghollywood 85, 91*n*11, 92*n*19, 148*n*8
Glamour Girls (1994) 16, 19, 66, 68
global network of Nigerian cinema **120–2**
 alternative global networks 122, 127, 152
 diaspora 124–5
 distribution: online **132–42**; physical **127–32**; television **142–4**
 foreign funding 123–4
 global production input **123–7**, 146
 informal nature 144–6
 training 125
globalisation 22, 152–3, 158
 of entertainment industry 28, 151–2
Gotter, Bastian 134, 148*n*11
guilds 42–6, **110–14**
 as alternative distribution system 113–14
 as contract substitute 112–13, 117
 leadership 40, 112
 membership 60*n*5
 system 111–12

Hallencreutz, Daniel 25–6
Hausa (ethnic group) 2
Haynes, Jonathan 28*n*1, 29*n*2, 64, 80, 91*n*8, 91*n*10
  on geography of Nollywood 33–4
Himpele, Jeff 91*n*7
Hollywood 3
  early history 22
  geography 150
  global dominance 2, 150–1
  informality in working relationships 45
  interaction with Nollywood 123, 129
  neglect of African market 88, 147*n*2, 150
  straight-to-video movies 92*n*14

Idigbogwu, Bruce *see* 'Natty Bruce'
Idumota Market 33
  comparison with Alaba market 35
Igbo (ethnic group) 2
  role as marketers 35–6
  role in business 15–16
Igodo: Land of the Living Dead (1999) 65
Igwe, Amaka 14, 18
Independent Television Producers Association of Nigeria (ITPAN) 111
Indigenisation Act 1972 98
Infant Malaria (1935) 71
informal business practice
  alternative global networks 61
  contracts 113
  definition 31–2
  in distribution 47, 127, 129
  as impediment to growth 47
  power cycle 53
  reliance on external infrastructure 32
  role in distribution 59
  as tool of resistance to global markets 7, 56, 60, 151–2
  when funding films 39
  see also trust-based business
International Monetary Fund (IMF) 59
iROKOtv 8, 48, 56, 59–60, *133*, *135*, 143, 145, 147, 156
  business partners 132–3
  buying rights 139–40
  change of location 61*n*16, 136, 148*n*10
  competition with Alaba Market 141–2
  development **134–6**
  domestic audiences **136–41**
  fees 135–6, 144, 155
  investment 132, 138–39
  popularity with diaspora 85, 132, 136
  prime viewing hours 81–2
  pronunciation 148*n*9
  reliance on infrastructure 140–1
Isikaku, Emmanuel 39, 76, 101, 103, 107–8, 124
Isong, Emem 37, 82, 129, 139, 143

Jaiyesinmi (1983) 12
Jamaican music industry 25–6
Jedlowski, Alessandro 130–1
Jénífá (2008) 66, 90*n*2
Jonathan, Goodluck 103, 116, 124, 159*n*1

Kannywood 85
Kelani, Tunde 37, 82
Kenyan cinema *see* Riverwood
Kinnevik 132
Kongi's Harvest (1970) 75
Krings, Matthias 86–7
Kuti, Fela 71

labour organisation *see* guilds
Lady Gaga 69
Lady Gaga (2012) 69
Lagos
  as centre of production **39–42**
  civil unrest 13
  colonial past 10
  as creative city **20–2**, **122–3**
  demographics 10–11
  diversity 11
  geography 33
  growth 32
  as hub of alternative global markets 146, 154–5
  importance to Nollywood 5, 57
  infrastructure 24, 40, 148*n*15
  as movie setting 64
  population 33
  role in development of Nigeria 21
Larkin, Brian 6, 20, 28*n*1, 29*n*8, 55, 56–7, 121
Last Flight to Abuja (2012) 67
Laval Decree 72, 74
LeadDog Entertainment 1
Living in Bondage (1992) 16, 19, 65–6
Lobato, Ramon 32, 79
Los Angeles Film Festival 1

M-Net (satellite television company) 48, 142, 147
MainOne 137, *138*
marketers
  as backbone of industry 35–5
  background in electronics trade 56

marketers *cont.*
  competition with unlicensed distribution 54, 55
  control of financing and distribution 45, 124
  dominance of domestic market 37, 39, 116
  as financiers 38
  rancour between 36, 38–9
Martins, Isaac 61*n11*
Mba, Emeka 102–3, 104–5, 107–8, 152
Mboti, Nyasha 59
Meyer, Birgit 91*n11*, 92*n19*
Ministry of Cooperation 73
Ministry of Culture 98
Ministry of Information 98
Mission to Nowhere (2007) 67
Mister English at Home (1940) 71
Mohammed, Rabiu 83–4, 128, 131, 139, 143
MOPICON **108–10**, 115
movie stars in Nigerian film 61*n14*, 79–80
  fees 44
  use in marketing 45, 81
  use of social media 83–4
MultiChoice (satellite television company) 104–5, 142–3, 145
music industry
  Jamaica 25–6, 28
  Sweden 25–6

National Association of Nigerian Theatre Arts Practitioners (NANTAP) 111
National Film and Video Censors Board (NFVCB) 7, 29*n5*, 94, **97–8**, 102–3, 104–8, 109–10, 115, 152
  increase in use 19

'Natty Bruce' (Bruce Idigbogwu) 17–18, 119*n14*
Netflix 37, 140
Network Society definition 24
New Distribution Network 97, 103, **104–8**, *106*, 110, 113, 115
'New Nollywood' 78
  aim to gain control of profits 59
  blockbusters 141
  composition 36, 156
  departures from traditional Nollywood 37
  funding 37
  global distribution 129
  increased budgets 64
  international attention 37, 149*n23*
  investment in cinema construction 46
  plot differences 64
  scarcity of titles 45
  target audiences 82
  use of film festivals 36–7
New York Film Academy (NYFA) 125
Nigeria
  corruption 96, 114
  cultural exports 71
  currency 9
  demographics 94
  economic crash 13
  economy 156
  ethnic groups 2–3, 117*n1*
  expatriate population 87
  global perception 124
  homophobia 20
  imports 126
  independence 95
  infrastructure 24–5, 103, 116–17, 119*n16*, 136–7, 140–1, 145
  languages 92*n16*

  political history 59, **95–6**, 115, 118*n3*
  population 2
  separation from global economy 57
Nigeria Bank of Industry 116
Nigeria Bank of Investment 159*n1*
Nigerian Broadcasting Commission 103
Nigerian Copyright Commission (NCC) 7, **99–102**, 115
Nigerian Energy and Power Authority (NEPA) 40
Nigerian Enterprises Promotion Decree 1972 *see* Indigenisation Act
Nigerian Film Corporation (NFC) 7, 94, **98–9**, 102, 115
Nigerian film industry *see* Nollywood
Nigerian Foreign Ministry 124, 125
Nigerian Society of Cinematographers 42
Nigerian Television Authority (NTA) 10, 13–14, 17–18, 111
Nigerian traditional theatre *see* Yoruba theatre troupes
Njoku, Jason 37, 56, 132–4, 136, 148*n9*, 148*n18*, 152, 156
  education 134
Nnebue, Kenneth 15–16, 17–18, 85
Nollywood
  aesthetic 37, 46, 58, 64
  budgets 38, 64
  business model 3
  categorisation 62, 77–8
  as cultural industry 8

as cultural product **2–3**, 6, 80, 153
disparate goals of industry 115
as distinct from African cinema 77
domestic focus 82
dubbing 84
emergence 25
funding difficulties 28
geography **33–5**, 151
global context **3–5**, 7
governance of industry 7, 58
languages 16
origin of term 78
origins 6
plot 62, 77
political cinema 7, 40
pricing of movies 52
relationship to global film industry 28, 120
royalties 38
scale of business 31
style 3, 62
see also audience for Nollywood film; distribution; employment in Nigerian film industry; financing in Nigerian cinema; future of Nigerian cinema; genre in Nigerian film; global network of Nigerian cinema; movie stars in Nigerian film; origins of Nigerian film industry; regulation of Nigerian film industry; setting in Nollywood; sister industries to Nigerian cinema; structure of Nigerian cinema; technology in African cinema; themes in Nigerian cinema
Nollywood North American Film Festival 124

Obazele, Paul 112
October 1 (2014) 37
Ogum, Yinka 113
Ogundaisi, Yinka 107, 118n9
Ogunde, Hubert 11–12, 90
Ogunleye, Foluke 28n1
O'Jez's (bar) 33
 role in employment 44
Okereke, Stephanie 125
Okome, Onookome 28n1, 76
Okoye, Gabriel *see* Gabosky
Okri, Ben 71
Olusola, Segun 14
Onwochei, Francis 93, 124
origins of Nigerian film industry 6, **9–13**, 76, 93–4
Osuofia in London (2003) 68–9

P-Square 71
Packer, George 58
Phone Swap (2011) 36, 37
piracy 17, 53, **55–7**
 Bollywood movies 56
 Hollywood movies 56
 international 129, 144, 146–7
 see also black market
Post Office Savings Bank (1935) 71
post-production 41–2
Power, Dominic 25–6
Power Holding Company of Nigeria (PHCN) 40, 61n10
producers *see* marketers
profits
 average number of copies sold per movie 52
 secrecy 31
Pype, Katrien 144

regulation of Nigerian film industry **93**
 development **98–9**

governmental agencies **96–102**
 interventions 102–10, 155–6
 lack of oversight 94
 as legitimising tool for state 115
reproduction process 50–2
The Rich Also Cry (2009) 14
rights, theatrical 1
Riverwood 86

Sanga Entertainment **128–32**
Saul, Mahir 91n7
Scott, Allen J. 150
Sembéne, Ousman 74, 75
setting in Nollywood **63–4**
 urban settings 65–6
Shashore, Ruth 125
Silicon Valley 21, 136
Silverbird 158
Simone, AbdouMaliq 23, 120–1
sister industries to Nigerian cinema **85–8**, 90, 147–8n5, 153
soap operas 13
 influence on early Nollywood 18, 80
 popularity in Nigeria 80
SONY 146
 as dominant industry supplier 40–1, 58, 125–6
 explanation of market dominance 61n11
 Lagos store 8, 41
 role in training film-makers 125
South African film industry *see* Vollywood
Soyinnka, Wole 71
State of Emergency (2004) 67
straight-to-video industry 78–80, 156
 defining features 78
 distribution 36

straight-to-video industry *cont.*
  formulaic nature 80
  television and online viewing 92*n*15
Structural Adjustment Program (SAP) 9–10, 13, 14, 18, 28
  see also World Bank
structure of Nigerian cinema **35–8**
sub-Saharan Africa
  dominance of Nollywood movies 150
  driving forces behind video industry 87–8
  exclusion from global society 23
Surulere (neighbourhood) 20, 33, 93, 114
  as production hub 30

Tanzanian film industry
  Nollywood influence 3
  see also Bongowood
technology in African cinema
  changes of video format 41
  expense of equipment 126
  lighting 41
  purchasing equipment 41
  salvage 126
Telenovelas 88, 153
  influence on Nollywood 14
  see also soap operas
themes in Nigerian cinema **69–70**

Tiger Global Management 132
trade unions *see* guilds
Transerve Disc factory 50, 51
trust-based business
  in guilds 110
  between marketers and directors 39
  policing 45
  repeat collaborations 44
  see also informal business practice
Tsika, Noah 29*n*8, 79–80

Uganda
  language 143
  popularity of Nollywood 143
  television 143–4
Ukadike, Frank 73, 75
United Bank of Africa (UBA) 114

VCR *see* video home system (VHS)
Victoria Island 33
video, as medium 3
  as defining factor of Nollywood 77–8
  dominance of Nigerian film industry 13
  negative perception 78
  see also straight-to-video industry
video compact disks (VCDs)

  benefits compared to VHS 50
  dominant replication technology 49, 140
  failure in western markets 49
  successor to VHS 49
video home system (VHS) 15
  global decline 10
  introduction into Nigeria 14
  role in enabling growth 27
video parlours 47
video rentals 47
Vollywood 86

Waliaula, Solomon 92*n*18
World Bank 9–10, 13, 29*n*10, 59
  loans to Nigeria 34
  statistics report on Nigeria 25, 29

Yoruba (ethnic group) 2
  heritage 89
Yoruba theatre troupes 10, **10–12**, 14, 21, 71
  composition 12
  emergence 89
  films 12, 75, 76
  influence on Nollywood 80, 89–90
  video movies 15–16
YouTube 132–3, 134, 140, 141

LIST OF ILLUSTRATIONS

While considerable effort has been made to correctly identify the copyright holders, this has not been possible in all cases. We apologise for any apparent negligence and any omissions or corrections brought to our attention will be remedied in any future editions.

Living in Bondage I, Kenneth Nnebue; *Phone Swap*, Golden Effects; *Edikan*, Emem Isong Production; *Blackberry Babes*, Simony Productions; *Last Flight to Abuja*, Nollywood Film Factory; *Before the Light*, Denziot Productions; *Beyonce and Rhianna*, Simony Productions; *Daybreak in Udi*, Crown Film Unit.